Ethics and the Arts

GARLAND STUDIES IN APPLIED ETHICS
VOLUME 5
GARLAND REFERENCE LIBRARY OF SOCIAL SCIENCE
VOLUME 993

GARLAND STUDIES IN APPLIED ETHICS

ALAN GOLDMAN, *Series Editor*

JUSTIFICATION AND EXCUSE
IN THE CRIMINAL LAW
A Collection of Essays
edited by Michael Louis Corrado

ETHICAL ISSUES
IN SCIENTIFIC RESEARCH
An Anthology
edited by Edward Erwin,
Sidney Gendin,
and Lowell Kleiman

DRUGS, MORALITY, AND THE LAW
edited by Steven Luper-Foy
and Curtis Brown

THE ETHICS OF SUICIDE
by Victor Cosculluela

ETHICS AND THE ARTS
An Anthology
edited by David E. W. Fenner

ETHICS AND THE ARTS
AN ANTHOLOGY

EDITED BY
DAVID E. W. FENNER

GARLAND PUBLISHING, INC.
NEW YORK AND LONDON
1995

Library of Congress Cataloging-in-Publication Data

Ethics and the arts: an anthology / edited by David E.W. Fenner.
        p.   cm. — (Garland reference library of social science ; v. 993)
(Garland studies in applied ethics ; v. 5)
   Includes bibliographical references.
   ISBN 0-8153-1847-2
   1. Arts and morals.   I. Fenner, David E. W. II. Series. III. Series:
Garland studies in applied ethics ; v. 5.
BJ46.E79   1995
701—dc20   95-17455
                                            CIP

Printed on acid-free, 250-year-life paper
Manufactured in the United States of America

SERIES PREFACE

The aim of this series is to make available texts and collections of essays on major moral issues. Each volume will be devoted to a single issue of contemporary interest. Such in depth treatment will transcend the usual superficial presentation of such topics in general applied ethics texts. Background will be provided by classic statements in articles or detailed definitions in texts of the problems, and opposing sides on the issues will be given ample development.

The series will include authored texts on topics that have not been discussed extensively in the philosophical literature before, as well as contemporary advancements on earlier treatments. Collections of essays will bring together articles that have previously been scattered in the recent proliferation of journals that address these issues.

The present volume is the only collection I know of that focuses exclusively on diverse moral issues connected with the arts: censorship and subsidy, authenticity and ownership, and the connections between moral and aesthetic values and evaluative judgments. The collection is not only unique, but timely. It appears in a period when the National Endowment for the Arts is under fire and the government's role in the arts is a hotly debated political issue, when the connection between moral or political content in art and its aesthetic value remains at the forefront of debate in aesthetics, and when ownership and commercialization of artworks continue to exercise the sociology of art.

David Fenner has collected some of the best recent writings on these issues and provides a clear and useful overview of them in his introduction.

Alan Goldman

Contents

Introduction   1

I. Censorship

Art and Censorship   29
Richard Serra

Protected Space:
Politics, Censorship, and the Arts   41
Mary Devereaux

Aesthetic Censorship:
Censoring Art for Art's Sake   59
Richard Shusterman

II. Creations and Re-Creations

Art and Inauthenticity   77
W.E. Kennick

Forging Issues from Forged Art   97
L.B. Cebik

No Dance Is a Fake   115
Kenton Harris

III. Artistic Property

Why Artworks Have No Right to Have Rights   143
Francis Sparshott

A Defense of Colorization   163
James O. Young

Worldmaking:
Property Rights in Aesthetic Creations   171
Peter H. Karlen

IV. The Sponsorship of Art

Can Government Funding of the Arts
Be Justified Theoretically?   201
Noël Carroll

Not with My Tax Money: The Problem of
Justifying Government Subsidies   219
Joel Feinberg

Should the Government Subsidize the Arts?   249
Ernest van den Haag

The Politics of Culture: Art in a Free Society   261
Gordon Graham

V. Aesthetic Values and Moral Values

Serious Problems, Serious Values:
Are There Aesthetic Dilemmas?   279
Marcia Muelder Eaton

Taste and the Moral Sense 293
Marcia Cavell

The Inter-relationship of Moral
and Aesthetic Excellence 303
Ron Bontekoe and Jamie Crooks

Contributors 319

Introduction

If there is but one best word to describe the world of art in the twentieth century, it is the word *challenge*. Art, artists and the artworld have provided challenge in all manner of ways. Impressionism, pointalism, abstract expressionism and cubism challenged just what representation in art means and how mimetic art need be. Dadaism, Pop Art, and "Ready-Mades" challenged the presumed unassailable line between the world of art and the ordinary world of work-a-day life, between the aesthetic world and the functional one. Now, in the latter half of the twentieth century, the line between art and the obscene or prurient has been challenged; one need only think of the uproar created by the late Robert Mapplethorpe. In general, art has become substantially less harmless. Art today not only challenges; in some ways, art literally threatens.

The obvious challenges in defining art are perhaps the most glamorous of the group, but the twentieth century artworld challenges also in ways more subtle yet certainly every bit as provocative. What now counts as originality? Can an artist add a mustache and goatee to (a copy of) the *Mona Lisa* and have a new artwork? Marcel Duchamp, in a 1919 work entitled *LHOOQ*, apparently did so. Can I simply *erase* the work of another artist and have the product of that erasure considered art? In 1959, Robert Rauschenberg, with the help of Willem de Kooning, did it.

Each time a challenge is laid down, audiences must assess how they will respond. The custom of late is that almost anything goes. But "almost anything goes" within a certain context. Apparently still one can mow one's lawn without being accused of destroying the work of art that was the unmown lawn. One can still throw away paper napkins at the end of a meal without harming the artworld. One can still highlight college textbooks without defaming art. Apparently, so long as one is in the right frame of mind, or in the right building, or with the right people, or perhaps *is* the right person or recognized as the right person . . . so long as there is an accepted context, almost anything goes.

But twentieth century art does not merely offer challenges that make connection to artists, aesthetes or aesthetic attention. Many of the aforementioned challenges purposely go outside the boundaries of the aesthetic to make their most provocative statements. Audience members are now forced—because of the moral, spiritual, patriotic challenges in art—to consider works under their attention more broadly. How one ought respond to a work of twentieth century art is not merely an aesthetic matter. If it were simply an aesthetic matter, then many of the most provocative and engaging works of recent art would be innocuous and facile.

Simply put, it is precisely decisions which call viewers (hearers, etc.) to question in themselves how they ought respond that make the challenges of art today ethically arresting and morally exigent. Ethics is a matter of deciding what to do given a certain situation. Ethics is about action. And situations calling for audience responses of ethical sorts are in abundance.

This book will address those artworld situations that call for ethical answers in five areas: censorship; the creation and re-creation—as in reproduction, copying and forgery—of artworks; ownership, copyrights and artistic property; the preservation, sponsorship, and value of artworks, or artforms; and the relationship between the aesthetic and the moral.

I

The first chapter is on censorship. This, perhaps more than the topics of the other chapters, has the virtue of being one of the most discussed themes in the first half of this decade. What is censorship? Who censors? Why do these individuals or agencies censor? Why should they censor? Under what conditions and through what means should censorship occur? How deliberate or direct must an effort be to effectively constitute censorship? If one can err by censoring too much, can one also err by censoring too little? Censorship can come in many different forms and for many different reasons.

One may censor on religious grounds; an object or event may be sacrilegious or sufficiently offensive to a religious body or perhaps even to common religious sentiment—perhaps even to spirituality itself—so as to be judged censorable. Serrano's *Piss Christ*, the photographic work, incidentally funded by the government, of a plastic crucifix suspended in a jar of urine, was the subject of religious and spiritual calls for censorship, or at the very least for national funding to be withdrawn (a kind of censorship in itself?).

One may censor on social grounds. In direct cases, a work may threaten national security (imagine a work that incorporates state secrets that were acquired surreptitiously by the artist) or a work may threaten by inciting a group of people to riot or harm others, either manifestly or covertly. In some cases, a work may even have the effect of promoting one to harm oneself (as certain rock music has been alleged to do; Mary Devereaux discusses this). In indirect cases, censorship may be deemed appropriate where the work in question attacks the moral fibre of the society or the community. If an artwork makes us less good than we would be, or were, before experiencing that work, then such a work might rightly be censored. Allegedly, pornography (which, let us stipulate here, is not art) has effects other than simply the satisfaction of prurient interests on the parts of those who experience it. Could art which has themes that could be seen to appeal to sexual interests have the same ill side effects? Should such photographic works such as those of Robert Mapplethorpe be censored—kept from children? kept from the public? kept from everybody at all times?

Besides the sorts of venues in which censorship is practiced, there are many forms of censorship. When a government dictates that a work not exist or never be opened to an audience, this is the most overt form of censorship. Currently our government "censors" acts that could incite riots, the public display of sexual themes, yelling fire in a crowded theatre, and all acts which in their creation would seriously harm the participants. If any of these items were incorporated into bona fide artworks, then they would be candidates for direct censorship. More subtle forms of censorship exist as well. If the N.E.A. elects never to fund a given art movement or artform, this may be viewed as a form of censorship. Some would argue, however, that for such an action to be censorship, that action on the part of the N.E.A. would have to be deliberate and intentional with the purpose of not allowing this movement or artform a chance for exposure; just because the N.E.A. does not fund every artist is no reason to suggest that the N.E.A. is censoring all those unfunded. Nevertheless, the government does take a moral responsibility, and so is morally accountable, when it delivers to some artists and artforms funds that others do not receive.

Decisions are being made as to what is to happen with the public's money, and these decisions almost of necessity will involve more than simply what an accountant would do. These decisions will involve what the government, or agents acting on behalf of the government, decide is worthy of funding, is culturally or socially important, is valuable as art.

Censorship can happen in still other forms. If a gallery owner elects not to show a particular artist or artform, if a community elects not to allow such a showing, if the local school board withdraws from school library shelves certain books—books traditionally found on school library shelves—if the local television station refuses to carry certain network shows, if an exhibit is picketed . . . there are many ways that censorship of artworks can occur. And in some communities it is clear that such means of censorship are overused and taken advantage of.

Beyond deciding exactly what censorship is, there are, it seems, three central questions making up the core of the issue of censorship: First, who ought censor? Second, what should they censor? Third, how should censorship be carried out?

The first question can be answered in several different ways:

    (1)   The Local Community.

    (2)   The Religious Community.

    (3)   The Moral Community.

    (4)   The Society. The state has the responsibility to protect us both domestically and from foreign invasion; does it also have the responsibility to protect us from things properly censored? On other hand, does the state have the responsibility, given a mandate to educate its populace, to provide us with access to art? What about the possibility that some of that art may be thought properly censorable by some of that populace?

The second question can be answered more simply. *What harms* should be censored. But, of course, the interest is in the details:

    (1)   What harms physically

        (a)   What harms the artist's subjects, persons, property or the environment.

        (b)   What harms another artist's work.

    (2)   What harms morally

    (3)   What harms spiritually or religiously

(4)   What harms socially or divisively
(5)   What harms societally or nationally
(6)   What harms psychologically
    (a)   Explicitness in violence
    (b)   Explicitness in sexual themes

The last question is, How should one censor? First, it is important to understand that all censorship is on a continuum with all other censorship. While authoritarian societies may censor more, and more frequently, than liberal states, each society is on the same continuum because every society, no matter how liberal, enlightened or psychologically stable, censors something. The trick is to understand where on that continuum is the proper place to draw a line—or, more modestly, where on that continuum is the proper line drawn for *this* society at *this* time.

The old adage about obscenity—"I can't define it, but I know it when I see it"—is almost entirely useless as a means of deciding where the line is to be drawn. Clearly in many cases—all?—the artist's intuitions about the propriety of a work disagree with the intuitions of those who seek to censor that artist or her/his work. It is probably the case that those who are in the most central position to enact governmental censorship, legislators and politicians, are in less of a position to act as the best judges of such things than are others. Shall the lawyers rule the artists? And yet, if the politicians are simply acting on the interests of their constituents, then we might ask why the artists ought think themselves immune from the commonality of the views of the populace of which they are but a part?

Liberal positions—though today there exists more interest among self-described liberals for censoring items that bespeak at all of ethnic or gender disenfranchisement—have traditionally held that adults, given that they are adults, ought serve as their own judges of what is and is not appropriate for themselves and their families. Some have held that the only appropriate group to be subject to the effects of censorship are children. In the privacy of one's home, or in the privacy of a closed location, adults have the right to experience almost anything they seek to experience. So long as there exists no overt physical harm of the subjects or the audience, adults can make up their own minds.

Furthermore, some hold that censorship, in concert with the liberal position described above, ought only to be practiced with regard to the *creation* of artworks. Only those works that in their creation involve harm to their subjects, as would so-called "snuff films" and child pornography, should be properly censored. All else ought be available for the decisions to view or not to view of free and thoughtful adults.

Finally, we have not discussed, except in passing, the problem of the mutability of the appropriateness of censorship for a given society or community. It may well be that what is properly censorable today will not be so tomorrow. While it was right and proper for Victorians to hide the legs of tables from potentially inflamed and subsequently scandalized onlookers, we today can brave bare-legged furniture without succumbing to its temptations.

Moreover, what is properly censorable here may not be so in other societies or communities. Amsterdam's tolerances may not be the sort that could be practiced, without negative social repercussions, in cities in America or Britain. And American tolerances may not be the sort that could be countenanced in Singapore or Iran. If there are such differences among place and time, then the task of censorship is an ever present one.

The articles collected here on the topic of censorship are three: (1) Richard Serra's "Art and Censorship," taken from a speech he gave in Des Moines, Iowa, on 25 October, 1989, seven months after the government dismantled his architectural sculpture, *Tilted Arc*, from its place beside the Federal Plaza in New York City; (2) Mary Devereaux's "Protected Space: Politics, Censorship, and the Arts"; and (3) Richard Shusterman's "Aesthetic Censorship: Censoring Art for Art's Sake."

Much of Serra's speech has to do with an earlier speech given by then-*New York Times* art critic, Hilton Kramer. In an article that has become famous in its own right, "Is Art Above the Laws of Decency?"[1] Kramer argues that galleries that elect to cancel exhibitions of highly controversial works, as the Corcoran Gallery in Washington did in the case of a Mapplethorpe showing, are acting rightly. "Should public standards of decency and civility be observed in determining which works of art or art events are to be selected for the government's support?" Kramer asks. " . . . [I]s everything and anything to be permitted in the name of art?"

Kramer then goes on to specifically discuss Serra's *Tilted Arc*:

> What proved to be bitterly offensive to the community that *Tilted Arc* was commissioned to serve was its total lack of amenity—indeed, its stated goal of provoking the most negative and disruptive response to the site the sculpture dominated with an arrogant disregard for the mental well-being and physical convenience of the people who were obliged to come into contact with the work in the course of their daily employment.

Kramer's position is clear: public, social standards of morality and taste rightfully play a role in the determination of which artworks the government funds and perhaps which artworks the public is made to look at. The tax dollars spent to fund projects like Serra's sculpture are *public* tax dollars. Why oughtn't the public, then, have their interests met in deciding how those public funds should be spent?

Although Kramer's position may stand alone in this anthology on the use of censorship and restriction of public funds to insure that social standards are not transgressed, there are articles included in chapter four which also question the parameters of governmental funding of the arts.

Serra's speech is in large measure an answer to the claims of Kramer. What Kramer fails to understand, charges Serra, is that for all the claims of uncivility of *Tilted Arc*, the reaction which was to destroy the sculpture was even more uncivil. *Tilted Arc*'s removal and destruction was a violation, says Serra, of his First Amendment rights to freedom of speech. The removal of the work on the part of the government served the government's interest in laying a precedent for future censorship.

In short, Serra claims that the General Services Administration which ordered the removal of *Tilted Arc*, a sculpture it had commissioned ten years earlier, violated his freedom of speech and acted on arbitrary standards in the destruction of a work of art.

While the GSA bought from Serra the sculpture, the GSA still did not have the right to destroy it. How far do the rights of buyers of artworks go? This is a question we address in chapter three. Serra claims that artists always have the right not to have their works destroyed, regardless of the property ownership of that work. The right the artist retains is not an economic right, insofar as the work has been bought and paid for by another, but a moral right of authorship.

Mary Devereaux's article, "Protected Space: Politics, Censorship, and the Arts," was a piece written for the fiftieth anniversary edition of the *Journal of Aesthetics and Art Criticism*. In it, she notes that art today is frequently politically contextualized. This occurs not only by the political right but also by liberals. While the right wing is concerned that standards of decency and morality are upheld, the left is concerned that intolerance as portrayed in artworks be eliminated. While formalist strategies of attending to works in the absence of considering their political ramifications, to thinking of artworks as "aesthetically autonomous," have been popular in the past, the answer lies not in reducing works to political vehicles nor to merely formal objects or line and color. The answer lies in striking a balance between the various facets of artwork consideration.

Devereaux writes

> Current Anglo-American aesthetics is embroiled in two debates: one centered on the National Endowment of the Arts and taking place in the "real world" of politics and art; the other centered on specifically philosophical issues and taking place within the progression of aesthetics. Both debates manifest an underlying struggle between the political and non-political conceptions of art. Both debates give rise to the same dilemma: forcing us to choose between *either* a formalist conception of art which protects art from the exigencies of changing political fashion but isolates art from life, or various political conceptions of art which integrate art with life but sacrifice its autonomy. This dilemma turns on a misunderstanding of autonomy, a misunderstanding that can, I argue, be resolved by a reconceptualization of autonomy as "protected space."[2]

Richard Shusterman's article, "Aesthetic Censorship: Censoring Art for Art's Sake," is the last of the three articles in this section. Shusterman's piece considers censorship of artworks on grounds other than political or social. He considers *aesthetic* censorship of artworks.

He argues that no case has been made against censorship which would preclude the propriety of censoring for reasons that are aesthetic in nature. Shusterman argues that, (i) aesthetic censorship would have the effect of highlighting the best work, (ii) it would not dull our aesthetic sensibilities with less-good work, (iii) if economic constraints will necessarily act as a censor, better we censor on aesthetic grounds so that the best work is assured support.

He writes

> Censorship has always been regarded as essentially and necessarily inimical and harmful to art, and antithetical to aesthetic autonomy and interests. My paper challenges this still popular dogma which stems from an oversimplified notion of censorship and its possible forms and motives. The concept of censorship not only allows the possibility of censoring works of art (or parts thereof) on *aesthetic* grounds, i.e. because they are aesthetically objectionable, but such aesthetic censorship would most likely promote superior art and appreciation.[3]

II

The second chapter is entitled "Creations and Re-Creations." Here we will discuss the problems of Fakes and Forgeries, Copies and Reproductions. While the latter two are obviously necessary in the creation and re-creation of many artworks and in some artforms, the former two labels are distinctly pejorative. Why? What is the difference between a copy and a forgery?

There are many works of art which exist, at least in a form that can be sensed, only through copies. Literature, poetry, symphonies, operas, dances, plays, lithographs, monoprints, etchings, and so forth and so on, can only be experienced by an audience through a performance, reproduction or copy. These works are different in kind, then, from artworks like paintings, sculptures and architecture, of which there can only exist a single instantiation. There are many copies of Joyce's *Dubliners*, all of them sharing in common a text, though only some sharing in common such things as print and binding. There can be many copies of an etching, though all, given that each is signed and numbered, are different in some respect. There can be a great number of performances and productions, and there are, of the ballet, *The Nutcracker*. But unlike *Dubliners*, each may be markedly different from the others. Even within a single score, a single choreography, a single company, and a single production run, there will be differences in each and every performance.

These differences are expected and, by aficionados today, embraced as a means of understanding and appreciating the artwork more deeply through being able to experience variations and being in the position of comparing copies one with another. Copies are essential to the work's existing in a sensory form. And they are important in their differences to presenting the artwork in detail and variation enough to add to the experiences of audiences who see or hear more than a single copy.

Forgeries and fakes, however, do not share in the nobility of diversity which informs copies and reproductions. Forgeries and fakes, in the very naming, have an ethical dimension. These items are made with the intention that at some time they will deceive. Whether they deceive a curator, art patron, viewer, or all three, they present themselves as something they are not. Indeed, there need not be specific physical work that is copied for such a deception to take place. For many years, works of Van Meegeren were taken to be authentic works of Vermeer. Van Meegeren's works were not copies of actual Vermeer works; Van Meegeren's works were simply very closely in the Vermeer style. How such deception is accomplished, and whether fakes and forgeries suffer in respect of their aesthetic appreciation, is not at issue here. What we mean to explore is the ethical aspect of the deception that seems a necessary part of any forgery or fake.

But what of an artist "borrowing" from another artist? "Variations on a theme," "Musical Sampling," and creating artworks "after so-and-so" or "in the style of so-and-so" are all of this kind. It has become commonplace to see the works of some artists taken over by other artists, either in collaboration of efforts, sometimes in homage to the first artist for offering inspiration or a great work, sometimes in mimicry of the former artist, and sometimes in outright appropriation of the first artist's work in the creation of that of the second artist. As is evident, the moral implications of the use of another's work in one's own can run the gamut from being highly flattering to stealing.

Ethically speaking, how far may one go? How much of the work of another artist can one appropriate and still refer to her own work as original and separate from that of the latter?

This, of course, raises the following question: What do terms like 'original', 'novel', and 'creative' mean? Without defining such terms at the outset, the point at which the demarcating line between flattery and stealing is to be drawn remains in question. Should a work, to be considered original, incorporate at least fifty percent new work? Line-drawing in percentages is problematic. Should a novel work simply include some new thought, some new expression not in the original from which it was inspired? How modest or how dramatic need be this new expression?

In this chapter, we will explore these and other questions. Included here are: (1) W.E. Kennick's "Art and Inauthenticity"; (2) L.B. Cebik's "Forging Issues from Forged Art"; and (3) Kenton Harris' "No Dance Is a Fake."

W.E. Kennick's "Art and Inauthenticity" obviously takes the inspiration for its title from the 1976 Nelson Goodman work, "Art and Authenticity."[4] Kennick's paper is first and foremost a sorting out of the correct classifications that ought be applied to forgeries, fakes, copies, etc. He avoids a discussion of the aesthetic value of forgeries in deference to defining the terms that we use to class what I call here "re-creations." The work that Kennick does is absolutely basic to sorting out questions of, say, the aesthetic merit of a forgery or, say, the moral status of a fake.

He writes

> Before the question whether there is an aesthetic difference between a fake and authentic artwork can be given an univocal answer, it must be given a univocal sense. To do this one must spell out not merely what an aesthetic difference is but also the differences between the authentic and the fake. Confining itself largely to painting, this paper deals with the last question only, particularly with the difference between forgeries and copies.[5]

L.B. Cebik's paper, "Forging Issues from Forged Art," is the second of the three in this chapter. Instead, Cebik suggests, of asking about the *aesthetic* value of a forgery, ask first about what forgeries say

about art theory. Perhaps forgery is less primarily an aesthetic problem
and more a problem of what Cebik calls the art realm.

Cebik writes

> The question, "Do art forgeries have any aesthetic
> value?" has produced numerous insights into the
> concept of forgery. Exploring the nature of the
> concept of forgery yields the conclusion that it says
> little or nothing about the possibility of aesthetic
> values in forged works. The presence or absence of
> such value depends upon the art theory the analyst
> brings to the study of the forgery.[6]

The last paper in this chapter is Kenton Harris' "No Dance Is a
Fake." After laying out a definition of dance to be used as a touchstone
for discussion of dance identity—that is, what makes two dances the
same—Harris explains that two dances are the same only when both
follow the rules of reproduction that govern the use of the name of the
dance that both claim to be. Two productions of *Swan Lake* are really
two productions of the same dance when each follows certain rules,
rules that are pliable and evolving, that govern calling each of those
two productions *Swan Lake*. Since each dance production will be
different from every other dance production with regard to what rules
a given production chooses to follow and which to discard or adapt, no
dance can be a "fake" of another. But while this is the case with regard
to dance productions or performances, this is not the case with dance
styles. Styles may be able to be forged.

III

Chapter three is on ownership, copyrights and artistic property. While
this chapter heading may suffer from sounding too legalistic, it
encompasses some of the most interesting moral dilemmas facing the
art world today.

Few of us, no doubt, have not had the opportunity to see a film
that was originally shot in black and white *colorized*. While it is
undeniable that film colorizers are becoming better at their craft—the
first colorized films were caricatures of themselves—this does not
address the point about whether they are doing a disservice to an

original black-and-white film in the first place. Woody Allen, for one, has taken a strong stance against the colorizing of films. And it is easy to see from where his sentiment is born. The nuance of shading, of the play with light and dark that is apparent in so many films of the thirties and forties would be severely limited in affect if colorized. Orson Welles' *Citizen Kane* is a prime example of a work that uses light and shadow in an integral way to the aesthetic nature and story of that film. Would the film be destroyed, or at least very much harmed, by colorization? What about more contemporary films like Allen's *Manhattan* or Spielberg's *Schindler's List*?

Or is it the case that artworks, like any other real properties, are possessions of their owners? If I own a table, and it is too high for my purposes, I have a right to cut the legs a bit in order to make it more functional. It is my table, and I can do with it as I like (within limits, of course; I cannot, for instance, use it to fashion stakes with which to kill the vampires I take to be sleeping in the house next to mine—actually, I suppose I can make the stakes; I simply cannot use them in the manner for which they were intended). Suppose I purchase an inexpensive copy of a painting, the sort always sold in museum bookshops and euphemistically called a print. I have the right, once I get the copy home and discover that it does not fit the frame I own, to cut bits off each side to make it fit. This may be aesthetically suspect, but it is still my right.

What if I own a film? What if, in the manner of Ted Turner, I purchase a film and its rights, and wish to colorize that film? If the film is my property, why ought I not have the right to do with it as I see fit? I can, for instance, decide only to show my film ("my" film) once a decade. Few will challenge my right to do that. I can have the film formatted to fit a television screen and to fit within a two-hour time period, and I can cut the film up with dozens of commercials. Few will challenge my right to do that. And if I want to colorize it?

The *Mona Lisa* is not for sale. It has reached that point as one of the most central members of the canon of western art that it will most probably never again be in the position where it could be sold and owned by a single patron or set of patrons. It, to employ the cliche, belongs to the world. But suppose that one could purchase it. If one did, would she be able to treat the *Mona Lisa* in any way she wished? On one side of the intuitional line about what is appropriate would be that patron's right to privately house the work; it is her right that she not allow the work to be shown. She may decide to house the work in a non-climate-controlled room. This would be very foolish in terms of her investment, and would no doubt offend museum owners and aesthetes, but it may be her right to do so. She may wish to illuminate it brightly; she may wish to lock it in a safe. In each case, the right seems hers. May she destroy it? That is, is it her right to dispose of it in such a way as to destroy it? Is it her right to paint on top of it, or draw on it, or remove the canvas from the stretchers? Can she chip away at the paint, or pinprick the canvas? These latter questions test the intuition that what one possesses, what one owns, can be treated in any way that the owner believes fit. Even if the Louvre decided to illuminate the work too brightly, many would be up in arms over such effrontery. Artworks seem to have a protection and a right to such protection that few other possessions enjoy. One may do whatever one wishes to one's table, but one cannot torture one's livestock or pets, one presumably cannot dump down the sink the cure for cancer, and one cannot draw on the *Mona Lisa*. These are not legal encumbrances; they are moral.

Yet another topic for this chapter is that of how material may be published and released. This book, for instance, enjoys a certain protection, and no publisher other than Garland Publishing has a right to produce copies of it. Each of the previously published articles collected herein also enjoys a certain protection, and alongside each such essay is mentioned the party from whom permission was sought and obtained to reprint those articles here. This protection, these copyrights, are in place to ensure that the work of authors and their agents, in this case philosophers and publishing houses, are not exploited for gains that the authors, etc., will not see. One's labor is one's own, and so benefits accruing from that labor should rightfully go to the deserving.

But what if a professor finds that there is no suitable anthology of articles available on the topic of her upcoming course? May she, for the sake of that single group of students, fashion one together for their use? May she copy just enough sets of those articles for those students and no others? What if a major in her department asks for an additional copy? Copyright law, as any teacher who uses copyrighted material can attest, is wide-ranging and not uncomplicated. The protections we enjoy as authors are in kind the nuisances we find as teachers.

In this chapter the following articles relating to these issues are included: (1) Francis Sparshott's "Why Artworks Have No Right to Have Rights"; (2) James O. Young's "In Defense of Colorization"; and (3) Peter Karlen's "Worldmaking: Property Rights in Aesthetic Creations."

Francis Sparshott claims that artworks do not have rights nor can they. While we may initially believe that artworks have certain rights—the right not to be vandalized, for instance—it is not actually the artwork that is the bearer of a right; it is rather we who have an obligation to treat the work in a certain way. We have this obligation not because of the artist so much as because of the future viewing audience that will come to appreciate the work in question. The rights are not borne by the artwork; they are rights that the future viewers hold.

Sparshott writes

> The rights and interests centered on artworks are radically heterogeneous. The temptation to consolidate them by thinking in terms of rights of artworks as such should be resisted. The value of human rights depends on human freedom and especially on human morality, which is not the same as the fragility of an artwork. The museum mentality that increasingly demonstrates the way American philosophers think about art bespeaks a fetishism that deserves sympathy but not respect.[7]

James Young tackles a problem that is very timely, the colorization of originally black and white films. This topic has gotten lots of press lately, with one of the most noteworthy opponents to the colorization of films being the director Woody Allen. Allen has claimed that the aesthetic merits of a film originally filmed in black and white can suffer if the film is colorized. And even with the advent of better and better means by which films are colorized, examples where black and white photographic effects are aesthetically very important, as in the case of Welles' *Citizen Kane* or a contemporary film like Spielberg's *Schindler's List*, still persuade that the colorization of originally black and white films, especially ones where it seems clear that such films would be aesthetically harmed by colorization, ought not be subject to colorization. On the other hand, of course, if Ted Turner buys a film and its rights, isn't it his to do with as he likes? This harkens back to the Serra case.

Young recognizes the strong pretheoretical intuition that one ought not tamper with the work of another artist; he also recognizes that there may be aesthetic reasons against the colorizing of a film, at least in the case of some originally black and white films. But he argues that since the only candidate for colorization is not the original film footage, but simply a *copy* of the film, which by definition is not the single instantiation of that artist's work, we do not destroy the artist's original by colorizing that copy.

Young writes

> I consider the claim that the colorization of films is an unjustifiable tampering with the artist's work and argue that it is not. I distinguish between artworks which are instantiated in only one object and works that are instantiated in many. I argue that modification of the second sort of artworks is unobjectionable. In fact, modification of works instantiated in many objects is the source of good art in many cases.[8]

The last paper of this chapter is Peter Karlen's "Worldmaking: Property Rights in Aesthetic Creations." Karlen is a practicing attorney. His work in aesthetics, then, is informed to some degree or other by legal concerns as well as aesthetic ones. In "Worldmaking," Karlen questions what the artistic copyright holder really owns. It is naive to suggest that the copyright owner owns something connected to the artwork, as a physical or sensible instantiation, in question. Rather, the copyright owner owns something that covers "a set of relationships" into which that artwork may enter. After outlining what a right to intellectual property means, Karlen suggests that the copyright ownership really extends in a limited way to the whole world, which is to say that no one may shape anything that will mimic, copy or create in viewers the same imaginative experience as the copyrighted artwork.

IV

The fourth chapter is on the issues of the preservation of art, state-sponsorship, and the social and/or cultural value of art. In this chapter, instead of focusing on the individual, be that the artist, patron or viewer, we focus on the society, or, more precisely, on the state or nation. What does the state owe art, artists and the art world? Do the obligations that the state bears towards its citizenry compel it to diligently oversee the cultural and artistic life of that society?

Many answer yes to this question. If a society is wont to call itself civilized or advanced, then it must look after the education of its inhabitants. Part of the educational aims of such a society may be cultural in content, and so part of the state's obligation may be to provide not only for the exposure of its populace to that society's cultural and artistic history, but to provide for the continuance of the traditions and institutions that have made up the content of that history. The state must collect monies from its citizenry for education; and since artistic education is a facet of that necessary education, the state must fund art exhibitions, art institutions, artists and art movements. In short, the state must fund art.

But how is it to accomplish this? While it is easy enough to create taxes for the benefit of art and to create agencies for the distribution of these funds, it is very difficult in the face of the number of artists working—and deserving—to decide who gets funding and who does not. Some argue that the state agencies, then, to accomplish their missions, must be in the position of being able to judge artistic and cultural value. These agencies must be able to, in a sense, look into the future to see what will be of lasting value, aesthetically as well as socially, to the society and its populace. This is a tough trick, but one that must be done *if* a society deems the funding of art to be among its responsibilities (as ours does).

The other side of the coin, of course, is that art is not properly part of the education content of a society. If art, might say those holding this position, is to flourish, it must be a thing embraced by the populace, and to be embraced is to be supported. If the citizens want art, let them fund it themselves, in the way perhaps that the great patrons of renaissance Florence, the Medicis, and the Vatican, did. Americans pay a great deal for entertainment. If art is essentially for the purposes of pleasure, as some contend, then it is a pleasure that must rely on its own attraction for its own life. The film industry is flourishing, as is the rock music industry. If the opera or ballet is valued by the citizens, or enough of them, then the opera and ballet will flourish likewise. If they are not, then they will go the way of other artforms that are no longer practiced today. To governmentally support artforms that are not popularly supported may result in the isolation of those artforms from the very public they are intended to benefit. Such artforms may become insulated from public criticism and in doing so the governmental support may succeed in stifling and inhibiting the artistic growth of those artforms.

The key, then, is to determine, first, what role government support of the arts should take, and, secondly, exactly what value the arts, or particular artforms or movements, hold for a society. To ask the latter, one first must inquire into what context this question ought be asked. Should the value of art be merely to strengthen the society as a political body? Should the value of art be for educational purposes only? Should art always uplift and moralize? Should art simply mirror the society, its strengths and weaknesses? Should art always challenge?

If any positive answer is forthcoming to the question about whether the state ought support the arts, then we must ask about the nature of such an obligation. Certainly the concerns mentioned above must be addressed, but beyond these concerns lie those regarding what the state is supposed to do with the product of its investment. If the state funds art, then what is created is either the property of the state or not. In the American case, the property is that of the artist, and is his to dispose of as he sees fit. But if the value of the funding of art is social, then there is reason for suggesting that the property, the created art, ought be looked after by the state: used in exhibitions, used for educational purposes, and stored away for continued use as the history of that society progresses.

National museums may see it as part of their mission to do just this, to house the most valuable of the works created by artists of that society (or one related in some way to that society). But what about the plethora of works that are funded and created but are not deemed valuable enough to house in national galleries?

The Netherlands are having this difficulty today. As a nation, the Dutch have funded a great deal of art, with the consequence that the state is now responsible for that work. In 1992, a report came out in *The New York Times*[9] that the Dutch state was trying to "give away

215,000 works of art," which the state had funded and was currently housing. This body of work had been collected from the 1950s to the 1980s in programs where the Dutch government purchased the hitherto unsold works of Dutch artists. The government will not sell the works, for this would flood the market, ruining it for artwork currently being produced in the Netherlands. Neither will the government destroy the work, at least not until such time as all other options have been attempted, because this would suggest that the work had no value. For the same reason, then, the government will not simply give the work away. Instead, the Dutch state is trying to find homes for their vast collection in schools, hospitals, clinics, police stations, government buildings and the like.

The Dutch are carefully attempting to assess the aesthetic and cultural merits of the works, insuring that they are not "donating the Rembrandts and Van Goghs of our time." While governments are perhaps qualified to judge the economic and social worth of objects, theirs is an inescapably controversial task in the assessment of the aesthetic and cultural merits of artworks. But perhaps it is not so unique. The United States' NEA is charged with judging, at least partly on aesthetic or cultural grounds, the relative worth of projects brought to their attention for possible governmental funding. The Dutch simply have a much larger task in their hands, different in degree but perhaps not in kind from what the NEA does.

Four articles relating to these questions, those of the responsibilities of the state to fund art, and what its further, though implicit, obligations are, are included in this chapter: (1) Noël Carroll's "Can Government Funding of the Arts Be Justified Theoretically?"; (2) Joel Feinberg's "Not with My Tax Money: The Problem of Justifying Government Subsidies"; (3) Ernest van den Haag's "Should the Government Subsidize the Arts?"; and (4) Gordon Graham's "The Politics of Culture: Art in a Free Society."

Noël Carroll's "Can Government Funding of the Arts be Justified Theoretically?" clearly lays out many of the issues involved in creating a case for governmental funding of the arts. The first case that Carroll considers as possible justification for governmental funding of the arts is the case wherein the government's concern for the welfare of its citizenry mandates public arts funding. This case can be made out in terms of the basic goods that address the needs of the populace, including the artists themselves; this case can also be made out in terms of the "aesthetic welfare" of the society. Although the state may not be justified in treating the funding of arts with the same degree of importance as securing (other) basic goods to its populace, the state may still have a secondary duty to provide for arts funding. This may be in part due to understanding the populace as in part having *aesthetic* needs. But then of course only those art projects, or perhaps we ought say those aesthetic projects, which meet the aesthetic needs of human beings would be the sort justified for governmental support. Beyond this, Carroll considers economic reasons for funding art. He ends the article with a consideration of the possibility that the development of aesthetic sensitivities in the society may foster moral awareness as well.

Joel Feinberg's paper, "Not with My Tax Money: The Problem of Justifying Government Subsidies," is the most recent of the papers on state funding of the arts. He argues that there is a *prima facie* case not to have citizens pay for what they may not be able to share in. One possible answer is the *Benefit Principle*, which suggests that art will benefit some of the populace directly—as education, even if one is not in school, has a direct benefit—or that it will benefit indirectly. But the case for the universality of benefit is very difficult to make. A second possible answer is what Feinberg calls *Rotational Justice*, where some people, even though they constitute a minority, get what they really want, because others, even when they find themselves in minorities, will get the things they really want. We all win for the important things, so we are willing to lose for things that are important to others. Feinberg complements this with a discussion of the intrinsic value (some) works of art possess; cashing out the intrinsic value of artworks in terms of their ability to offer viewers valuable experiences (regardless of whether they actually do this, since that would make the value purely instrumental).

The fourth paper in this chapter is Gordon Graham's "The Politics of Culture: Art in a Free Society." What is the place of government intervention, including government support, of the arts in a free society? First, it depends on the theory of the value of art. (i) The *Pleasure Theory* holds that art is good as it offers pleasure to viewers—but then so does sports, and we might find that sports offers greater pleasure. (ii) The *Understanding Theory* holds that art is good as it furthers our understanding of the world and ourselves—but science does this as well. Any government intervention will violate a strict conception of orthodox liberalism: coercion of people to pay for something that they might not wish to be coerced to pay for. What must be recognized for this coercion to be at all justified is that in funding the arts, the state increases the overall wealth of that state.

Graham writes

> This essay considers the place of state support for
> the arts in a free society conceived along traditional
> liberal lines. It argues that this question cannot be
> addressed adequately without considering the value
> of the arts. Once this is recognized, a defense of
> state involvement can be made in terms of art as
> wealth creation.[10]

The third paper in this chapter is Ernest van den Haag's "Should the Government Subsidize the Arts?" Van den Haag argues that the case for government support of the arts is not made on the basis of the public benefit of pleasure. Even though historical precedent shows government support of the art throughout the ages, this does not justify subsidies today. Why should the few who go to the opera expect the many who do not to subsidize the opera? Art does not have enough social benefit to be socially supported. Further, how should the government judge the deserving of such support? Finally, subsidies might promote mediocrity in art by rewarding half-hearted artists who only work because there is government support, *or* government support might reward imitation: "copy what gets support." Prices might go up without governmental funding of the arts, he argues, but art will survive through private support.

V

The final chapter is entitled "Aesthetic Values and Moral Values." This chapter deals with the relationship between these two sorts of value. How is excellence of one kind, say aesthetic, related to excellence of the other? Can an increase in one sort of value complement a paucity of the other? For example, can a strong moral message make up for a lack of aesthetic merit in assessing the overall value of a work of art? On the other hand, does an increase in the focus on one sort necessitate a decrease in the other? For instance, does a greater focus on the aesthetic merits of an artwork lead to the unawareness of the moral standards of a work? Does a formalist consideration of a work, for example, allow in that work a greater moral latitude? Or, on the other hand, does a greater emphasis on the moral facet of a work curtail the aesthetic freedom present in a work?

Yet another question in this vein is whether art can morally illuminate or instruct. Some philosophers of art working today believe the answer to this question is yes. We grow as moral persons through exposure to art. If this is the case, then is this instruction at the hand of the artist, or is it a function of the art object itself? Do artists have a responsibility regarding the moral enrichment of their audiences? Can a work displaying immoral themes, or incorporating immoral aspects, nonetheless be uplifting? Is all art properly criticized from a moral perspective?

The articles included in addressing this somewhat broad topic are: (1) Marcia Muelder Eaton's "Serious Problems, Serious Values: Are There Aesthetic Dilemmas?"; (2) Marcia Cavell's "Taste and the Moral Sense"; and finally, (3) Ron Bontekoe's and Jamie Crooks' "The Interrelationship of Moral and Aesthetic Excellence."

Marcia Muelder Eaton explores, in "Serious Problems, Serious Values: Are There Aesthetic Dilemmas?" whether there are aesthetic dilemmas in the way that there are moral dilemmas, that is, if indeed there are moral dilemmas. What would constitute an aesthetic dilemma? What would be the similarities between aesthetic dilemmas and moral ones? Would there be, and what would be, the connections between aesthetic dilemmas and moral dilemmas?

She writes

> One way of approaching the question of whether or not there is a significant connection between aesthetic and ethical value is by investigating apparent analogies and disanalogies between moral and aesthetic activities. In this paper I ask whether any aesthetic tests for the presence of a moral dilemma—a logical test and an emotional test—are applicable to aesthetic problems discussed. Several categories fail to meet the tests that moral dilemmas meet; some qualify as genuine dilemmas. Finally I argue that since moral dilemmas arise due to the existence of moral obligations, aesthetic dilemmas imply the existence of aesthetic obligations. A way of interpreting "aesthetic dilemma" is suggested.[11]

The second paper in this chapter is Marcia Cavell's "Taste and the Moral Sense." Though there is much argument for the separation of moral and aesthetic considerations when it comes to art, there is common ground between moral and aesthetic activity. As aesthetic consideration is not rule-guided, moral sensibility cannot be truly rule-guided either. Furthermore, as moral considerations are contextualized, so are aesthetic considerations.

Cavell writes

> It is argued that while there are important differences between moral and aesthetic judgments, there are also important similarities. In particular, certain kinds of moral judgments are as little concerned with rules and principles as are critical judgments about particular works of art; and questions of purpose and context are equally important—contra Stuart Hampshire in *Logic and Appraisal*—to an understanding of action and art. The critic attempts to describe and judge the work of art on its own terms; but what these terms are, in any given case, or what is *internal* to the work and what is *external*, is a complicated question.[12]

The last (but, of course, not least) paper in this collection is Ron Bontekoe's and Jamie Crooks' "The Inter-relationship of Moral and Aesthetic Excellence." They argue that a mishandling of moral matters in an artwork is an aesthetic defect. A bad moral vision in a work hurts that work. An artist must be sensitive to moral matters, though this does not mean that the artist's moral vision must be worn on the sleeve of his/her artwork (so to speak). Preaching is not of aesthetic merit. Being concerned, however, with the overall moral character of the work, is of importance to the worth of the resulting artwork.

Bontekoe and Crooks write that

> The process of artistic creation is a matter of progressively narrowing in on some worthwhile experience the possibility of which the artist has caught a glimpse. This process involves the artist in an attempt to capture the inner necessity governing her subject. Because a bad moral vision is one which gets something significantly wrong about the

human condition, if an artist chooses to deal with
moral issues, and does so badly (i.e. fails to do
justice to the inner necessity governing her
subject), her work can be criticized as having failed
to meet *aesthetic* as well as moral criteria of
excellence.[13]

With this paper the collection is completed. It of course must be
acknowledged that not every question of the relationship of the moral
to the aesthetic, not every ethical question that can be posed about art,
artworks, artists, the art world, gets a hearing in this collection.
Indeed, not every question raised just in this brief introduction gets a
hearing. But what has been attempted is to collect together some of the
most lively and thoughtful treatments of some of the most timely ethical
matters relating to art. Certainly this volume suffers by being too short.
But perhaps that might be said of all collections which strive to present
such a far ranging topic as ethics and the arts.

Notes

1. Hilton Kramer, "Is Art Above the Laws of Decency?" *The New York Times*, July 2, 1989, Section Two.

2. This abstract first appeared in the *Philosopher's Index* (Philosophy Documentation Center, Bowling Green, Ohio, 1993). It is reprinted here by permission of the publisher and the author.

3. This abstract first appeared in the *Philosopher's Index* (Philosophy Documentation Center, Bowling Green, Ohio, 1985). It is reprinted here by permission of the publisher and the author.

4. Nelson Goodman, *Languages of Art* (Indianapolis: Hackett Publishing, 1976).

5. This abstract first appeared in the *Philosopher's Index* (Philosophy Documentation Center, Bowling Green, Ohio, 1986). It is reprinted here by permission of the publisher and the author.

6. This abstract first appeared in the *Philosopher's Index* (Philosophy Documentation Center, Bowling Green, Ohio, 1989). It is reprinted here by permission of the publisher and the author.

7. This abstract first appeared in the *Philosopher's Index* (Philosophy Documentation Center, Bowling Green, Ohio, 1984). It is reprinted here by permission of the publisher and the author.

8. This abstract first appeared in the *Philosopher's Index* (Philosophy Documentation Center, Bowling Green, Ohio, 1989). It is reprinted here by permission of the publisher and the author.

9. Marlise Simons, "Dutch State Dumping Some Non-Masters' Artwork," *The New York Times*, September 14, 1992, National Education Section.

10. This abstract first appeared in the *Philosopher's Index* (Philosophy Documentation Center, Bowling Green, Ohio, 1992). It is reprinted here by permission of the publisher and the author.

11. This abstract first appeared in the American Society for Aesthetics Newsletter 14 (2), Fall 1994, p. 4. It is reprinted here by permission of the author.

12. This abstract first appeared in the *Philosopher's Index* (Philosophy Documentation Center, Bowling Green, Ohio, 1975). It is reprinted here by permission of the publisher and the author.

13. This abstract first appeared in the *Philosopher's Index* (Philosophy Documentation Center, Bowling Green, Ohio, 1993). It is reprinted here by permission of the publisher and the author.

I

Censorship

Art and Censorship

Richard Serra

The United States government destroyed *Tilted Arc* on 15 March 1989.[1] Exercising proprietary rights, authorities of the General Services Administration (GSA) ordered the destruction of the public sculpture that their own agency had commissioned ten years earlier.[2] The government's position, which was affirmed by the courts, was that "as a threshold matter, Serra sold his 'speech' to the Government. . . As such, his 'speech' became Government property in 1981, when he received full payment for his work. An owner's '[p]roperty rights in a physical thing [allow him] to possess, use and dispose of it.'"[3] This is an incredible statement by the government. If nothing else, it affirms the government's commitment to private property over the interests of all free expression. It means that if the government owns the book, it can burn it; if the government has bought your speech, it can mutilate, modify, censor, or even destroy it. The right to property supersedes all other rights: the right to freedom of speech, the right to freedom of expression, the right to protection of one's creative work.

In the United States, property rights are afforded protection, but moral rights are not. Up until 1989, the United States adamantly refused to join the Berne Copyright Convention, the first multilateral copyright treaty, now ratified by seventy-eight countries. The American government refused to comply because the Berne Convention grants moral rights to authors. This international policy was—and is—incom-

Richard Serra is known for his large-scale site-specific works in landscapes, urban environments, and museums. This article is based on a speech given in Des Moines, Iowa, on 25 October 1989, and first appeared in *Critical Inquiry* 17, Spring 1991, pp. 574-581. It is reprinted by permission of the publisher and the author.

patible with United States copyright law, which recognizes only economic rights. Although ten states have enacted some form of moral rights legislation, federal copyright laws tend to prevail, and those are still wholly economic in their motivation. Indeed, the recent pressure for the United States to agree, at least in part, to the terms of the Berne Convention came only as a result of a dramatic increase in the international piracy of American records and films.

In September 1986, Senator Edward M. Kennedy of Massachusetts first introduced a bill called the Visual Artists Rights Act. This bill attempts to amend federal copyright laws to incorporate some aspects of international moral rights protection. The Kennedy bill would prohibit the intentional distortion, mutilation, or destruction of works of art after they have been sold. Moreover, the act would empower artists to claim authorship, to receive royalties on subsequent sales, and to disclaim their authorship if the work were distorted.[4] This legislation would have prevented Clement Greenberg and the other executors of David Smith's estate from authorizing the stripping of paint from several of Smith's later sculptures so that they would resemble his earlier—and more marketable—unpainted sculptures. Such moral rights legislation would have prevented a Japanese bank in New York from removing and destroying a sculpture by Isamu Noguchi simply because the bank president did not like it. And such legislation would have prevented the United States government from destroying *Tilted Arc.*

If Senator Kennedy's bill were enacted, it would be a legal acknowledgement that art can be something other than a mere commercial product. The bill makes clear that the basic economic protection now offered by United States copyright law is insufficient. The bill recognizes that moral rights are independent from the work as property and these rights supersede—or at least coincide with—any pecuniary interest in the work. Moreover, the bill acknowledges that granting protection to moral rights serves society's interests in maintaining the integrity of its artworks and in promoting accurate information about authorship and art.

On 1 March 1989, the Berne Convention Implementation Act became law.[5] On 13 March 1989, on learning that the government had started to dismantle *Tilted Arc,* I went before the United States District Court in New York City, seeking a stay for the destruction so that my lawyers would have time to study the applicability of the Berne

Convention to my case. I expected—as would be the case in other countries that were signatories to the treaty—to be protected by the moral rights clause, which gives an artist the right to object to "any distortion, mutilation or other modification" that is "prejudicial to his honor and reputation," even after his work is sold. I learned, however, that in my case—and others like it—the treaty ratified by Congress is a virtually meaningless piece of paper in that it excludes the key moral rights clause. Those responsible for the censorship of the treaty are the powerful lobbies of magazine, newspaper, and book publishers. Fearful of losing economic control over authors and faced with the probability of numerous copyright suits, these lobbies pressured Congress into omitting that part of the Berne Convention Implementation Act which provided moral rights protection.[6] Thus, publishers can continue to crop photographs, magazine and book publishers can continue to mutilate manuscripts, black-and-white films can continue to be colorized, and the federal government can destroy art.

A key issue in my case, as in all First Amendment cases, was the right of the defendant to curtail free speech based on dislike of content.[7] Here the court stated that the aesthetic dislike is sufficient reason to destroy a work of art: "To the extent that GSA's decision may have been motivated by the sculpture's lack of aesthetic appeal, the decision was entirely permissible."[8] Hilton Kramer has asked, "Should public standards of decency and civility be observed in determining which works of art or art events are to be selected for the Government's support?"[9] He answers his rhetorical question affirmatively and insinuates that *Tilted Arc* was uncivil and comes to the conclusion that it was rightfully destroyed:

> What proved to be so bitterly offensive to the community that "Tilted Arc" was commissioned to serve was its total lack of amenity—indeed, its stated goal of provoking the most negative and disruptive response to the site the sculpture dominated with an arrogant disregard for the mental well-being and physical convenience of the people who were obliged to come into contact with the work in the course of their daily employment. ["A," p. 7]

Kramer goes on to say that it was my wish to "deconstruct and otherwise render uninhabitable the public site the sculpture was designed to occupy" ("A," p. 7).

All of Kramer's statements concerning my intentions and the effect of the sculpture are fabricated so that he can place blame on me for having violated all equally fabricated standard of civility. *Tilted Arc* was not destroyed because the sculpture was uncivil but because the government wanted to set a precedent in which it could demonstrate its right to censor and destroy speech. What Kramer conveniently sweeps under the rug is the important fact that *Tilted Art* was a First Amendment case and that the government by destroying *Tilted Arc* violated my right to free speech.

In the same *New York Times* article, Kramer applauds the Corcoran Gallery for having canceled an exhibition of Mapplethorpe photographs. The photos Kramer objects to render men, in Kramer's words, "as nothing but sexual—which is to say, homosexual—objects." Images of this sort, according to Kramer, "cannot be regarded as anything but a violation of public decency." For those reasons, Kramer concludes, the National Endowment for the Arts (NEA) should not have contributed its funds to support its public exhibition ("A," p. 7). Once again he accused the artist of having violated a public standard, which in Mapplethorpe's case is the standard of decency. The penalty for this violation is the exclusion of his speech from public viewing and the withdrawal of public funds to make the work available to the public.

Kramer's article is part of a larger radical conservative agenda. The initiative Kramer took in *The New York Times* was called for by Patrick Buchanan in May and June of 1989 in the *New York Post* and the *Washington Times* where he announced "a cultural revolution in the 90's as sweeping as the political revolution of the 80's." It's worth quoting Buchanan at length:

> Culture—music, literature, art—is the visible expression of what is within a nation's soul, its deepest values, its cherished beliefs. America's soul simply cannot be so far gone in corruption as the trash and junk filling so many museums and defacing so many buildings would suggest. As with our rivers and lakes, we need to clean up our culture; for it is a well from which we all must

> drink. Just as poisoned land will yield up poisonous
> fruit, so a polluted culture, left to fester and stink
> can destroy a nation's soul. . . . We should not
> subsidize decadence.[10]

Let me quote another leader of a cultural revolution:

> It is not only the task of art and artists to
> communicate, more than that it is their task to form
> and create, to eradicate the sick and to pave the
> way for the healthy. Art should not only be good
> art, art must reflect our national soul. In the end,
> art can only be good if it means something to the
> people for which it is made.[11]

What Buchanan called for and what Kramer helped to justify,
Senator Jesse Helms brought in front of the Senate. He asked the
Senate to accept an amendment that would bar federal arts funds from
being used "to promote, disseminate, or produce indecent or obscene
materials, including but not limited to depictions of sadomasochism,
homoeroticism, the exploitation of children, or individuals engaged in
sex acts."[12] The Helms amendment was replaced by the supposedly
more moderate Yates amendment.[13] Nonetheless, Helms's fundamental
diatribe was successful in that the Senate passed an amendment which
gives the government the right to judge the content of art.

The Yates amendment, which was approved by the Senate, calls
for denying federal money for art deemed obscene. It is based on a
definition of obscenity as given by a 1973 Supreme Court decision in
Miller v. California.[14] In *Miller,* the Supreme Court prescribed three
tests for obscenity: a work must appeal to prurient interests, contain
patently offensive portrayals of specific sexual conduct, and lack
serious literary, artistic, political, or scientific value.[15] The decision
about whether something is obscene is to be made by a local jury,
applying community standards. Does this mean that the material in
question can be tolerated by one community and another community
will criminalize its author? What about Salman Rushdie?

Conservatives and Democrats agree that taxpayers' money should
not be spent on art which carries an obscene content; Kramer wants
publicly funded art to conform to the standards of decency and civility;
Helms does not want the NEA to fund indecency and obscenity; and the

Democratic majority in the Senate supported an amendment that will enable the government to deny federal money for art deemed obscene. The central premise in all these statements, proposals, and amendments is that obscenity can be defined—that there is actually a standard of decency which excludes obscenity. The assumption of a universal standard is presumptuous. There aren't any homogenous standards in a heterogeneous society. There is no univocal voice. Whose standards are we talking about? Who dictates these standards?

It seems a rather extreme measure to impose an arbitrary standard of obscenity on the whole of society. Gays, as one group of this heterogeneous society, for example, have the right to recognize themselves in any art form or manner they choose. Gays cannot be denied their images of sexuality, and they cannot be denied public funds to support the public presentation of these images. Gays are a part of this public. Why should heterosexuals impose their standard of "decency" or "obscenity" on homosexuals? The history of art is filled with images of the debasement, torture, and rape of women. Is that part of the accepted heterosexual definition of decency? It is obvious that the initiative against obscenity in the arts is not directed against heterosexual indecencies but that its subcontext is homophobia. Jesse Helms, in particular, makes no effort to hide the fact that part of his political program is based on homophobia. In an earlier amendment Helms wanted to prohibit federal funds from being used for AIDS education; he argued that the government would thereby encourage or condone homosexual acts. He also stated publicly that no matter what issue comes up, if you attack homosexuals, you can't lose.

The position I am advocating is the same as Floyd Abrams, a noted constitutional lawyer, who stated:

> While Congress is legally entitled to withdraw endowment funding, the First Amendment doesn't allow Congress to pick and choose who gets money and who doesn't. You can't punish people who don't adhere to Congress's version of art they like. Even if they want to protect the public, the basic legal reality is that funding may not exclude constitutionally protected speech.[16]

The argument ought not to be about assumed standards. We should not get involved in line drawing and definitions of decency and obscenity.

There is no reason to participate in this fundamentalist discourse. Taxpayers' dollars ought to support all forms of expression as guaranteed by the First Amendment. Gays pay taxes. Taxation must include the right to representation. Ideas, images, descriptions of realities that are part of everyday language cannot be forbidden from entering into the discourse of art. All decisions regarding speech ought to be made in a nondiscriminatory manner. Government agencies allocating funds for art cannot favor one form of speech over another. Preferences or opinions, even if shared by a majority, are nonrelevant judgments and improper grounds for exclusion. To repeat: If government only allocates dollars for certain forms of art and not others, the government abolishes the First Amendment. If anything, the First Amendment protects the diversity of speech. Government cannot exclude because to exclude is to censor.

Kramer, as well as Helms and Yates, argued that the introduction of obscenity clauses into the NEA funding guidelines was not an attempt at censorship because there was no effort to prevent publication or distribution of obscene material. Instead, they argued that they were merely barring the use of taxpayers' money for such projects. Taxpayers' money ought to be spent to protect the standards of the Constitution and not to protect bogus standards of decency and civility.

Previously the NEA panels were required only to recognize "artistic and cultural significance" and "professional excellence." Now the head of the NEA must add to these intentionally and exclusively art-related criteria the politically charged criterion of obscenity. I question that obscenity is a matter for the judicial system, but I am certain that it is not for the NEA and politicians to determine. The NEA is no longer politically independent and there is no doubt that its independence will erode even further once the Senate's commission begins to review the NEA's grantmaking procedure and determine whether there should be standards in addition to the new obscenity standard that has been forced on the NEA. The twelve-member commission reviewing the NEA guidelines is a purely political commission. It consists of four members appointed by the Speaker of the House, four by the president pro tempore of the Senate, and four by the President. For the time being, John E. Frohnmayer, chairman of the NEA, has taken it upon himself to reverse peer panel recommendations on grants to artists who might use the grant money to produce potentially obscene material. Those artists considered "harmless" and worthy of NEA funding are asked to sign away their right to free speech by signing a guarantee that they will not use the NEA monies to produce obscenities.

It is obvious that the Mapplethorpe case set in motion for the NEA what the *Tilted Arc* case set in motion for the GSA. The *Tilted Arc* case was used to change fundamentally the guidelines of the GSA's Art-in-Architecture Program. The peer panel selection was weakened because every panel will now select under community pressures or will try to avoid community protest. The contract between the artist and the GSA was changed. The new guidelines now overtly favor the government, which can cancel the contract at any stage of the planning process, and it excludes the realization of site-specific projects in that it explicitly states that artworks commissioned by the GSA can be removed from their federal sites at any time. Every artist who agrees to have a work commissioned by the GSA or funded by the NEA will thereby become a collaborator and active agent of governmental censorship.

Notes

1. On 15 March 1989, *Tilted Arc* was dismantled and removed from its site at the Federal Plaza in New York City. *Tilted Arc* was specifically created for this site, and its removal from this location resulted in the work's destruction.

Site-specific works

> are determined by the topography of the site, whether it is urban, landscape or an architectural enclosure. My works become part of and are built into the structure of the site, and often restructure, both conceptually and perceptually, the organization of the site. . . . The historical concept of placing sculpture on a pedestal was to establish a separation between the sculpture and the viewer. I am interested in a behavioral space in which the viewer interacts with the sculpture in its context. . . . Space becomes the sum of successive perceptions of the place. The viewer becomes the subject. [Richard Serra, "Selected Statements Arguing in Support of *Tilted Arc,*" in *Richard Serra's Tilted Arc,* ed. Clara Weyergraf-Serra and Martha Buskirk (Eindhoven, 1988), pp. 64-65]

2. For the court's affirmation of the government's proprietary rights, see *Serra v. United States General Services Administration* 847 F.2d 1045, 1051 (2d Cir. 1988); reprt. in *Richard Serra's Tilted Arc,*" pp. 259-68. The court's position turns in part on an understanding of the contract for *Tilted Arc*'s commission. For additional information on this contract, see Serra, "Selected Statements Arguing in Support of *Tilted Arc,*" p. 66. The inadequacies of the GSA's contract are detailed in Barbara Hoffman's complete legal analysis of the case, *"Tilted Arc:* The Legal Angle," in *Public Art, Public Controversy: The "Tilted Arc" on Trial,* ed. Sherrill Jordan et. al (New York, 1987), pp. 35-37. For a history of the GSA's Art-in-Architecture Program, see Judith H. Balfe and Margaret J. Wyszomirski, "The Commissioning of a Work of Public Sculpture," in *Public Art, Public Controversy,* pp. 18-27. See also "General Services Administration Factsheet Concerning the Art-in-Architecture Program for Federal Programs," in *Richard Serra's "Tilted Arc,"* pp. 21-22.

3. "Brief Filed by the Defendants, United States Court of Appeals for the Second Circuit, January 26, 1988 (edited)," in *Richard Serra's "Tilted Arc,"* p. 253.

4. Although this section appeared in the original version of Kennedy's bill, the current version provides for a study of resale royalties.

5. In October 1988 both the United States Senate and the House of Representatives passed the Berne Convention Implementation Act of 1988 (P. L. 100-568), which made the necessary changes in the United States copyright law (17 USC §§ 101-914 [1978]) for adherence to the Berne Convention. On 20 October 1988, the Berne Convention was ratified, and on 31 October 1988 President Reagan signed into law the copyright amendments, making the United States the seventy-eighth member of the Convention.

6. The moral rights provision of the Berne Convention states:
Article 6bis.

(1) Independently of the author's economic rights, and even after the transfer of the said rights, the author shall have the right to claim authorship of the work and to object to any distortion, mutilation or other modification of, or other derogatory action in relation to, the said work, which would be prejudicial to his honor or reputation.

(2) The rights granted to the author in accordance with the preceding paragraph shall, after his death, be maintained, at least until the expiry of the economic rights. . . .

(3) The means of redress for safeguarding the rights granted by this Article shall be governed by the legislation of the country where protection is claimed.

This section of the Berne Convention was ratified by Congress in this fashion: "The provisions of the Berne Convention, the adherence of the United States thereto, and satisfaction of the United States obligations thereunder, do not expand or reduce any right of an author of a work, whether claimed under Federal, State, or the common law--(1) to claim authorship of the work; or (2) to object to any distortion, mutilation, or other modification of, or other derogatory action in relation to, the work, that would prejudice the author's honor or reputation." [P. L. 100-568, § 3]

7. See "Appeal Filed by Richard Serra in the United States Court of Appeals for the Second Circuit, December 15, 1987," in *Richard Serra's "Tilted Arc,"* pp. 225-50. For example, counsel drew an analogy to *Board of Education, Island Trees Union Free School District v. Pico* (1982), which held that library books could not be removed simply because the board disliked the content of the texts (ibid., pp. 243-45).

8. *Serra v. United States General Services Administration,* in *Richard Serra's "Tilted Arc,"* p. 266.

9. Hilton Kramer, "Is Art Above the Laws of Decency?" *The New York Times,* 2 July 1989, sec. 2; hereafter abbreviated "A."

10. Patrick Buchanan, "Losing the War for America's Culture?" *Washington Times,* 22, May 1989, sec. D.

11. Joseph Goebbels to Wilhelm Furtwangler, 11 Apr. 1933, in Hildegard Brenner, *Die Kunstpolitik des Nationalsozialismus* (Hamburg, 1963), pp. 178-79; my translation.

12. 135 Cong. Rec., 101st Cong., 1st sess., 29 Sept. 1989, S12210.

13. Ibid., S12211.

14. *Miller v. California,* 413 U.S. 15 (1973).

15. Ibid.

16. Grace Glueck, "A Congressman Confronts a Hostile Art World," *The New York Times,* 16 Sept. 1989.

Protected Space:
Politics, Censorship, and the Arts

Mary Devereaux

Anniversaries are appropriate times for reflection. On this, the 50th anniversary of the American Society for Aesthetics, I want to explore a complicated and confusing situation currently facing Anglo-American aesthetics. Works of art were once esteemed as objects of beauty.[1] In the past several years, however, artists have been accused of encouraging teenage suicide, urban rage, violence against women, and poisoning American culture. Museum directors have been indicted on obscenity charges, and artists and organizations receiving federal grants have been required to sign pledges that they will not promote, disseminate, or produce materials that may be considered obscene. Today in America, as in other times and places, artists face demands for their art to conform to religious and moral criteria. These demands are not new, but they challenge the view that artistic expression falls under the protection of speech guaranteed by the First Amendment.[2]

Also in the past several years, aestheticians have had to face a theoretical assault on the division between art and politics. That division is sacrosanct to the formalist aesthetics that has largely dominated the ASA since its founding. Now, the idea of aesthetic autonomy, so dear to professional aestheticians, has itself come under attack.

Mary Devereaux's article first appeared in the *Journal of Aesthetics and Art Criticism* 51 (2), Spring 1993, pp. 207-215. It is reprinted here by permission of the publisher, the American Society for Aesthetics, and the author.

We can begin to bring some order to these chaotic and disturbing events if we cast them in terms of two debates. The first is taking place in the "real world" of politics and art, outside professional aesthetics. It centers on the role the National Endowment for the Arts (NEA) plays in providing federally financed support for the arts. The second debate is taking place within the profession of aesthetics. It centers on a specifically philosophical issue, namely, the adequacy—even feasibility—of an aesthetics built around the idea of art's autonomy.

The two debates might at first appear to be completely unconnected. One takes place in the world of politics outside the academy, the other within it; moreover, whereas the NEA debate appears to be concerned with wholly practical matters such as the allocation of tax dollars and the role of government in supporting the arts, the autonomy debate is primarily philosophical and theoretical in character. But in fact, the two debates are connected. Both are concerned with the issues of art, politics, and autonomy. And both present us with a choice between the same unattractive alternatives: either we embrace the political character of art and risk subjecting art and artists to political interference, or we protect art and its makers from political interference by insisting upon their "autonomy," but at the cost of denying the political character of art and its broader connection with life. If we are ever to get beyond these stale alternatives—both of which require the sacrifice of something essential to the understanding of art—we must look closely at what is meant by the autonomy of art.[3]

Suggesting that we reconsider the autonomy of art may make it sound as if I plan to take the standard liberal line against the politicization of the art world. I don't. I want to argue, on the contrary, that political art—the work of Hans Haacke, Barbara Kruger, Judy Chicago, Faith Ringgold, Vito Acconci, Scott Tyler, David Hammonds, and others—is important, both for political reasons and for artistic ones. But, whether or not one agrees with this judgment, political art is at the center of what is happening in contemporary art. Thus, I will demonstrate, it is increasingly important to understand the challenge that political art presents to aesthetic theories which analyze art in primarily nonpolitical terms.

I will show that the current situation in the arts can be understood in terms of the two debates I have mentioned. In Section I, I lay out the issues that divide the opposing camps. In Section II, I aim to do two things: first, to show in detail where the two debates intersect and, second, to show that they pose a common problem. Having explained what this common problem is, I then conclude, in Section III, by suggesting the direction we must move if we are to solve this problem.

I

Turning first to the real world, I want to begin by observing that concerns about art have, in recent years, come to the center of political debate in questions about the value and limits of freedom of expression, the role of government in the enforcement of morals, the function of art, and the direction of public arts policy. The NEA controversy came to public attention in 1989 when questions were raised over the funding of Robert Mapplethorpe's homoerotic photographs of a gay subculture and his innocent but sexually candid portraits of children, and Andreas Serrano's *Piss Christ,* a photograph of a crucifix submerged in urine. However, concern over what kind of art the government was funding emerged as early as 1972 when then first-term Senator Jesse Helms objected to NEA support for Erica Jong's "obscene book," *Fear of Flying.*[4] These and subsequent demands for restricting the content of federally financed art stand opposed to the "climate encouraging freedom of thought, imagination, and inquiry" called for by the 1965 legislation creating the NEA.[5]

The NEA's conservative opponents are, of course, primarily concerned with art as a vehicle of moral and social education. Their understanding of "good art" has less to do with artistic value than with "decency" and the promotion of a certain (largely Christian fundamentalist) conception of ethical life. From this perspective, modern art reflects the spiritual degeneracy of 20th century America. On the other side of the debate, naturally enough, are artists (concerned with protecting their work from interference), civil libertarians and "classic" liberals (concerned with First Amendment issues and the freedom of expression), gay rights advocates (concerned with the civil rights of homosexuals), and traditional aestheticians (concerned with defending the formalist division between art and politics).

Art has emerged as an important political issue not only for these groups, but also for the general public. That it has is striking especially in light of the common view that art really "doesn't matter." The continuing public debate, charted in editorials and "letters to the editor" from *The Washington Post* to the *Cincinnati Enquirer,* demonstrates quite unexpectedly that art *does* matter. It matters not only to artists and museum directors, but also to record store owners, politicians, and "ordinary taxpayers"—even perhaps to policemen.

How art matters is less clear. To some, art matters because it is—or they take it to be—of irredeemable value. To others, art matters because it is—or they take it to be—pernicious, something we must guard against and control. Furthermore, art has become a litmus test of beliefs about sexuality, public decency, obscenity, and the limits of tolerance. It has also become a battleground on which competing groups fight to define (or redefine) America's view of itself as a nation.

In brief, the political battle over art is interesting because of its suddenness and depth. It is also interesting because behind the clamor about when art is obscene and whether it merits public funding lies what amounts to a *philosophical* discussion about the nature of art. I suggest that the real world battles fought over the photographs of Robert Mapplethorpe, performance art, and political art in general are actually driven by a theoretical conflict between two opposing conceptions of art. According to the now familiar, modern conception, art is intrinsically valuable, deserving of a separate "autonomous" sphere within which artists can be guaranteed protection from government and other forms of outside interference. Aestheticians will readily associate this position with Kant, 20th century modernism, and formalist theories of art.

According to a second, more traditional conception, the value of art is inextricably linked to political considerations. Thus, for example, art cannot be evaluated apart from considerations of its ideology and social value. In one version of this political conception of art. if a work offends the state, the state may—indeed should—control or suppress it. This offense may take different forms, so, for example, a work may be censored because it is seen as socially disturbing or frivolous even if not politically threatening. The view that such offenses warrant restriction is a position associated with the Plato of *The Republic* and with Marxist theories of art.[6]

The theoretical discussion underlying the NEA controversy thus concerns a conflict between political and nonpolitical conceptions of art. On the one hand, a formalist conception of art does not allow art to be seen politically; on the other hand, political conceptions of art require that it must be.

Now, admittedly, this is a complex debate and, like most frameworks, the one I'm introducing here is somewhat artificial. For one thing, so-called nonpolitical conceptions of art may themselves rely upon political assumptions and have political implications. (This charge has been made repeatedly, for example, with respect to formalism.) So, obviously, there is a question here concerning just how nonpolitical "nonpolitical" conceptions of art are. And, of course, there are participants in the NEA debate who do not espouse simply one or another of these views. The advantage of setting things up in this way is that it makes the main lines of debate visible.

Alternatively, someone might object that, by framing current art world controversies as a struggle between two underlying conceptions of art, I make the debate appear overly theoretical. This is not my intent. Clearly, the outcome of the battle over political and nonpolitical conceptions of art has real consequences for artists and the art world generally.[7] Let's consider what these consequences are.

In the wake of anger over public funding for work by Mapplethorpe and Serrano, Helms convinced Congress to pass legislation that threatened artists with loss of support for work deemed obscene or indecent. "Obscene" or "indecent," according to the Helms Amendment, meant depictions of sexual activity, material deemed homoerotic, material that denigrated the objects or adherents of a particular religion, and other offenses which, if committed, would result in the artist's loss of funding. As was widely reported, this amendment was ruled unconstitutional by a federal court in January 1991, further legal restrictions on art have also been strongly opposed by civil libertarians and many members of the arts community. What effect, then, aside from increasing vocal opposition to certain forms of art, have Helms' efforts had on artists? Should we simply dismiss Helms as a hypersensitive, but harmless, critic of contemporary art?

The answer, I think, must be "no." Although Congressional restrictions on federally funded art have not withstood judicial scrutiny, Helms and his supporters have nevertheless managed to control the funding process through other, more subtle means, e.g., partisan appointments to the NEA directorship and boards. They have also succeeded in creating a *climate* in which artists and those who exhibit, publish, and sell art feel threatened in ways having little to do with the availability of public funding. Thus, to give two examples, an obscenity complaint was brought against artist Richard Bolton for his exhibition

The Emperor's New Clothes: Censorship, Sexuality, and the Body Politic, and the Boston television station WGBH was investigated by the FCC for broadcasting certain Mapplethorpe photographs on its Ten O'clock News program.[8] In neither of these cases were federal tax dollars at issue.

The increasing public suspicion of, and perhaps even hostility toward, art centers on the moral rather than artistic failings of contemporary art. So, in the Mapplethorpe controversy, public outrage centered not on the question of artistic value (that question being largely left to art world "experts") but on whether the funded art was obscene (the assumption being that obscene art can't have been worth the money the taxpayers "paid for it").

A related sign of the threatening climate toward art is the growing number of court cases directed at artists, museum directors, and commercial distributors of art. Recent court cases have targeted not only the authors of "offensive" opinions such as Ice T, the author of "Cop Killer," but also those who display and sell such material. Thus, Charles Freeman, a Florida record store owner, was charged and convicted for selling the music of the rap group, 2 Live Crew. Art has even come under attack for its so-called "subliminal message," as in the suit brought by parents of an adolescent suicide against the heavy metal band, Judas Priest. The band's repeated lyric "do it," they alleged, was responsible for their son's decision to end his life.[9]

The result of such cases is to discourage and penalize certain forms of art: art dealing with sexuality (especially gay or lesbian sexuality); explicitly political art; offensive, obscene, or irreligious art, and so on. As one observer of the Endowment noted, what we are seeing is a "very real attempt by conservatives to stop certain kinds of art dead in its tracks."[10] What I am suggesting is that such efforts now extend far beyond the Endowment and the arena of public funding. The effort to penalize those who make, distribute, or promote difficult or disturbing art has now broadened to include privately funded art, such as the Bolton exhibit mentioned above, and commercial work, such as the music of 2 Live Crew and Ice T.

One thing, then, about the present political situation is clear. Artists can no longer rely on the indulgence of a public convinced that art and artistic autonomy are worth protecting at all costs. Nor can they assume that works that challenge the status quo will have a chance at even the modest support offered by the NEA or at winning public exhibition. Of course, from the standpoint of the history of art, guarantees that art will be protected or funded are a relatively recent phenomenon. No government needs to have publicly funded arts programs. But, once such programs are in place, the demand that artists meet content restrictions is arguably a form of censorship. In the present climate, the financial, artistic, and personal costs of using certain words, representing certain body parts, or advocating certain beliefs effectively threaten to relegate whole bodies of opinion to silence.

Let's step back for a moment. So far, Helms and his opponents appear to be simply replaying an old debate between the perceived needs of the republic and the demands of art. Seen in these terms, Mapplethorpe and his photographs offended Senator Helms and members of Congress by seeming to promote homoeroticism, sadomasochism, and the sexual exploitation of children. Mapplethorpe's opponents argued that the acts these photographs depict, and the values they endorse, have a negative effect on individual conscience and the quality of public life.[11] In response to this perceived threat, Helms attempted to use the power of the state and the political force of outraged taxpayers to bring the NEA (and indirectly, artists concerned with these or related issues) in line with the conservative values of the political party in office. This aspect of the current situation makes it natural to associate a political conception of art with those on the political right. While not wrong, this association can be misleading. Although art *is* under attack from the right in the NEA controversy, the situation is more complicated.

Elsewhere in the public arena, art is also under attack from the left, that is, from feminists and progressive social theorists generally. Here the claim is not that art is "obscene," or "indecent," but that it is misogynist, racist, violent, or exclusionary. Thus those on both the right and the left of the present political spectrum may be seen to link art inextricably to political considerations. A "political conception of art" thus defines a generic conception of art held by people who (may) possess opposing political beliefs.

Both conservatives and radical feminists—odd bedfellows though they may be—have advocated restrictions on certain kinds of art. And both have political agendas they wish to see reflected in the reading lists of literature courses and the criteria used to fund public art. Of course, the first-order political views of Jesse Helms and Catharine

MacKinnon are different. And this first-order difference is obviously important. But, the point I'm trying to make here is that, despite their first-order disagreement with Helms, many feminists agree with him about the second-order point concerning the relevance of political considerations to the evaluation of art. That is, they *agree* with Helms in holding that it is appropriate to judge art by *political* standards.

I want now to turn to the second debate, the debate within aesthetics over the autonomy of art. As an academic discipline, aesthetics is witnessing a growing challenge to the old notion that art is, or should be, independent of politics. The separation of the aesthetic from other values—moral and religious as well as political—has, since Kant, largely defined the discipline of aesthetics. At least within the Anglo-American philosophical tradition, aesthetics has come to mean "autonomous aesthetics."

It is this traditional autonomous aesthetics that is under attack, largely by feminist theorists advancing a political conception of art.[12] From a feminist perspective, the charge against traditional aesthetics is that it (a) isolates art from the contextual and historical factors that, in this view, its proper understanding requires; (b) confuses the interests of particular groups (mainly the interests of male property owners of European descent) with universal human interests, wrongly attributing universality to partisan artwork; and (c) disguises standards of evaluation, which are implicitly if not explicitly committed to existing power relations, as "purely aesthetic."

In adopting a politics of art, feminist theorists confront traditional aesthetics head-on.[13] First, in place of an autonomous but isolated art, they substitute a conception of art rooted in life, rooted, for example, in social movements and immediate cultural concerns. Thought of in these terms, art moves from a separate, protected realm to the everyday world of social and political praxis. It gains a history that transcends the bounds of art history, as they have been traditionally understood. Second, feminist theorists challenge art's claim to speak for all of us. Traditional aesthetics may be right that art speaks for "mankind," but, as feminist critics point out, mankind includes only some of us. To question art's autonomy and universality need not imply that art lacks value—quite the contrary—but this questioning may yield answers that differ from what we once supposed. Lastly, having sought to show that "purely aesthetic" standards of evaluation are not politically neutral, feminist theorists urge a third proposal. They ask that we rethink our relationship to established artistic traditions in terms that do not assume such traditions are uniformly enlightening and liberating.

In summary, aesthetics within the academy finds itself embroiled in a debate between two main camps: feminist theorists advocating a political conception of art and traditional aestheticians defending a non-political, basically formalist, conception of art.

II

If we stand back from this somewhat rarefied philosophical debate, we can see that it mirrors in interesting respects, the grittier NEA debate. For at the heart of the debate between traditional aestheticians and feminists lie the same three issues—art, politics, and autonomy—that underlie the conflict between Helms and his opponents. In both cases, the conflict centers on the nature and function of art.

These debates have more in common than a shared set of issues. They also share a common situation: the intrusion of politics into what were formerly believed to be "apolitical" arenas. In both the arena of Helmsian-inspired debate and the academy, American aesthetics and its practitioners face the erosion of the line dividing art from politics. On both fronts, politics has intruded into what were once "purely aesthetic" deliberations. To be sure, political considerations have always played a role, however inadvertent or unacknowledged, in the deliberations of the art world. But what we have now, at least with feminist theorists, is the overt assertion that the role politics plays in aesthetic deliberations is necessary and desirable.

Within the academy, and to some extent in the culture at large, what we are seeing is evidence of a change from the prevailing non-political conception of art to a political one. The growing recognition of art's political dimensions (and the corresponding shift to a more political conception of art) is the result of the interplay of many factors. Dissatisfaction with the limits of formalist art criticism, the growth of interest in more broadly cultural approaches to art, the end of the dominance of analytic philosophy, the influence of postmodernism, and most especially, the impact of feminism—both as a social movement and as a theoretical discipline—have all shaken the conviction of mainstream analytic aestheticians that political considerations have nothing to do with art. Those who remain committed to the separation of the artistic and the political, and the theory of aesthetic autonomy which demands it, now find themselves called upon to defend what they could once assume with little or no argument.

What are we to make of this transformation? The most welcome feature of adopting a political conception of art is in broadening the framework in which art is discussed and evaluated. Expanding this framework has had several positive consequences. The first is that it immeasurably enriches our understanding of representation, the pleasures and powers of art, and aesthetic experience.

A second, related consequence of adopting a political approach to art is the increased potential for art to arouse controversy and engage widespread public interest. As a result of the NEA controversy, the museums were packed—many of the people who were there, were there for the first time.[14] Of course, not everyone who came to see this work came out of "pure," i.e., aesthetic, motives. Yet even those who came to gape, leer, or express moral outrage found themselves face-to-face with questions about whether *anything* is a legitimate subject for art and whether publicly funded art should have limits that are not imposed on art in general.

Lastly, the sudden infusion of politics into discussions of art has initiated important reflection at the level of public policy. Questions about the role of art in a democratic and pluralistic social order, the value of "public art," and the responsibility of the artist, once funded, to render his or her creative expression intelligible, and to whom, are now engaging participants on all sides of the NEA controversy.[15] Quite unintentionally, Helms' efforts to bring art into line with conservative values—again, like feminist attempts to bring art criticism into line with "progressive" values—have brought to public attention issues which lie at the root of thinking about artists and their role in society.

If, therefore, one function of art is to broach issues, to force us to look at ourselves and to ask deep questions, we might conclude that the intrusion of politics into the art world has been beneficial—reinvigorating and broadening interest in the arts as well as provoking reflection on what role the arts play in our individual and communal lives.

In the academy, too, the growing acceptance of a political conception of art has resulted in welcome changes. The merging of art and politics evident in feminist theory provides an attractive alternative to the formalism of traditional aesthetics. As a wide variety of critics of formalism have successfully argued, the exclusion of political or any considerations other than narrowly formal ones leaves us ill-equipped to understand or explain the kinds of issues posed by contemporary works such as Judy Chicago's *Dinner Party* or Mapplethorpe's *X Portfolio.* These works and countless others—Marion Rigg's documentary film about gay black men, *Tongues Untied,* Karen Finley's angry performance pieces—are themselves part of a political debate, partly fueled by arguments about the NEA and driven by powerful questions about homosexuality and homophobia, reproductive choice and women's issues, AIDS and the politics of AIDS. These works can't be understood—can't be understood as the works of art they are—in terms of the critical preoccupations of Modernism, i.e., in terms of formal values. But then, neither can much of art. The arguments against approaching Duchamp's *Fountain* or most of the history of art prior to this century in these terms are too well-known to need repeating. What we need and what we get, once political considerations are allowed to play a role in the discussion of art, is a way of recognizing the tensions between aesthetic responses and a whole range of complicated human responses: sexual or erotic, emotional, religious, moral, or political.

Thus, within the academy, as outside it, the shift from a nonpolitical to a political conception of art has resulted in a more complex and nuanced understanding of the various purposes and functions of art, and the complex emotions it is capable of arousing. For these as well as other reasons, the appearance of a viable alternative to formalism is a welcome occurrence.

Less welcome, however, are certain other features of this shift. As we have seen, one characteristic of a political conception of art is a blurring of the distinction between strictly artistic issues and political ones. In blurring this distinction, a political conception of art poses two risks, neither of which arise with formalism.

The first risk is that in emphasizing the political character of art we lose sight of or underestimate the many "nonpolitical" elements that make art art. It would be difficult, if not impossible, to give a definitive list of these "art-making" elements, but the general idea is familiar enough. One wants to be able to talk about stylistic or formal features, not only "what the work says," but "how." The worry is that in abandoning the separation of art and politics, we reduce art to propaganda.

The second risk posed by a political conception of art is that art may be exposed to various forms of political interference. The worry here is that once art is thought of, and evaluated, in political terms, it loses its independence. In discussing the risks of political interference in the arts, it is government interference that often comes first to mind. Equating "political interference" with government interference uses "political" in its strict sense. A second threat to art's independence involves political interference more broadly understood—what Mill calls the "tyranny of the majority." Like government action, this sort of activity is designed to restrict or suppress art of certain kinds—art that is obscene, indecent, unpatriotic, racist, misogynist, and so on. Consumer boycotts, like the one implemented by police organizations against Ice T's anti-police lyrics, fall into this category.

Thus, while bringing art to public attention and integrating it more closely with life, a political conception of art risks making artists and their works dependent on popular opinion and the whims of political fashion. Traditionally, artists and their supporters have responded to government-enforced "standards of decency" and other forms of political interference by appealing to a principle of aesthetic autonomy. It is this autonomy, they argue, that makes such interference illegitimate.[16] The irony of the current situation is that just when artists find themselves most in need of the protection that appeals to autonomy traditionally provided, art theorists are struggling to discredit the very idea of aesthetic autonomy.

I do not mean to imply that advocates of a political conception of art—feminist or otherwise—are responsible for the current plight of artists. Nor do I mean to imply that individual theorists intend to align themselves with Helms' political agenda. But I am suggesting that in attacking the idea of aesthetic autonomy, feminists are attacking a conception of art that provided certain principles to which artists and their supporters could appeal when forced to defend themselves against government-enforced "standards of decency" and the tyranny of public opinion. Hence, abandoning autonomy has important practical consequences—consequences its critics have not clearly thought out.

Aesthetics thus faces a double dilemma. At the level of theory and criticism, we seem forced either to recognize art's political character and sacrifice its specifically artistic character or to recognize its specifically artistic character and ignore the political. At a more practical level, we seem forced to choose between a formalist conception of art which protects art from the exigencies of changing political fashion but isolates art from life, and various political conceptions of art which integrate art with life but sacrifice its autonomy.

This dilemma appears insoluble, for what we want is to combine two apparently incompatible things: the recognition of the political character of art and the recognition of its artistic character. And we also want to separate two apparently inseparable things: the autonomy of art and formalism. This dilemma is, as I have been suggesting, at the heart of current aesthetic concerns.

I want to conclude by arguing that this dilemma turns on a misunderstanding—a misunderstanding of what autonomy demands. This misunderstanding is shared by both traditional aestheticians and many feminists.

III

In this final section, I want to clarify this misunderstanding by offering what I take to be a correct account of aesthetic autonomy. At its core, the autonomy of art refers to the idea that art deserves a protected space. By "protected space," I don't mean the obvious safeguards needed to preserve artworks from vandals and the overly curious, such as railings, velvet ropes, and alarm systems. Nor do I mean a domain cut off from the social and political world. If we interpret autonomy as a demand for an "apolitical" or otherwise disengaged art we would be right to reject it.

By "protected space" I mean the principle of granting artists control over both their subject matter and means of expression. It is this figurative space, that is, the space in which artists can work without outside interference, which the literal spaces of the museum and gallery concretely embody. Historically speaking, the idea that artists deserve such control is recent; the separation of artistic institutions from institutions of church and state did not occur until the eighteenth century and then primarily in Europe.[17] In the past, artists were not granted independence. What, then, explains the modern view that artists deserve independence? What is the basis of the idea that this independence ought to be protected?

One source of this idea, of course, is the liberal democratic conception of individual liberty whereby artists, like everyone else, have a right to individual expression. It is this concept of individual expression that is embedded in the American Constitution. So artistic liberty *can* be protected by appealing to Constitutional guarantees. Here the independence of art is simply a consequence of Constitutional protections of free speech. An appeal to the First Amendment does not, however, distinguish art from any other form of expression. It thus cannot explain the idea that artists deserve *special* protections. The demand for special protections rests on the intuition that art is not just any kind of expression—in burning all the existing copies of *The Grapes of Wrath* we lose more than just Steinbeck's opinions.

In seeking an explanation for the idea that artists deserve *special* protections, we might do better to look to a concept of genius that has its roots in Kant, namely, the view that artists possess an inborn imaginative talent that enables them to "see" in ways others cannot. In this conception, the genius has a natural capacity for originality, i.e., for breaking with tradition and making his or her own rules. Romantic tradition comes to understand artistic vision as transcending ordinary experience or penetrating beneath it to a realm deeper or more primordial than ordinary reality. The artist becomes a god-like visionary, or even a "mad genius," who is due extraordinary indulgence. From this problematic perspective, the talents of Gauguin or van Gogh exempt them from the normal demands of family life or social responsibility.

Basing the argument for the special protection of art on the madness of the artist is vulnerable to the objection that such "madness" deserves not more liberty, but less. However, the argument for special protection needs only the assumption that artists possess talent and training that make them capable of showing us what we might not otherwise see or see clearly. This is *a* conception of genius, but it is a modest and, indeed, a familiar one.

Artists may not be the only people who can do these things. But if we accept that artists *are* specially equipped—technically and imaginatively—to help us see things, then they naturally have a special social role to play. They can function as critics, reformers, revolutionaries—or even, as defenders of unappreciated aspects of the status quo. Historically, of course, artists have often served these functions.

Seen in this way, art has a high social value. It makes us think twice, think differently, relive the past, imagine the future. It is this social value, not the mad genius of its makers, that warrants protection, according to the principle of autonomy. In allowing art the independence to function in these ways, we seek to protect a political good.

What does it mean to grant the principle of the autonomy of art? And what are the consequences of doing so? Well, one thing it means is that, where artistic and government interests conflict, the presumption should be in favor of the artist. The autonomy of art, properly understood, takes this principle as fundamental. But it is not absolute. You can have yourself shot and wounded in the service of art, as Chris Burden did in a performance piece entitled *Shoot,* but you can't expect the government to sit still while you have someone else shot. The point of advocating autonomy is not, as Helms and his supporters have charged, to grant artists absolute license, but rather to make it clear that in cases of conflict, the presumption should be in favor of the artist.

One important consequence of granting the principle of the autonomy of art is that we cannot demand that the government impose our own partisan agendas with respect to art. Thus, we cannot consistently endorse autonomy and also pass legislation requiring that publicly funded art promote conservative family values. Nor could we endorse laws prohibiting phallocentric works of art.

So far, there is little in this account of autonomy to which traditional aestheticians would object. But what of the feminist objection that adopting autonomy commits us to a non-political conception of art? Doesn't autonomy go hand in hand with formalism? I want to end by suggesting that the principle of the autonomy of art, properly understood, does *not* commit us to formalism. Of course, autonomy does not *preclude* formalism; it does not, however, *require* it. One can both insist on the importance of a protected space for art *and* maintain that an apolitical, disengaged art is undesirable. There is no inconsistency here. Indeed, one good reason for endorsing the principle of autonomy is precisely *because* one thinks art has a political function, i.e., because one thinks the kind of independent, critical voice art often provides is worth protecting. Thus, a political conception of art need not leave art unprotected against political interference.

Nor, I might add, does commitment to a political conception of art require that criticism become solely the assessment of the ideological import of art. One can allow that art has political content and that its content is important in discussing and evaluating it without giving *priority* to political considerations, as Helms does in dismissing artistic questions in favor of judgments about decency.

Politics does have an explicit role to play in evaluating art. But we need not determine the political value of art *simply* by the content of the work. In ignoring not only Mapplethorpe's style, but also the interrelationships between his photographs and the context in which they appeared, Helms parts ways with both formalism and the far more sophisticated politics of art advanced by feminist critics like Linda Nochlin, Lucy Lippard, Rita Felski, and others.[18] Their work demonstrates how political criticism can take stylistic innovation and the changing meaning of textual forms into account.

In valuing creativity and the stylistic values of art, these feminist theorists are closer to traditional aesthetics than one might initially suppose. This is not to say that political conceptions of art run no risk of reducing criticism to politics. But it is to say that we now have examples of sophisticated feminist criticism that point in the direction of a politics of art that is not reductionistic.

In sum, I have argued, we need not accept the narrow critical constraints of formalism in order to guarantee artistic liberty. The autonomy of art, properly understood, does not *require* formalism. We can banish formalism and still protect art and artists from political interference. And given that we can, we should.[19]

Notes

1. The idea that art reflects nature at its best and most perfect is prevalent among the Greeks and during the Renaissance. I am not claiming that art has been regarded as an object of beauty throughout the history of art. My aim here is simply to draw a broad contrast between the current suspicion of art and the veneration of art typical of periods such as the Renaissance.

2. For the judicial opinion that obscenity law exempts the classics and works of art, see The United States of America vs. Samuel Roth, The U.S. Court of Appeals, Second Circuit, reprinted in *Pornography and Censorship,* eds. David Copp and Susan Wendell (Buffalo: Prometheus Books, 1983): 343-344.

3. See my "The Philosophical and Political Implications of the Feminist Critique of Aesthetic Autonomy," in *"Turning the Century": Feminist Theory in the 1990s,* ed. Glynis Carr, *Bucknell Review* 36 (1992): 164-186.

4. *Culture Wars: Documents from the Recent Controversies in the Arts,* ed. Richard Bolton (New York: New Press, 1992), p. 333.

5. Bolton, *Culture Wars,* p. 332.

6. Whether we should attribute to Plato himself the desire to banish the poets raises complex questions of interpretation. See, for example, Julius A. Elias, *Plato's Defense of Poetry* (State University of New York Press, 1984).

7. Here and throughout my discussion, I am using the term "artist" generically, to include writers, musicians, filmmakers, and dancers, as well as painters and sculptors.

8. Bolton, *Culture Wars,* p. 359.

9. Those who object that "Cop Killer" or "As Nasty As I Wanna Be" aren't art simply confuse the classificatory use of the term "art" with its evaluative use. "Cop Killer" is provocative, outrageous, entertaining, and moving. It's a good song; the music of 2 Live Crew is junk. In any case, nothing in my argument rests on classifying heavy metal or rap music as art since, at this point in the paper, I am claiming only that "commercial art" is also under attack. Part of the problem with formalist theories of art is that they make it difficult to see what makes a song like "Cop Killer" good art.

10. Christopher Belden, "Letters to the Editor," *The New York Times* (Aug. 16, 1992).

11. For a version of the argument that Mapplethorpe's art threatens the body politic, see the editorial "Body Politics," *Commonweal* CXVII, no. 19 (Nov. 9, 1990).

12. Devereaux, "Autonomy," pp. 173 ff.

13. Here I draw on analysis developed in my earlier essay, "Oppressive Texts, Resisting Readers, and the Gendered Spectator, the 'New' Aesthetics," *The Journal of Aesthetics and Art Criticism* 48 (1990): 337-347.

14. How many people would have seen Mapplethorpe's *X Portfolio* or a performance by Karen Finley were it not for Helms' well publicized objections to this art? This is the irony of Helms' campaign.

15. Rachel Newton Bellow, "What artists want," in *Deciding What to Do. An Occasional Paper of The Center For Effective Philanthropy* (Dec. 1986). It was condensed and revised from "The Needs of the Individual Creative Artist, A White Paper," prepared for the American Council for the Arts (Jan. 1985).

16. One can also, as in the case of 2 Live Crew, defend art on traditional, liberal, democratic grounds. Here the appeal is to Constitutional protections of free speech.

17. For an analysis of how artistic practice emancipated itself from religious and ritual practice, see Lydia Goehr, *The Imaginary Museum of Musical Works: An Essay in the Philosophy of Music* (Oxford: Clarendon, 1992).

18. See Linda Nochlin, *Women, Art, and Power and other Essays*, (New York: Harper & Row, 1988); Rita Felski, *Beyond Feminist Aesthetics: Feminist Literature and Social Change* (Harvard University Press, 1991); Lucy Lippard, *Mixed Blessings: New Art in a Multicultural American* (New York: Pantheon, 1990).

19. For helpful comments and criticism, I thank Michael Hardimon, Catherine Blair, Deborah Lefkowitz, and the copy editor for this special issue.

Aesthetic Censorship:
Censoring Art for Art's Sake

Richard Shusterman

Artists and art lovers have always been among the most frequent and fervent opponents of censorship, and a dominant theme in their support of freedom of expression is, of course, its crucial importance for art. Art's quarrel with censorship seems as old as its ancient quarrel with philosophy; and ever since Plato's proposal to ban mimetic art for its moral and epistemological evils, the champions of art have tried to protect art's freedom and right to exist. Originally, art's apologists tried to refute or extenuate the moral and epistemological censure of art by stressing its cathartic and didactic value. But as art's status grew stronger, the claim was pressed for art's complete autonomy and for total freedom of expression, which its creative nature allegedly requires. Romanticism decried anything that would restrain the imagination of aesthetic genius, and aestheticism deplored any outside interference in the free and pure pursuit of "art for art's sake." Even throughout the twentieth century, artists in both East and West have had to denounce and struggle with the censor. It is therefore generally accepted that censorship is not merely an ancient bogeyman of art's infancy, but a principle which is fundamentally and quintessentially inimical and harmful to art, and antithetical to aesthetic autonomy.

Such a view, I think, is mistaken and stems from an oversimplified notion of censorship and its possible forms and motives.

Richard Shusterman's article first appeared in the *Journal of Aesthetics and Art Criticism* 43 (2), Winter 1984, pp. 171-180. It is reprinted here by permission of the publisher, the American Society for Aesthetics, and the author.

In this paper I shall argue that acceptance of the autonomy of art does not entail the rejection of censorship, and further, that aesthetic censorship could be more beneficial than harmful to art.

I introduce the expression "aesthetic censorship" advisedly, and not in the merely elliptical sense of censorship of aesthetic material, because I wish to maintain that censorship can be aesthetic in the sense of serving aesthetic ends. We are apt to identify censorship, especially in the context of art, with moral censorship. But obviously there are other kinds, e.g., political and military. Indeed, the dictionary sanctions an open list of kinds of censorship, defining the censor as suppressing what is "objectionable on moral, political, military or other grounds."[1] Among those other grounds for censorship can there not be aesthetic ones? For surely things may be aesthetically objectionable. If so, aesthetic censorship is not a meaningless, self-contradictory notion, and we should not be shocked to find an aesthetic censor in the art world or "Republic of Art" lately so often envisaged and discussed.[2]

However, having meaning does not entail having justification; and perhaps aesthetic censorship, if it existed, would merely be one of the Republic's evils. Certainly some critics of the institutional theories of art raise the objection that institutionality threatens art's freedom and creativity, any restraint of which is allegedly pernicious to art.[3] (But it is important to note here that institutional theories of art have only recently emerged when extreme artistic liberties have much more frequently been taken, and that, moreover, such theories typically base themselves on and endorse these radical innovations or liberties of artistic expression.)

In any case, similar objections concerning freedom and creativity would undoubtedly be raised with greater force at the notion of aesthetic censorship, and we shall have to consider them in assessing the case for such censorship. But first we should try to get a better idea of what aesthetic censorship might be. For though the notion does not seem meaningless through self-contradiction, its having meaning is no proof of its actual practice. Indeed, it would seem that there are no actual practices or actions which we would naturally label or give as an example of aesthetic censorship. However, we can (and should) at least make some clarificatory remarks about the concept of censorship itself, which is far from clear, and suggest some actual cases that may be on the margins of aesthetic censorship and perhaps may shed some light on this notion and its likely effects on the welfare of art and art appreciation.

II

Censorship can be narrowly construed as suppression by prevention (of publication or distribution), or more widely to include also suppression by repressive punitive means.[4] To make our test for the value of aesthetic censorship both simpler and more severe, let us concentrate on the narrower and stricter sense of prevention, and examine what activities at least approximate such a notion of aesthetic censorship and whether they are intrinsically inimical to art.

The (preventive) suppression of art on aesthetic grounds might be very crudely classified according to two factors: whether all or only part of the work is suppressed and whether it is suppressed by the author or by some other person or group. There are, of course, many tales of artists destroying or suppressing entire works because they were aesthetically dissatisfied with them. And the creating artist's deletion or suppression of aesthetically damaging parts of his work is undoubtedly extremely common, if not ubiquitous. Such criticism is, as Eliot noted,[5] an essential part of the creative process; and this should give a preliminary indication that creativity and censorship are no more incompatible than creativity and criticism.

It might be argued that such self-censorship is not real censorship at all, which may be alleged to require suppression by an outside force. Yet this objection is problematic since in one of the central forms of censorship, the military censorship of intelligence reports, the body authoring the report may well be the same body which censors it and prevents its publication. But again, to make the case for aesthetic censorship more difficult, let us discount all cases of self-censorship.

We are thus left with nonauthorial censorship of either entire works of art or parts thereof which are aesthetically objectionable. Ruskin's suppression, indeed destruction, of some of Turner's drawings because he thought them aesthetically bad clearly illustrates the former possibility.[6] Perhaps the closest actual approximation to the latter case is when the literary editor suppresses through deletion aesthetically objectionable parts of an otherwise publishable work. Moreover, literary editors may be seen as also approximating the aesthetic censorship of entire works. Though their rejection of manuscripts is often presented as owing to "lack of space" or "lack of financial viability," it is hard not to believe that some works are refused publication simply because they are judged to be aesthetically inadequate or objectionable. (Generally a work of art [or part thereof] is aesthetically objectionable only if it is aesthetically bad, i.e., has very low or even negative aesthetic value. However, there may be cases of aesthetic censorship where something that is granted some aesthetic merit in itself is nonetheless judged aesthetically objectionable be very damaging or dangerous in effects, e.g., in corruption of the direction of style. Eliot's early condemnation of Milton for his deep influence on English poetry, greatness, is a good example of aesthetic objectionability.[7])

One might well object here that refusing to publish something is not the same as preventing or suppressing its publication. The editor's or publisher's rejection of a work does not prevent the author from publishing it elsewhere or at his own expense.[8] This is surely true, but the difference may be only due to insufficient power to suppress it elsewhere. One can easily imagine an editorial board judging that a particular work of art is aesthetically not worthy of publication and should not be published by anyone whether or not space and money are available. Such a judgment seems to employ a principle of aesthetic censorship, though their censoring verdict need not be accepted by other firms or printers through which the work may succeed in being presented.

But does not censorship mean and require the complete or effective suppression of the work? We have reason to doubt this when we recall that censorship by Church and even by State often did not and cannot wholly prevent authors from issuing and distributing their censored works, at their own risk and that of their readers. Of course, the risks here are definite legal or spiritual sanctions, and there is a clearly defined censoring body who issues the exercitive censoring pronouncement; while the Republic of Art, as described by its exponents, may be too loosely and informally organized to provide formal acts of censorship or official enforcement of sanctions.

Yet are such formal and explicitly formulated acts and sanctions always necessary for institutional censorship, particularly if the institution is very loosely and informally organized as the art world is said to be? I see no compelling reason to suppose them necessary, and perhaps not even institutionality itself is necessary for censorship; perhaps mere power of suppression without institutional endorsement would be enough. Resolution of all these issues seems to hang on how precisely the concept of censorship is to be defined, a complex task of analysis which, regrettably, cannot be undertaken here.

The main purpose of this paper is neither to define censorship (aesthetic or otherwise) nor to determine to what, if any, extent aesthetic censorship is actually practiced or approximated in our culture (say, in the form of harsh criticism that obstructs dissemination of artworks), but rather to question the established dogma that any censorship of works of art is in principle necessarily pernicious to art. In other words, if we can imagine an autonomous Republic of Art, dedicated entirely to the pursuit of aesthetic aims above all others, would such a Republic necessarily ban all censorship or would there not be room for aesthetic censors to protect aesthetic interests, much as the ancient Roman censors (from which we take the term) served to protect the morals of the state? I fancy that the aesthetic censor might well find a place in such a Republic. And if, as I shall suggest, censorship is neither intrinsically nor always harmful to art but rather can in a certain (aesthetic) form actually serve aesthetic and artistic needs, then it would follow that contrary to accepted dogma, censorship of the arts cannot be rejected on aesthetic grounds, as it traditionally has been. This iconoclastic claim, of course, requires close consideration, so let us then examine the aesthetic arguments for and against opposition to the censorship of art.

III

Morse Peckham, whose *Art and Pornography* concentrates not on aesthetic but on moral censorship of art, briefly suggests the two main aesthetic arguments against censorship: "the artist must have freedom of expression so that he may discover artistic truth, or, alternatively, create great art."[9] Let us examine these arguments one at a time and see whether they are valid against aesthetic censorship.

1. Peckham, who rejects both arguments, dismisses the first far too glibly and inadequately.

> Either artistic truth . . . cannot be uttered except in
> the form in which it is uttered, or artistic truth can
> be uttered in a nonartistic form. In the first case, it
> is of no importance to the principle of freedom of

> expression; since artistic truth cannot be uttered in
> another form, it is impossible to tell whether or not
> the artist's freedom of expression has been
> infringed upon. In the second case, if it can be
> uttered in another form, . . . the attribute "artistic"
> is improperly ascribed to it.[10]

Peckham seems to be arguing (roughly in the form of a constructive dilemma) that if artistic truth is ineffable in another form, then we can never know if it has been suppressed and can therefore never blame censorship for its suppression. But if, on the other hand, it is expressible in another form, then its censorship in art does not deny its expression elsewhere; and to object that its suppression in art nonetheless reduces art's value is to move already to the second aesthetic argument against censorship.

Peckham's argument has serious problems and fails to show that censorship does not hinder the discovery of artistic truth (if indeed there is such a thing). First of all, the first part of the argument makes the very questionable assumption that that which cannot be expressed in another form (i.e., not the ineffable but merely the ineffable in another form) cannot be known and therefore cannot be known to be suppressed. Though skeptical of the notion of artistic truth, I still see no reason to maintain that we cannot know a truth unless it can be adequately expressed in more than one form. Moreover, even if we grant that we can never know whether censorship has suppressed artistic truth, our mere ignorance does not mean that such truth has not been suppressed and that art or our experience has not consequently suffered a depletion. One might wish to draw a distinction between the discovery of artistic truth and its dissemination, and then perhaps try to maintain that censorship would only disturb the latter. But such a strategy is unsuccessful, since an artist's discovery of artistic truth would often clearly seem to be essentially dependent upon the dissemination of other artists' discoveries.

Finally, with regard to the second part of Peckham's argument, one might object that even if an artistic truth were to some degree expressible in another form, its artistic formulation might be so much more powerful and convincing that to deny its expression in art might entail failure to recognize its truth. But a likely rejoinder to this might be that censorship is being opposed to here more on cognitive than aesthetic grounds. Peckham, I think, is right that if artistic truth can be nonartistically expressed, its *aesthetic* claim against censorship can only be in terms of its aesthetic value. But his treatment of the entire issue suffers by considering only the aesthetic grounds against censorship of the nonaesthetic kind and thus failing to recognize the possibility of a form of censorship which is *aesthetic,* serving aesthetic ends and endorsed on aesthetic grounds.

This suggests that we might bring a better argument than Peckham's to the effect that censorship on aesthetic grounds will not hinder the discovery of artistic truth, such truth (whether or not otherwise expressible) being alleged to have great aesthetic value. For if artistic truth is aesthetically so valuable, any work of art that expresses it is bound to have some aesthetic value, and therefore there would seem to be no reason to censor it on aesthetic grounds. If, on the other hand, artistic truth has no real aesthetic value, then surely we cannot use it as an aesthetic justification for opposing censorship.

Against this line of argument, the opponent of aesthetic censorship might object that even if artistic truth confers enough aesthetic value to a work that contains it as to preclude the work's censorship on aesthetic grounds, there may be works which are aesthetically bad and contain unsuccessful attempts to attain artistic truth but whose failures are nevertheless very instructive and can be very helpful in the pursuit of artistic truth. Therefore, it would be argued, if we censor such works, we shall hinder the discovery of artistic truth.

However, a defender of aesthetic censorship could handle this objection in two ways. First, he might argue that if aesthetically blemished works may be very instructive or essential to the discovery of new artistic truth, this will only be because such artistic failures (often called noble or notable failures) approximate artistic truth and have some significant degree of aesthetic merit. If it be objected that, strictly speaking, it is possible that even a total aesthetic failure could stimulate the discovery of an artistic truth, our defender of aesthetic censorship would have to employ a second, probabilistic strategy; maintaining that while *anything* might conceivably further the discovery of artistic truth, given the alleged close connection between artistic truth and aesthetic value, it is far more likely that attention to aesthetically worthy works will further this discovery than will attention to the aesthetically insufferable. Given that the artist's or appreciator's time is limited and that he cannot in his search for artistic truth examine everything claimed to be art, it is most prudent that he consider works having aesthetic value since they are more likely to advance his search (as well as be more satisfying aesthetically) rather than spend his time on inferior works of art. It could be further argued that since in many, if not all, arts it takes some time to discern the aesthetically good from the aesthetically worthless (e.g., it takes time to read a novel or hear a symphony), it would be of great value for the worthless works to be removed or withheld from access to our aesthetic consideration so that we may avoid wasting our time and energies on them. Aesthetic censorship could provide this service and thus promote artistic truth.

I think, therefore, that no powerful case can be made against censorship by appeal to its hindering the discovery of artistic truth, even if we assume that there indeed is a special thing such as artistic truth, a very questionable assumption in itself. Commitment to such truth and its pursuit would rather make us more sympathetic to aesthetic censorship, just as commitment to scientific truth would make us condemn a scientific journal for wasting and misleading our attention by publishing theories and experiments that are hopelessly inept and methodologically unsound or illegitimate. Let us then leave the notion of artistic truth and see whether the advocate of full artistic freedom can refute the validity of aesthetic censorship through appeal to its harmful effects on the production and appreciation of Feat art.

2. The basic argument here seems to be that the artistic genius cannot suffer external limitations, both in the sense that it naturally rebels against them and in the sense that it tends to be seriously harmed by them. Artistic genius, according to romantic myth, needs and tolerates no rule but its own; it demands and flourishes under absolute freedom. This myth, though it may seem innocuously absurd and outdated, is surprisingly deeply entrenched in much of our aesthetic thinking and emerges in a variety of contexts. Thus Weitz, hardly a romantic aesthetician, defends the undefinability of art and the need to keep "art" an open concept by arguing that to close the concept by definition would be to "foreclose on the very conditions of creativity in the arts."[11] If the aesthetician's abstract definitions can be seen as a threatening limitation on the creativity of art, the very concrete limitations imposed by censorship would surely seem insufferable and pernicious to the creation of great art. But is this really the case? Does great art require complete freedom? Is censorship on whatever grounds intrinsically harmful to the production and appreciation of great art? I think the answer to these questions is a firm and definite "No," and I

shall later go on to suggest that one form of limitation, aesthetic censorship, is more likely to support great art than to hinder it.

First of all, we can reject as obviously false the radical romantic premise that great art requires absolute freedom. For even if sense can be made of the notion of absolute freedom (especially with regard to a mortal, hence limited creature like the artist), the plain and simple fact is that most (perhaps all) of the great art we have was created under very real and definite constraints or limitations. Painters, sculptors, and architects have always been limited by the availability and amenability of their materials and the capabilities of their technologies. Artists of all kinds have created masterpieces under the constraint of having the subjects of their works determined by the persons who commissioned them. Great art has further been produced under the aesthetic limitations of genre rules and aesthetic traditions.

Moreover, central to the concept of art is the notion of form, and form implies order, limitation, and lack of absolute freedom. It has been cogently argued that good art requires some control or limiting framework to impose structure on the artist's creative impulse. In many expression theories of art, it is this control and imposition of limiting structure (for example, by the artistic medium) which distinguishes artistic expression from mere "letting off steam."[12] It has also been argued that limiting rules, forms, and conventions help promote great art even when such art sometimes consists in stretching them, wavering from them, or even dramatically violating them.[13] Deprecators of contemporary art not infrequently blame its alleged inferiority on its excessive liberties. Thus, it seems that great art does not at all require absolute freedom. It rather seems that (paraphrasing Eliot's remarks on verse) no art is free for the artist who wants to do a good job.

One might object that though refuting art's need for absolute freedom, I have not refuted its need for immunity from all censorship. Even if art is more likely to prosper under certain aesthetic constraints, one could maintain that there is a crucial difference between such structuring constraints or rules and the ogre of censorship which does not mold or form but rather cruelly suppresses. The latter, it would be argued, surely is pernicious to great art. Here again we must face the sobering fact that many of the greatest masterpieces of English literature, e.g., the works of Spenser, Marlowe, Jonson, Shakespeare, and Donne, were created under the conditions of strict censorship of the Court of Star Chamber, where "no book was to be printed unless first licensed by royal authority or by the Archbishops of Canterbury

and York or other specified censors."[14] Can we assume that we would
have had more or greater masterpieces without this censorship? Has the
end of licensing produced works of greater value? I doubt it. But, in
any case, the censorship exercised then was religious, political, and
moral, while my concern here is rather with the aesthetic harm or
benefit of censoring art on *aesthetic* grounds. Nonetheless, such facts
do show that there is nothing incompatible about the suppression of
some art and the creation of good or great art.

IV

Thus far my case for aesthetic censorship has been mainly defensive,
showing that such censorship need not result in aesthetic evils. Let me
now offer some more positive arguments, which maintain that
censorship on aesthetic grounds is apt to foster the production and
appreciation of great (or simply good) art and thus increase aesthetic
value in our culture.

The first argument is based on the view that the understanding and
proper appreciation of great art, indeed of any art, requires
appreciation within an artistic tradition. In Eliot's famous words: "No
poet, no artist of any art, has his complete meaning alone. His
significance, his appreciation, is the appreciation of his relation to the
dead poets and artists. You cannot value him alone, you must set him
for contrast and comparison among the dead."[15] This, of course, holds
equally for the artist's individual works, whose meaning and
appreciation depend on their relation to the important works of the
artistic tradition. Now, from the view that a work of art's meaning and
appreciation depend on its having a place in an artistic tradition, it
seems to follow that great art can only be produced and appreciated in
relation to such a tradition; not necessarily slavishly aping it, but
somehow conforming to it, even if developing and extending it. The
essentially historical and traditional character of art has recently been
powerfully emphasized by many aestheticians of various philosophical
persuasions, and there is no need (or space) to rehearse their arguments
here.[16]

If the maintaining of a tradition is essential to both the
appreciation and the creation of great art, then that which protects and
preserves the tradition from decay, destruction, or abandonment would

be promoting art and aesthetic value. Aesthetic censorship, it could be argued, can and does serve this important protecting and preserving role. If all works of art, no matter how aesthetically foul and inimical to our artistic tradition, are allowed to circulate freely and claim our serious attention as art, our aesthetic tradition will be seriously threatened with corruption and loss. For even if our taste is currently capable of sorting out the worthy from the chaff or the diseased, how could we maintain this discriminating sensibility under the relentless pressure of an uncontrolled inundation of bad art, especially considering how heavily such selection drains our strength and time? (We shall return to this presently.) Moreover, even if we grant that our good taste is firm enough to withstand any onslaught of the aesthetically horrible and corrupting what about our children's taste, still unformed and very susceptible? Corruption of that is equally pernicious to tradition and thus equally dangerous to aesthetic production and appreciation.

A second argument for censorship on aesthetic grounds is based on man's finite nature and limited capacities. The argument is that an overabundance of and overexposure to poor (or even mediocre) works of art will dim the value or dull and hinder the appreciation of great works of art, since it will divert and drain one's attention from the comparatively few works of real aesthetic worth. Bad and mediocre works of art are not labelled as such, and it takes time, often considerable time, for one to realize that the work he is considering is of no real value. Man's time for aesthetic pursuits is already very limited and should not be so wasted on the worthless. This goes for the artist as well, who typically contemplates and assesses art so that he may create it, and thus with him there is the additional danger that his creation will bear the unhappy influence of the bad art on which he wasted his time.

Moreover, not only is one's time limited, but so are one's energies. The art lover who in his quest for beauty is too often faced with the aesthetically foul or mediocre will tend to weary of the search if not abandon it in despair. Furthermore his taste and sensibility are apt to be dulled by such extensive exposure to the aesthetically inferior. In order to prevent the wasting of our precious time and the dissipation and dulling of our aesthetic energies and sensibility, it would seem advisable on purely aesthetic grounds (and considering no other grounds) to suppress aesthetically unworthy works of art or at least clearly brand them.

This line of argument may seem radical and surprising, but it is not really new. Already in 1856 Ruskin propounded it with characteristic vehemence:

> With poetry second-rate in *quality* no one ought to
> be allowed to trouble mankind. There is quite
> enough of the best, much more than we can ever
> read or enjoy in the length of a life, and it is a
> literal wrong or sin in any person to encumber us
> with inferior work. . . . Nay, more than this; in all
> inferior poetry is an injury to the good, inasmuch
> as it takes away the freshness of rhymes, blunders
> upon and gives a wretched commonalty to good
> thoughts; and in general, adds to the weight of
> human weariness in a most woeful and culpable
> manner.[17]

One might also pursue the idea, latent in Ruskin's remarks but not really part of his argument, that essential to artistic value and appreciation (at least in Western culture) is the notion of the uniqueness or specialness of a work of art; and this would seem to be gravely threatened by the uncontrolled mass production of inferior art.

There is perhaps yet another argument for aesthetic censorship, somewhat similar to the second but still, I think, distinguishable. The argument starts with the recognition that art is not and cannot be created and circulated in a context of absolute freedom. There will always be limiting factors and controlling influences, e.g., social, religious, economical, etc. Thus, even in our comparatively tolerant culture, where moral, religious, and political censorship of art hardly exists, the production of art is still not free from control, but, at least in literary art, is rather significantly controlled by economic factors. Many good books, publishers sadly tell us (often truthfully), are not published simply because they are not economically viable. The cost of their production and their marketing would not be adequately compensated by their potential sales. Artistic or aesthetic *laissez-faire* is thus in effect tantamount to economic censorship or control. To be more successful economically, a book must appeal to a wider market, which generally means a lowering of artistic standards to insure the accessibility to the largest audience.

The argument then maintains that if the production of art must in some way be regulated and restricted, it is aesthetically better that it be restricted by aesthetic considerations and controls than by those of the marketplace. One might further suggest that if only good books were allowed to circulate, there would be enough demand for this limited supply to make their publication economically renumerative. But this is not the crucial consideration here. The crux of the argument is that aesthetic censorship (suppression of the aesthetically unworthy), will free us from the heaps of economically but not aesthetically adequate art which is fostered by the economic control of art production. Aesthetic control of art thus would reduce the power of nonaesthetic, nonartistic controls that are otherwise likely to wield a potent and pernicious influence on artistic production.

V

Thus far I have argued that the traditional attacks against all censorship which are based on aesthetic grounds are in fact extremely unconvincing. I have further argued that on the basis of purely aesthetic considerations we can make a good case for one type of censorship of art, censorship on aesthetic grounds.

It might be objected here that though I may have successfully established the first thesis and demonstrated that there is nothing in the essential nature or principles of art that entails that aesthetic censorship will be (or even tend to be) harmful to art, I have failed to prove the second point, viz., that in principle aesthetic censorship will tend to promote art. This objection could maintain that my arguments for the beneficiality of aesthetic censorship all draw, at least ultimately, on the history of art rather than on theoretical principles concerning the essential nature or necessary character of art.

My arguments are indeed based on considerations that are ultimately historical in character, relating specifically to the history of art (its past reliance on firm tradition, its past flourishing in conditions of censorship, its current chapter of history concerning the sad effects of aesthetic *laissez-faire* and consequent free-market economic regulation of publication of art), and also to more general socio-historical conditions of modern man (i.e., his rather limited capacities of time and energy facing the mass of aesthetic objects which claim his attention). They are not based on ahistorical, purely theoretical considerations concerning the unchanging essence of art and its principles, nor is my conclusion that aesthetic censorship of art is more likely to promote than harm art's welfare a necessary, immutable inference from such essence or principles. I am perfectly willing to admit that should great changes occur in the practice of art and its production, consumption, and appreciation, aesthetic censorship may prove more a bane than a blessing.

In short, I plead guilty to the charge that my aesthetic theorizing here is in some sense historically dependent, conditional, and empirical. However, I deny that this removes it beyond the pale of philosophical aesthetics. For art, as so many aestheticians have come to realize, is an essentially historical phenomenon, whose nature and concepts have changed with time; and to confine aesthetic theory to the elucidation of what follows from the ahistorical essence and immutable principles of art is certainly to beg the question that there are indeed such timeless verities to be elucidated, a very doubtful proposition.

Before concluding, I should offer a clarificatory caution. One is likely to infer from my arguments that I do (and must) support or justify the aesthetic censorship of art. But such a conclusion would be premature and erroneous. I emphatically do not recommend nor would I justify or excuse the censorship of art on mere aesthetic grounds. But this is not because such grounds or considerations are in themselves invalid or insignificant, but rather because they typically conflict with and are (to my view) overruled by other, viz., moral considerations. Thus, though for very good aesthetic reasons, indeed for every aesthetic reason, I may feel a work should be suppressed or destroyed, I should not accept that these reasons alone would justify its censorship; and this is because of my *prima facie* moral commitment to freedom of expression and to tolerance of the tastes of others.[18] It seems, therefore, that if censorship of art is intrinsically wrong and harmful, it is for moral rather than aesthetic reasons; since purely aesthetic considerations of "art for art's sake" would seem to endorse some (viz., aesthetic) censorship.

This should be a surprise to the innumerable artists, aesthetes, and aestheticians who denounce censorship of any form as being insufferable for art and who disclaim morality as being not only irrelevant to art but as being the traditional champion of censorship and thus the sworn foe of artistic freedom of expression. We seem to have reached the very different conclusion that the moral and *not* the aesthetic is the real protector of artistic freedom.

Notes

1. *The American College Dictionary* (New York, 1968), p. 194.

2. *See,* for example, T. J. Diffey, "The Republic of Art," *British Journal of Aesthetics*, 9, no. 2 (1969), 145-56; G. Dickie, *Aesthetics* (New York, 1971), pp. 98-108; and A. Danto, "The Artworld," *Journal of Philosophy*, 61, no. 19 (1964), 571-84.

3. *See,* for example, C. Lord, "Convention and Dickie's Institutional Theory of Art," *British Journal of Aesthetics*, 20, no. 4 (1980), 322-28.

4. Y. R. Simon, in "A Comment on Censorship," *International Philosophical Quarterly*, 17, no. 1 (1977), 3342, claims that censorship proper should be identified with the narrower notion.

5. T. S. Eliot, "The Function of Criticism," in *Selected Prose of T. S. Eliot*, F. Kermode, ed. (London, 1975), p. 73.

6. *See* A. Wilton, *Turner in the British Museum: Drawings and Watercolours* (London, 1975), p. 7.

7. *See* my discussion of Eliot's argument in R. Shusterman, "Evaluative Reasoning in Criticism," *Ratio*, 23, no. 2 (1981), 145.

8. A. Huxley maintains, however, that printing prices have become so exorbitant that such refusals to publish literary works do in fact prevent the publication of many works and thus constitute a form of censorship, i.e., economic censorship. *See* A. Huxley, "Censorship and Spoken Literature," in *Adonis and the Alphabet* (London, 1956), p. 117.

9. M. Peckham, *Art and Pornography* (New York, 1971), p. 5.

10. Ibid.

11. M. Weitz, "The Role of Theory in Aesthetics," in *Philosophy Looks at the Arts*, J. Margolis, ed. 2nd ed. (Temple University Press, 1978), p. 127.

12. *See,* for example, B. Bosanquet, *Three Lectures on Aesthetic* (London, 1915), pp. 8, 32-40.

13. Wittgenstein seems to affirm this view. *See* L. Wittgenstein, *Lectures and Conversations* (Oxford 1970), pp. 5-6.

14. A. Craig, in *Suppressed Books* (New York 1963), pp. 19-20, maintains in fact that apart from the brief period between 1640-1643, there was state control and censorship of books in England from the time of Henry VIII until 1695 (pp. 19-22).

15. T. S. Eliot, "Tradition and the Individual Talent," in Kermode, p. 38.

16. Among analytic aestheticians, *see,* for example, R. Wollheim, *Art and its Objects* (New York, 1968), pp. 160-67; T. J. Diffey, "On Defining Art," *British Journal of Aesthetics*, 19, no. 1 (1979), 15-23; and G. McFee, "The Historicity of Art," *Journal of Aesthetics and Art Criticism*, XXXVIII, no. 3 (1980), p. 307-24. One of the most recent and extreme versions of this view

is in M. Sagoff's "On the Aesthetic and Economic Value of Art," *British Journal of Aesthetics,* 21, no. 4 (1981), 318-29 where it is maintained that "to experience an object of art is... to perceive and share a history" and that the value of art is in its constituting and "maintaining our cultural heritage" (p. 327). A number of hermeneutic aestheticians, most notably Gadamer, also emphasize the essential historicity of art and the crucial importance of tradition in art's appreciation. For an admirably lucid discussion of their view of these matters, *see* D. C. Loy, *The Critical Circle* (University of California Press, 1982), pp. 95-166.

17. J. Ruskin, "The Pathetic Fallacy," in *English Critical Essays (Nineteenth Century),* E. D. Jones ed., (Oxford University Press, 1945), pp. 382n.-83n.

18. This does not mean that there are no cases or circumstances where censorship (either of art or nonart) may be morally justified and fully recommended.

II

Creations and Re-Creations

Art and Inauthenticity

W.E. Kennick

*Eine der schwersten Aufgabe des Philosophen
ist es zu finden, wo ihn der Schuh druckt.*

— Wittgenstein

Is there an aesthetic difference between a deceptive fake and a genuine, authentic, or original work of art?

This question cannot be given a univocal answer as it stands, for the simple reason that as it stands it is highly ambiguous. It involves three problematic concepts: those of an aesthetic difference (and, *pari passu,* of an aesthetic similarity or identity), of a fake, and of a genuine, authentic, or original work of art. Instead, therefore, of attempting to answer it, I shall here be concerned with an endeavor logically anterior to that of answering it, namely, some clarification of two of the problematic concepts cited: those of a fake and of a genuine, authentic, or original work of art. (The concept of an aesthetic difference is an intellectual Augean stable, and I lack the Herculean powers to clean it up.)

Others, of course, have tried to answer the question, but, as I see it, the best answers offered to date[1] are compromised by a failure not only to make clear just what constitutes an aesthetic difference between, say two or more paintings[2] (for which they can understandably be forgiven) but also to draw appropriate distinctions between various

W.E. Kennick's article first appeared in the *Journal of Aesthetics and Art Criticism* 44 (1), Fall 1985, pp. 3-12. It is reprinted here by permission of the publisher, the American Society for Aesthetics, and the author.

ways in which something may appear but fail to be a genuine, authentic, or original work of art, which is the chief topic of this paper. Let two examples of what I have in mind suffice.

(1) Although Sagoff recognizes, quite correctly, that "not every copy of a painting is a forgery,"[3] he holds, quite incorrectly, that "every forgery is simply a copy of a painting."[4] The notorious van Meegeren, whom he mentions, produced, as I understand it, only one forgery that was a copy—of Baburen.[5] His criminal masterpiece, *The Supper at Emmaus,* was not a copy of a Vermeer and can now be seen to imitate certain stylistic features of Vermeer only superficially at best. (2) In posing the problem addressed by the opening sentence of this paper, Goodman writes:

> The question is most strikingly illustrated by the case of a given work and a forgery or copy or reproduction of it. Suppose we have before us, on the left, Rembrandt's original painting *Lucretia* and, on the right, a superlative imitation of it. We know from a fully documented history that the painting on the left is the original; and we know from X-ray photographs and microscopic examination and chemical analysis that the painting on the right is a recent fake.[6]

What Goodman obviously has in mind is a true or exact *copy* of Rembrandt's *Lucretia,* and yet he uses five different words—"forgery," "copy," "reproduction," "imitation," and "fake"—as if it made little or no difference which he used; as if they were all, at least approximately, synonymous. This is especially surprising in Goodman's case, since he holds that "the aesthetic properties of a picture include not only those found by looking at it but also those that determine how it is to be looked at."[7] From the context I gather that a painting's being a forgery is a property that determines how it is to be looked at, and is thereby an aesthetic property of it; in which case a picture's being an innocent copy is also a property that determines how *it* is to be looked at, and is thereby an aesthetic property of it; in which case, since a forgery and an innocent copy are worlds apart, they are not to be looked at in the same way (which, I believe, is unmistakably the case) and are hence aesthetically quite different.

There is a set of expressions we use to indicate that a painting is not an original *N;* where, to keep matters simple, *"N"* stands for the name of a painter but does not stand for some such description as "fifteenth century Siennese painting." Any one of these expressions, on a suitable occasion, might be used to complete the following schema:

That is not an original *N;* it is a ____. Among these expressions are the following: "a forged *N,*" "a fake *N,*" "a copy of an *N,*" "a reproduction of an *N,*" "a picture in imitation of *N* (or of an *N),*" "a picture after *N* (or an *N),*" "a painting by a follower of *N,*" "a picture belonging to the school of *N,*" "a painting from the studio or workshop of *N,*" "a painting wrongly attributed (or misattributed) to *N.*" The only one of these terms that comes readily to mind as a generic term covering all the cases signified by the others in the use indicated for them is the term "fake" which, in one of its uses, as in "fake diamond," means simply not real, not genuine. A fake *N,* then, is a painting which is not an original *N* but which, in a given context, purports—innocently or fraudulently—to be an original *N.*

But this sounds odd. 'Fake' in the sense specified does not normally contrast with "original" but with "real," "authentic," or "genuine." Why, then, make it contrast unnaturally with "original"? Because, although an original *N* is a real, authentic, or genuine *N,* it would appear to be possible for a painting to be a real, authentic, or genuine *N* without being an original *N;* if by "a real, authentic, or genuine *N*" we mean simply a painting that has been executed by *N.* Because *N* might, for example, slavishly copy one of his own paintings. In this case the result would be a real, authentic, or genuine *N,* but it would not be an original *N* (the original *N* being the painting that was copied), anymore than a copy by someone other than *N* would be an original *N.* Sagoff apparently disagrees:

> Two paintings which look alike, even if they were created by the same artist, are not instances of the same work. No matter how many times Cezanne painted *The Card Players* and no matter how well the resulting paintings resemble one another, practice establishes each as an original work of art. Since these paintings have the same author, of course, they will belong, presumably, to all the same conventional reference classes. . . . Incidentally, the fact that an artist cannot forge his

> own work but creates an original with every copy
> suggests the truth that paintings are not classified as
> forgeries or as fakes if they can plausibly be
> counted in some other way.[8]

Reason will be given below for doubting the first sentence of this passage, but for the moment we can let it and the next two sentences stand, if by "created" Sagoff really means created and not simply made or fabricated.[9] His example of *The Card Players,* however, suggests that what Sagoff has in mind are two or more versions of the same subject, like Chardin's three (at least) versions of *Still Life with a Loin of Meat.*[10] But a second, or third, version of the same subject, even if it is superficially indistinguishable from the first, is not the same as a copy of an original. Hence it is not the case that an artist "creates an original with every copy." A copy of an *N* belongs to a different reference class from an original *N,* no matter by whom it may be produced. A skillful painter may or may not be a skillful copyist. If *N* creates a painting exhibiting a skillful handling of light emanating from three sources and then paints a skillful copy of that painting, it does not follow, for persuasive reasons offered by Sagoff himself, that the copy is a painting exhibiting a skillful handling of light emanating from three sources; although *ex hypothesi* it is a skillful *copy* of such a painting.

We might note further that there is a subtle ambiguity in the notion of an *N,* or even of a real, authentic, or genuine *N.* According to Alfred Moir,[11] the so-called *St. John the Baptist* in the Doria Gallery, Rome, is not an original Caravaggio (the original being in the office of the Mayor of Rome) but was probably "painted by a contemporary occasional imitator of Caravaggio named Angelo Caroselli who is recorded in seventeenth century literature as a very skillful faker of the master." Well, suppose that the Doria *St. John* was actually painted by Caroselli.[12] Clearly it is not an original—and *a fortiori* not a real, authentic, or genuine—Caravaggio. But is it a (real, authentic, or genuine) Caroselli? Now Caroselli was a painter in his own right, not merely a copyist, and it is certain that his original paintings are (real, authentic, genuine) Carosellis. But what, again, of his copies? By "an *N*" or "a real, authentic, or genuine *N*" one may, as we have noted, mean simply a painting that was painted, made, or executed, but not necessarily created, by *N*—although even this is treacherous, as we shall see shortly. In that case the Doria *St. John* is a Caroselli, even a real, authentic, or genuine Caroselli. Or by "an *N*" or "a real, authentic, or genuine *N*" one may mean a painting that was created *by N,* that is, an original *N;* in which case, although the Doria *St. John* was, *ex hypothesi,* painted by Caroselli, it is not a (real, authentic, genuine) Caroselli. It is simply a copy of a Caravaggio by Caroselli. To resolve this ambiguity if only for my own purposes, I shall mean by "an *N*" an original *N,* a painting created by *N;* in which case a real, authentic, or genuine *N is* always an original *N.* This will make the generic use of 'fake' more plausible.

But this matter is still further complicated by the fact that the creator or author of a painting need not be identical with the maker or fabricator of the painting, i.e., the person who actually painted it. For example, Moholy-Nagy tells us:

> In 1922 I ordered by telephone from a sign factory
> five paintings in porcelain enamel. I had the
> factory's color chart before me and I sketched my
> paintings on graph paper. At the other end of the
> telephone the factory supervisor had the same kind
> of paper, divided into squares. He took down the
> dictated shapes in the correct position. (It was like
> playing chess by correspondence.)[13]

Here we have five paintings by Moholy-Nagy. Each is an original, real, authentic, genuine Moholy-Nagy, of which there could be copies or forgeries. But, although Moholy-Nagy was the creator or author of the paintings, he was not the maker (the actual painter) of any of them.[14]

We may now turn to exploring some conceptual relations between some of the terms listed above, and we shall begin with the notion of forgery.

Unlike the other terms with which we have associated it, "forgery" belongs to what might be called the language of the morality of art. Forgery is something of which a person is guilty, whereas simply copying or painting in the manner of someone is not. The term is, I take it, borrowed from the law, so we may get clearer about what forgery in art is if we note how the term is used by lawyers. Turning to *Black's Law Dictionary* we find "to forge" defined as follows:

> To fabricate, construct, or prepare one thing in
> imitation of another, with the intention of

substituting the false for the genuine, or otherwise
deceiving and defrauding by the use of the spurious
article. To counterfeit or make falsely. Especially,
to make a spurious written instrument with the
intention of fraudulently substituting it for another,
or passing it off as genuine; or to fraudulently alter
a genuine instrument to another's prejudice; or to
sign another person's name to a document, with a
deceitful and fraudulent intent.[15]

Taking cues from this legal definition of "to forge," I would list at
least the following conditions as requisite to forgery in art:

(1) A forged *N* cannot be an *N* (in the sense of being an *N* I
committed myself to above). Does this mean that a painter cannot forge
his own work? Sagoff to the contrary, no. If *N* makes a slavish copy
(as opposed to another version) of one of his own pictures and passes
it off, e.g., sells it, as the original, as Rubens is said to have done on
at least one occasion, he is as guilty of forgery as someone other than
N would be were he to copy a work of *N*'s and pass it off as an
original *N*. The copy is, to be sure, the work of *N,* but it is not the
work of *N* it purports to be. Indeed, it is not an (original) *N* at
all—except in replica.

(2) Someone must pass off, or attempt to pass off, as an *N* what
is not an *N*, or is not the *N* it purports to be. Must the someone in
question be the fabricator of the inauthentic *N*? Yes. Suppose that a
copyist, C, like Angelo Caroselli with the copies he made and signed
with an AC cypher, copies an *N* with no intent to pass it off as a
genuine *N*, but subsequently, and unbeknown to C, an art dealer or
museum director, *D*, passes off C's copy as a genuine *N*, but does so
with deceitful or fraudulent intent. Is C guilty of forgery? Clearly not.
Well, is *D?* I think not. Consider a parallel legal possibility. I am
teaching a child how to write checks. I tell her to fill in the date and to
make the check out to me. "For how much?" she asks. "Oh, let's say
$150,000." "But who has that kind of money?" "David Rockefeller,"
I say. So, she writes "David Rockefeller" where one's signature
normally goes. Being thoroughly unscrupulous and seeing a golden
opportunity to make a fast buck, I take the check to the bank and cash
it. I am later found out. Am I guilty of forgery? I am not sure just
what the law would say, but I should be inclined in this case to say that
although I am not guilty of *forgery* because I have not *forged*

anything—and *ex hypothesi* neither has anyone else—I am guilty of fraud. The check in question is clearly a bogus or fraudulent check, and in the parallel case in art the picture in question should, I think, be properly described as a bogus or *fraudulent N*.[16]

(3) Whoever passes off, or attempts to pass off, as an *N* what is not an *N*, or is not the *N* it purports to be, must do so with deceitful or fraudulent intent. Again, a copyist who sells or exhibits his copy of an *N* as a copy is not guilty of forgery or of fraud, and his picture is neither a forged *N* nor a fraudulent *N*. Nor is an art dealer or museum director who sells or exhibits as an *N* what is not an *N*, honestly believing it to be an *N*, guilty of forgery or fraud. In the case of the copyist we are not dealing with a fake *N* at all, but in the case of the art dealer or museum director we are.[17]

In addition to these four requisites of forgery in art must there be at least a fifth, viz., that the inauthentic *N* be in the manner or style of *N?* I think not. It has been claimed[18] that van Meegeren's "Vermeers" are not really in the style or manner of Vermeer at all (or are at best only superficially so) and hence that visual analysis alone could have revealed that even *The Supper at Emmaus* was a fake.[19] To be sure, if one were to make a painting imitating the manner of Boucher and attempt to sell it to some ignoramus, claiming that it was a Rembrandt, and if he were to fall for the trick, it is hard to think of this as a forged Rembrandt. But what is hard to think of is anyone's being taken in by such a scam. If an act of forgery is to be completed or carried through, someone must be deceived or defrauded. And to be deceived or defrauded, he must believe that the inauthentic *N* he is offered is a genuine *N*. And in order for him to believe that it is a genuine *N*, it may have to look like an *N* to him. And for it to look like an *N* to him, it may have to be in the manner of *N*, or in a manner resembling, if only superficially, the, or a, manner of *N*. But it is not necessary that a forged *N* be in the manner of *N* or in a manner resembling the manner of *N*. It is requisite for an act of forgery's being completed or carried through only that the person deceived or defrauded believe, on whatever grounds, that the inauthentic *N* is a genuine *N*, but this is not requisite to forgery *per se*. Attempt to deceive or defraud is requisite to forgery *per se*, but the attempt need not be successful. If someone attempts unsuccessfully to pass off his copy of a Titian as the original, knowing it to be merely a copy, then he is guilty of forgery, and the painting in question is a forged Titian.

A forged or a fraudulent *N* is a fake *N*, but a fake *N* is not necessarily a forged or a fraudulent *N*. Imagine a set designer who is commissioned to design a set for a play about a wealthy art collector. To avoid populating the collector's drawing room with (copies or reproductions of) well known paintings, he paints several convincing "Cezannes," "Monets," "Renoirs," or what have you. Although there might be said to be an intention to deceive at work here, the kind of deception at issue would be simply that endemic or natural to a certain kind of theatre and would be as innocent as the deception practiced by a performing magician. So these pictures would not be forgeries or frauds, but they would be fakes. They would be as fake, say, as the marble of the fireplace over which one of them hangs.[20]

Some forgeries are copies, but many forgeries are not. As we noted above, most of van Meegeren's forgeries are not copies. They are often characterized, whether aptly or not, as being in the style of, say, Vermeer or de Hoogh.[21] And this raises the rather delicate question of when one painting is in the manner or style of another.[22]

First, there is a difference, I think, between being *in the style of* and being *in the same style as*. For example. Pissarro's *Spring Sunlight in the Meadow at Eragny* is in the same, or much the same, style as his *Peasant's House at Eragny* (both of 1887), but neither is in the style of the other, nor is either in the style of his *The Boieldieu Bridge, Rouen, Misty Weather* (1896); although both are in Pissarro's pointillist or neo-Impressionist style.[23] And, of course, *Boieldieu Bridge* is truistically in the same style as *The Boieldieu Bridge*, i.e., in the same style as itself, but it is not truistically, or even meaningfully, in the style of itself. Can pictures by two or more painters be in the same style as one another without being in the style *of* one another? I can see no reason why not, especially if we allow that two pointillist, or two analytical cubist, or two Caravaggesque pictures are in the same style simply in virtue of their being pointillist, or analytical cubist, or Caravaggesque pictures. For example, Bartolomeo Manfredi's *Musical* (Florence, Uffizi) and Orazio Gentileschi's *Crown of Thorns* (Varese, Lizza-Bassi Collection) are both Carravagesque paintings of approximately the same period and to that extent are in the same style. But neither is in the style of the other. Both are in the style of Caravaggio.[24] To say that x is in the style of *N* at least suggests that the style (certain prominent stylistic features) of x were adopted or borrowed from paintings by

N—perhaps even by N from earlier paintings of his own; whereas to say that x is in the same style as y is to make no such suggestion.

Secondly, two paintings can be more or less in the same style, and one painting can be more or less in the style of another. One painting can, for example, be more Caravaggesque than another, precisely because it is more in the style of Caravaggio than is the other. Indeed, Moir[25] feels called upon to divide the Caravaggesque works of the *Caravaggisti* into three groups: copies, variants, and imitations. Actually, copies ought not to be included, for reasons given below. As for variants, "neither by intention of their makers nor in fact are they to be mistaken by competent observers for Caravaggio's works. . . . Their makers treated Caravaggio's originals not as scores to be followed but as themes on which improvisations could be made." The works of the most famous *Caravaggisti*—Manfredi, Saraceni, Gentileschi, *et al.*—fall into this category. But what Moir calls "imitations" come so close in style to Caravaggio originals as to be scarcely discernible from them.

> These are neither copies of, nor specifically variants on, Caravaggio's own works. But with such excellence as to rival his in quality, they recreate his style so perfectly as to seem to be his own work. . . . Some may have been painted innocently. Others may have been painted as deliberate fakes. . . .

Thirdly, the question of what constitutes style is, of course, a vexed one in aesthetics, but according to Goodman (and I can think of no good reasons for parting company with him here) "a feature of style may be a feature of what is said [as opposed to merely 'how' it is said], of what is exemplified [which includes formal or structural features], or of what is expressed. Goya and El Greco characteristically differ in all three ways: in subject matter, drawing, and feeling."[26] Further, and more important for our purposes, all stylistic features of a painting are "who-when-where relevant":

> a property—whether of statement made, structure displayed, or feeling conveyed—counts as stylistic only when it associates a work with one rather than another artist, period, region, etc. A style is a

complex characteristic that serves somewhat as an
individual or group signature . . . . [I]n general
stylistic properties help answer the questions: who?
when? where?[27]

It would appear to follow from this that no painting that differs widely
in place and time from *N* can be in the style of *N,* because *its* stylistic
features cannot have the appropriate who-when-where relevance. As
Sagoff puts it, "no one can paint a Vermeer, a Van Gogh, or an
Impressionist painting today."[28] I cannot, for example, even if I had
the appropriate technical skills, paint a picture in the style of the
thirteenth century Chinese master Mu Ch'i (or Fa Ch'ang). The best I
can do is to *imitate* (ape, mimic) his style. Hence my set designer's
'Cezannes' are not merely fake Cezannes, they are also imitation
Cezannes. But just as there is a difference between adopting someone's
manner of speech, making it one's own, and imitating another's manner
of speech, so there is a difference between adopting and imitating a
painter's style. The *Caravaggisti,* because they were in the suitable
historical and geographical position to do so, adopted, *in parte,* the
style of Caravaggio; they did not merely imitate Caravaggio—which is
not to say that some early seventeenth century Italian painter could not
have imitated the style of Caravaggio, e.g., to make fun of it. It does
not follow from this Goodmanian conception of style, however, that,
in Sagoff's words, "no style predicate can apply both to an original and
a forgery in the strong sense."[29] It is just possible that the Prado
David attributed to Carravaggio—wrongly according to some
experts—is a forgery painted by some contemporary of Carravaggio,
say Caroselli. Assume that it is. Then, assuming further that the Prado
David is realistic in the sense of that term as it is applied to
Carravaggio,[30] then the Prado *David* and Caravaggio's *Entombment*
would be realistic in the same sense.

It should go without saying that the notion of being in the manner
or style of *N* is a vague notion. How close in time and place does one
painter have to be to another for the first's work to count as being in
the style of the second, as opposed to merely imitating the style of the
second? No answer is forthcoming. But this does not imply that the
notion is useless. It should also go without saying that not every
painting in the style of *N* is a fake, a fraudulent, or a forged *N.* And
the same holds for a painting after *N,* or an *N,* for a painting belonging

to the school of *N*, for a painting from the studio or workshop of *N*, and for a picture honestly but wrongly attributed to *N*.

Of all the concepts under discussion here, that of copying is probably the most troublesome. The question whether there is an aesthetic difference between a forgery or a fake and an original usually turns on thinking of the forgery or fake as a copy; otherwise the question is simply whether two paintings by two different artists can be aesthetically identical, e.g., whether there could be a Caroselli, whether painted as a forgery of Caravaggio or not, that does not differ aesthetically—whatever it is to do that—from a Caravaggio. Before turning finally to what I take to be responsible for this problem, some preliminary remarks about copies seem to me to be in order.

People have copied paintings for a variety of reasons, the most prominent of which has been to learn, not to forge. Although copying may no longer be a widespread pedagogical device, it was once one of the principal methods of teaching painting both in the West and in the East. The last of the Six *Canons of Painting* of the early Chinese master Hsieh Ho was, "transmission of the experience of the past in making copies,"[31] a rule Sherman Lee glosses by saying, "The making of copies was the discipline by which the painter, through the study of the brush of his predecessors, learned control of his own."[32] It is safe to say, then, that most of the copies of paintings that have been produced in the world have not been produced as fakes or forgeries, although some of them may subsequently have become fraudulent pictures, and therefore fakes, in the hands of others.

A copy of a painting need not itself be a painting. We possess copies of paintings in drawing, engraving, and even mosaic. Further, a copy need not be of the same size or in the same proportions as the original. Someone could, I suppose, copy Raphael's *Madonna della Sedia* on the head of a pin, or someone could produce a copy which is an anamorphosis of that same painting. This suggests that a copy is rather like a map, that it projects the original in some medium according to a rule or system of projection, which means that a copy need not "look like" the original, any more than an ordinary map of the state of New York "looks like" the state of New York—even from high in the air.

This must not mislead us into thinking that where a copy of a painting is itself a painting it is a painting of a painting. In the first place, x may be a painting of y even if there is no y of which x is a

painting (there may be paintings of purely imaginary paintings just as
there are paintings of purely imaginary persons and places), but if x is
a copy of y there must be or have been some y of which x is a copy.
In the second place, as Danto points out,[33] a painting of a painting is
"a different thing altogether" from a copy of a painting, "though it
might exactly resemble a copy," for another reason:

> A copy is defective, for example, insofar as it
> deviates from the original, but the question of
> deviation is simply irrelevant if it is a painting of a
> painting: much as we do not expect the artist to use
> chlorophyll in depicting trees. Now, if deviation is
> irrelevant, so is non-deviation.

But this is not quite right, for in the case of painting, drawing, etc. we
recognize a class of "free copies," copies which are copies of originals,
which do deviate, sometimes significantly, from the originals, but
which are not thereby branded as defective; perhaps because we think
of them as not *mere* copies—hence, *free* copies. For example, Panofsky
tells us that in 1494 Durer "copied several mythological engravings by
Mantegna," among these copies being Durer's famous drawing of
Mantegna's *Battle of the Sea Gods*. Of these drawings Panofsky writes:

> In these copies the contours are directly traced
> from the originals; only the modelling is entered in
> free hand. Yet, even while copying the outlines as
> mechanically as possible, Durer involuntarily
> strengthened their graphic energy, and to achieve
> the modelling he replaced Mantegna's schematic
> parallels by a pattern of curves and violent,
> commashaped hooks which endow the forms with
> vibrant life.[34]

Although at first sight or to the unobservant eye Durer's copy of
Mantegna's *Sea Gods* may appear to be an exact copy of that
engraving, when one notes the features Panofsky calls our attention to
he is inclined to suppose that Durer had more in mind than merely
copying Mantegna's work. For the result is not a botched or defective
copy, but a new and interesting work of art derived from or based on
Mantegna's—something it would usually be inappropriate to say, even
with "new and interesting" changed to "dull and uninteresting," of a

botched or defective copy. The difference would appear to lie not just in the visible results but in the actual or putative intentions of the copyist—intentions that may have to be imputed to the copyist from the visible results of his work. (From here on we shall confine our attention to copies that pretend to be no more than copies, i.e., to copies that strive or purport to be exact or slavish copies.)

What is the difference, if any, between a copy and a reproduction of the same painting? We may perhaps find an answer to this question by considering some remarks by Sagoff on the subject:

> A forgery copies another painting; a reproduction is not a painting but a print, photograph, or something of that sort, which represents a painting. A photographic reproduction—generally this is the kind found on posters, postcards, and in art books—represents a painting just as, for example, a photograph of Churchill reprinted on a poster, postcard, or whatever, represents him. . . . Thus, if a reproduction of a Cezanne landscape, for example, captures the strength and solidity of the original, it does so not by duplicating the original but by actually representing it. . . . The relation of the reproduction to the original is one of denotation not of similarity; the symbolic devices of photographs figure as much in this picture of a painting as they do in a picture of a sculpture or a picture of a man. The reproduction and the original differ in medium and in subject matter. . . . The relation between a *forgery* [i.e., a copy] and an original, on the other hand, is not one of representation but of similarity. Here the ancient ideal of *mimesis* is best fulfilled.[35]

To clear up some relatively minor matters first: (1) not every forgery, as we have seen, is a copy of an original. (2) There seems to be some confusion in Sagoff's mind between photographs and reproductions, especially photographic reproductions. The kind of thing generally found on posters, postcards, and in art books is not a photograph but a photographic reproduction, i.e. a reproduction of a photograph. It is at least twice removed from the object of which we say that it is a reproduction. That is, a photographic reproduction of an N is a reproduction of a photograph of an *N*: It has as *its* subject a photograph which in turn has as *its* subject an *N*. So if a photographic reproduction of a Cezanne landscape captures the strength and solidity of the original, it does so not by actually representing the original but by representing a photograph of the original, which captures the strength and solidity of the original by representing *it*. A photograph of a painting is not a copy of it, but neither is it a reproduction of it.[36] But let us ignore reproductions and concentrate on photographs and copies. It is the difference between these that Sagoff seems really to have in mind.

Although a photograph of a work of art and the work of which it is a photograph do differ in subject, so do a copy and the original: the photograph of an *N* and the copy of an *N* both have an *N* as their subject. But, as Sagoff will say, a photograph and a copy stand to an original painting in different ways: the relation between a photograph and an original painting is one of denotation, whereas that between a copy and an original is one of similarity. Although I am ready to concede that a photograph and an original painting of which it is a photograph and a copy and an original do stand to one another in different ways, I find Sagoff's account of the difference unpersuasive. The relation between a photograph of a painting and the painting of which it is a photograph is, to be sure, not one of similarity or resemblance—at least where similarity or resemblance counts. But neither is the relation between a copy and the original of which it is a copy one of similarity or resemblance—at least where similarity or resemblance counts. Copy and original may both be paintings (in some minimal sense of "painting"), although, as we have seen, they need not be; but they are not both works of art: "a copy of an artwork is not an artwork,"[37] any more than a statue of a man is a man. Copy and original may both be the same in size, although, again, they need not be. And so on. But copy and original are not the same, or even similar, in subject matter, in style, in expressive force, and so on; in short, in all the significant ways in which two originals—say, two versions of the same subject by the same painter—may be similar.

Further, although I am not as confident as Sagoff is that the relation between a photograph and that of which it is a photograph is one of denotation, any more than I am confident that the relation between a mirror image or a reflection in water and that of which it is an image or a reflection is one of denotation, I will grant this point for the sake of argument. But I would say that the relation between a copy and an original is one of denotation, or is at least analogous to denotation, which is a further reason—one in addition to those adduced by Sagoff—why copies and originals do not, or even cannot, share the same aesthetic properties.

An important clue to the nature of copies—and one which separates them from photographs—is provided by Danto's likening of copies to quotations.[38] Although to quote someone's words is not the same as to copy them (a secretary copies the boss's letter but in doing so does not quote it), to quote someone's words, correctly and accurately, is to reproduce them. A quotation, however, differs semantically, and therefore in other important ways, from the words quoted. According to Frege,[39] if I quote the words of another my words (those within quotation marks) designate or have as their reference *(Bedeutung)* the words of that other; they do not have their usual or normal reference. Thus if I say: "Panofsky says, 'Albrecht Durer was born in Nuremberg on May 21, 1471,'" the words within single quotation marks have as their reference Panofsky's *words:* 'Albrecht Durer' stands for "Albrecht Durer," not for Albrecht Durer, and 'was born in Nuremberg on May 21, 1471' stands for "was born in Nuremberg on May 21, 1471," not for the concept or property of being born in Nuremberg on May 21, 1471. Similarly, we might say, if only analogously or metaphorically, the reference or denotation of a copy is the original of which it is a copy, whereas the reference or denotation of the original (if it has one—and it need not have one, whereas a copy must) is say, Wivenhoe Park. Nor need a painting, again say, of Wivenhoe Park, be taken as *saying* or *asserting* anything about Wivenhoe Park, e.g., that this is the way it looked from such and such a spot; but a copy must be taken in some such way. And so a copy *qua* copy implicitly carries with it something analogous to "A said, ' . . . ,'" sometimes indicated by a label of the form "Copy of *N's* '*T*'," where '*T*' stands for a title; whereas the same is not true of a photograph, despite the superficial resemblance between "Photograph of *N's* '*T*'" and "Copy of *N's* '*T*'." One reason for this appears to be that, unlike a photograph, a quotation or a copy requires an *original.* One can quote only what someone (perhaps oneself) has originally said, and one can copy only what someone (perhaps oneself) has originally done.[40] But one can photograph just about anything, and if she photographs an original work of art that work is *not* the original of which the photograph is a photograph in the sense in which an *N* must be the original of a copy of that *N*.

A quotation may be incomplete, inaccurate, garbled. A copy may be defective in analogous ways: incomplete, inaccurate, crude, clumsy. But a photograph is defective in other ways: out of focus, over- (or under-) exposed, indistinct or fuzzy, distorted—defects that are closer to those of vision than to those that are the results of want of, or misapplied, skill.

More important, quotations "merely resemble the expressions they denote without having *any* of the artistically relevant properties of the latter: *quotations* cannot be scintillating, original, profound, searching, or whatever what is quoted may be,"[41] and similarly "copies (in general) lack the properties of the originals they denote or resemble."[42] But if a quotation cannot itself be original, scintillating, profound, and the like, it obviously can be the quotation of an original or profound remark; and the only way we may have of knowing whether the words quoted were original or profound is by way of the quotation. The words of the pre-Socratic philosophers, for example, are known to us only through (putative) quotations by Plato, Aristotle and the doxographers; just as the words of Jesus are known to us only through (putative) quotations by the authors of the Gospels. Likewise, many paintings are known to us only from copies, and the history of painting, Western or Eastern, would be very different from what it is were this not so. Often, indeed, we do not know whether we are dealing with a copy or an original,[43] and for certain purposes, if we are assured that the copy is a good one, this may make little or no difference. It is this fact, however, the fact that an accurate quotation or a good copy reproduces, and therefore may *preserve,* without *having* the qualities of its original, that leads, I think, to the view that there is no aesthetic difference between an original painting and an exact copy of it. Advocates of this view are impressed by the fact that one could, in principle, know just about all there is to know about an original *N*[44] from a perfect copy of it. But they fail to realize that there is still a world of difference between the two. Whether that difference is an *aesthetic* difference, however, is another matter.

Notes

1. Those of Nelson Goodman, *Languages of Art* (Indianapolis, 1968), Ch. III, "Art and Authenticity," and Mark Sagoff, "The Aesthetic Status of Forgeries," *The Journal of Aesthetics and Art Criticism*, 35 (1976): 169-80. Both of these essays have been reprinted in *The Forger's Art,* Denis Dutton, ed. (The University of California Press, 1983), but page references are to the original sources.

2. I shall, like Goodman and Sagoff, confine myself entirely to paintings. The question of fakery as it has to do with works of literature or music are different and more complicated.

3. Sagoff, 178.

4. Ibid., 176.

5. I owe the information about van Meegeren cited in this paper to Hope B. Werness's "Han van Meegeren*fecit,*" Dutton, pp. 1-57. Professor Werness delivered an earlier and shorter version of this paper ("The Falsity of Van Meegeren's *The Supper at Emmaus")* as part of a symposium on forgery in art at the 39th Annual Meeting of the American Society for Aesthetics, held at Tampa, Florida, October 28-31, 1981. A more rudimentary version of the present paper was my own contribution to the same symposium.

6. Goodman, *Languages of Art,* pp. 99-100.

7. Ibid., pp. 111-12. The natural way to read this sentence is: The aesthetic properties of a picture include all those found by looking at it as well as all those that determine how it is to be looked at. But Goodman may not have meant anything quite as strong as this.

8. Sagoff, 177-78.

9. On the distinction in question see my "Creative Acts," revised version, *Art and Philosophy: Readings in Aesthetics,* W.E. Kennick, ed., 2nd ed. (New York, 1979), pp. 163-85.

10. See Pierre Rosenberg, *Chardin* (The Cleveland Museum of Art, 1979), pp. 160-61, with illustrations.

11. In his (untitled) contribution to the symposium on forgery mentioned in note 5. This paper will be referred to hereafter simply as "Moir Paper."

12. For details of Caroselli's career see Alfred Moir, *The Italian Followers of Caravaggio* (Harvard University Press, 1967), Chs. II-III passim. Moir tells us that Caroselli "was a very skilled copyist" (p. 53). He copied Annibile Carracci, Titian, Corregio, Raphael, and Caravaggio "so well as to deceive such experts as Borgianni and Poussin." Usually he signed his copies with an AC cypher, thereby exonerating himself of forgery, although some of his copies seem to have been sold as originals, and some may have been intended to be so sold (ibid., n. 129).

13. Laszlo Moholy-Nagy, *The New Vision and Abstract of an Artist* (New York, 1947), p. 79. The long paragraph from which this is taken reveals a desire on Moholy-Nagy's part to eliminate the "unique," the "personal touch" in painting, the "naive desire" for which, he says, "can hardly be justified."

Incidentally, this practice of Moholy-Nagy's casts some doubt on Goodman's claim that painting is an autographic art. Goodman defines a work of art as autographic "if and only if the most exact duplication of it does not thereby count as genuine" (Goodman, p. 113). Suppose Moholy-Nagy ordered five of the same painting from the sign factory, all of them the same size. (He tells us (Moholy-Nagy, pp. 79-80) that he did order "one of the pictures . . . in three different sizes, so that I could study the subtle differences in the color relations caused by the enlargement and reduction.") Would each of these not be an exact duplicate of any of the others? And would they not all be instances of one and the same work of art? If so, painting would not necessarily be an autographic art, for each would surely be as "genuine" as any of the others. In that case, one might wish to say that in the imagined situation we do not really have five Moholy-Nagy's; only one.

14. For a similar phenomenon in sculpture, see John Canaday, "Magrittes That Magritte Never Saw," *The New York Times,* 22 November, 1969, p. 33.

15. Henry Campbell Black, *Black's Law Dictionary,* 5th ed. (St. Paul, Minnesota, 1979). Cf. also the definitions of "forgery," "to utter," and "fraud."

16. "Most of the seventeenth century paintings that became fakes [i.e. bogus or fraudulent *N*s] were probably not originally made with any intention to defraud. Instead they were made as innocent copies." Moir Paper.

17. So Goodman is dead wrong when he says, "A forgery of a work of art is an object falsely purporting to have the history of production requisite for the (or an) original work of art" (Goodman, p. 122). A picture innocently misattributed to *N*—and our museums contain many such objects—is "an object falsely purporting . . . etc.," but it is not a forgery, albeit it is a fake *N*.

18. Cf., for example, Werness, pp 35-37, 54-56.

19. There are also Goodmanian reasons as well for saying that van Meegeren's "Vermeers" *could* not be in the style or manner of Vermeer. See Nelson Goodman, "The Status of Style," *Critical Inquiry* 1 (1973): 799-811. These reasons are discussed briefly below.

20. In the context of the play, of course, they are real Cezannes, Monets, and Renoirs—just as it is Hamlet, and not the actor playing Hamlet, who, in the context of the play, says, "Get thee to a nunnery." Indeed, the plot of the play could involve the discovery that one of the pictures is a forgery, e.g., a forged Monet.

21. For example, in P.B. Coremans, *Van Meegeren's Faked Vermeers and De Hooghs* (Amsterdam, 1949), we find on pp. 28-29 a table listing

thirteen of van Meegeren's forgeries. One column is headed "Style of the Painting," and in it we find the names of Vermeer and de Hoogh.

22. "Style" and "manner" are usually used interchangeably by art historians and others. For certain purposes one might wish to draw a distinction between manner and style—working backwards, perhaps, from the fact that a mannerism of a painter and a stylistic feature of his work are not necessarily the same thing; but no such distinction will be invoked here.

23. For this—the original—use of "neo-Impressionist," see Ralph E. Shikes and Paula Harper *Pissarro: His Life and Work* (New York, 1980), Ch. 17. Reproductions of the Pissarros mentioned can be found on pp. 215, 217, and 292.

24. A Pissarro or a Caravaggio is not simply in the style of Pissarro or Caravaggio. It is just pointless to say, e.g., that Caravaggio's *Entombment* (Rome, Vatican Pinacoteca) is in the style of Caravaggio. It is not pointless, however, to say that it is in Caravaggio's mature, or post-1600, or religious style. And, of course, a Caravaggio is not a Caravaggesque painting.

25. Moir, *The Italian Followers of Caravaggio,* pp. 18-21.

26. Goodman, "The Status of Style," p. 806.

27. Ibid., p. 807. But "not . . . every property that helps determine the maker or period or provenance of a work is stylistic" e.g., its being signed by *N*. So every stylistic feature is who-when-where relevant, but not every feature of a work that is who-when-where relevant is a stylistic feature.

28. Sagoff, 178.

29. Ibid., 175. But merely in his words. For he has in mind "only forgeries which differ widely in place and time from the original."

30. By Caravaggio's "realism" or "secularism" is meant "the representation of sacred persons as common people and of sacred and miraculous subjects as human experiences, actions and events." Moir, *The Italian Followers of Caravaggio*, p. 302. As Moir points out, "among all the qualities of Caravaggio's art, its secularity . . . was the most objectionable."

31. Sherman Lee, *A History of Far Eastern Art* (Englewood Cliffs, N.J. 1964), p. 253.

32. Ibid., p. 255.

33. Arthur Danto, "Artworks and Real Things," *Theoria* 39 (1973): 13.

34. Erwin Panofsky, *Albrecht Durer* (Princeton University Press, 1955), pp. 31-32, figs. 47 and 48.

35. Sagoff, 176.

36. Nor need a photograph and an original differ in medium: a photograph of a photograph is a photograph—and a photographic reproduction of a photographic reproduction is a photographic reproduction.

37. Danto, 7.

38. Ibid., 7, 13.

39. "On Sense and Reference," *Translations from the Philosophical Writings of Gottlob Frege,* Peter Geach and Max Black, ed. (Oxford, 1952), pp. 58, 65.

40. To be sure, one can copy a copy. But a copy of a copy is like a quotation of a quotation, a quotation embedded in a quotation. If I quote myself as having said, "Panofsky said, 'S'," the reference of "S" is 'S', not S. A copy of a copy has as its reference another copy, not the original of which the other is a copy.

41. Danto, 7. This does not, as Goodman observes, mean that a copy cannot in some ways be superior to the original of which it is a copy: "An original painting may be less rewarding than an inspired copy; a damaged original may have lost its former merit [whereas a good copy may have preserved it?] . . ." *Languages of Art,* p. 119.

42. Ibid.

43. As, e.g., in the case of *The Admonition of the Instructress,* ascribed to Ku K'ai-chih. See Lee, pp. 255-57.

44. Apart, of course, from the usual supplementary materials employed by art historians, such as letters, biographies, legal documents, and the like.

Forging Issues from Forged Art

L.B. Cebik

For nearly a decade we have studied art forgeries in hopes of discovering something about their aesthetic impact. Since Nelson Goodman, the issues surrounding forgery have been framed in aesthetic terms. What is aesthetically wrong with artistic forgery?[1] If we judge a work on purely aesthetic criteria, why does a work of art become worthless when we discover it to be a forgery if once we found it moving and valuable?[2] Does knowing a work of art to be a forgery make an aesthetic difference between it and an authentic work?[3] What, if anything, makes authentic works aesthetically more valuable than copies or forgeries?[4] Do forgeries have radically different cognizable properties from authentic works and thus fail to have equal value to authentic works?[5] Are the origins and achievements of an artwork among the essential features of art so that to dismiss the importance of forging is to attack the very idea of art?[6] Can we aesthetically dismiss as irrelevant or merely extrinsic the moral, historical, and artistic disvaluation of forged artworks?[7]

These traditional ways of formulating the issues of art forgery continue unabated. Although the majority of discussants view the art forgery as tainted, at least a few have argued the reverse. Roger Clark, for example, concludes that "recent arguments have failed to establish the relevance of the origins or the history of production of an artwork

L.B. Cebik's article first appeared in the *Southern Journal of Philosophy* 27 (3), 1989, pp. 331-346. It is reprinted here by permission of the publisher and the author.

to its aesthetic value. Forgeries seem to deserve the same respect aesthetically as any other artwork . . ."[8] In contrast, David Goldblatt argues that "in the case of forgeries, there is only the *appearance* of having the same aesthetic predicates."[9]

The discussion approaches an impasse so long as we continue to formulate the basic questions in terms of a relationship between art forgery and aesthetic value. A much more fundamental question is whether we can learn anything about art itself from the analysis of art forgeries. Only when we can answer in the affirmative would it be time to return to the question of forged art's aesthetic value. However, what we learn about forgery and art may not necessarily direct us back to that question.

Forgery is not merely a concept. It is also and primarily a complex action and a complex of action performed by people for purposes within a special substructure of society in general. Thus, inquiries into forgery only begin with questions about the content and structure of the concept. They must go on to explore how we typically and atypically act toward forgeries. In this way, the inquiries uncover how we want to treat forgeries and for what reasons, giving us numerous clues to the nature and ramifications of the idea of forgery in art. Whether or not artistic forgery inextricably links to the very idea of art, as Denis Dutton so broadly suggests, is a question we shall leave open for the moment. It is at best a goal, and not a presumption, of our inquiry.[10]

Nevertheless, the debates over forgery and the aesthetic value of art have taught much about the concept of forgery. Almost every analysis of forgery has contributed something, if only instructive error. If the following discussion tends to focus around the work of Michael Wreen, it is because he has had some of the most sensible things to say about forgery.

Forgery, Deception and Fraud

Forgery necessarily involves at least the attempt to deceive.[11] In real forgery, the artist, his agent, or some other person in the chain between producer and consumer must represent the work of A as the work of B in an effort to deceive someone. Ordinarily we think of the artist, a Van Meegeren perhaps, as the author of the misrepresentation. The artist usually possesses the skills needed to make the misrepresentation convincing. However, we can conceive an agent who might doctor or have doctored an artist's study copy or a student's stylistic practice work or the work of an unknown derivative artist in order to convince a purchaser or expert that the work comes from an old or new master. Modern techniques of physical and chemical analysis make expert forgery more difficult than ever. But this only makes the process more complex in a world of 53 million-dollar Van Goghs.

We may note in passing that we tend to reserve the label "forgery" for cases in which we may bring to bear the most sophisticated methods of detection. Unloading a student copy of Mona Lisa upon a tourist counts as mere fraud. Extending these cases toward each other produces a vague territory between forgery and fraud, a territory that shifts with changing interests and techniques in analyzing artworks.

The effort to deceive implies an intention along with a consistent set of motivations. Economic gain and resentful embarrassment of critics count among potential motives for forging art.[12] Intentions, of course, are subject to evolving patterns of possibilities opened by the structures within which we produce artworks in any place and age. The Renaissance master who signs or releases a work done mostly or entirely by students in his school or shop commits no forgery. We may not say the same for all periods of painting, especially those in which we do not recognize the school or shop system of artistic production. What counts as deception or the intent to deceive, and thus what counts as forgery, carries within itself a decisive social element.

To this point, we have purposely categorized together forgeries perpetrated by an artist and those directed or conducted by others upon artistic works. Indeed, it would appear that a Van Meegeren belongs to a rare species of forger and that the latter practice is the more common.

Many would argue for a distinction at this point, noting perhaps that only the artist's attempt to pass off his work as that of another artist qualifies as true artistic forgery. An art dealer who alters or has altered an artist's signature commits a fraud. At most he forges or has forged the artist's signature.

The viability and the utility of this distinction depend upon the particular concern to which it might answer. Legally, we may prosecute the art dealer for fraud. Indeed, in this kind of case, if uncovered soon enough, we may be able to recover our economic loss.

From another perspective, the distinction hardly matters. More to the point is the fact that after a work has been accepted as authentic, the discovery of its true origin has many of the same consequences for both types of cases. The possessor of the work feels more than cheated; he or she feels chagrined at being fooled. The differences in style and technique, say between Vermeer and Van Meegeren, so obvious after the fact, should have been apparent before the fact: this point holds our attention even had Van Meegeren been innocent and his name changed to Vermeer by a dealer. Those originally certifying the work as authentic experience a loss of confidence in their expertise and judgment, if not worse consequences for their careers.

The work goes into hiding, and with it—hope the victims of the deception—the embarrassment. Forgetting embarrassment is difficult enough without the glaring reminder of the work itself hovering above us from a wall. Resentment and revenge, denial and denunciation, self-pity and self-righteousness all replace aesthetic concerns. The work itself matters little at all as a work of art. Anyone who focuses his or her attention on the consequences of deceit in art soon discovers that drawing lines between forgery and fraud only distracts from understanding those consequences.

Forgery as an Adjective

Forgery is an attributive rather than a predicative concept. As Wreen notes of his cat, Freddie, the predicative adjective "ten-pound" carries through truly in claims that Freddie is a ten-pound cat and he is a ten-pound animal. The attributive "large," however, allows Freddie truly to be a large (house) cat and falsely a large animal.[13] Moreover, the applicable class of attributive adjectives calls for two-term (or more complex) nouns.[14] Thus, one forges not just a painting and not just a Vermeer, but a Vermeer painting.

Understanding this much about attributive adjectives permits some understanding of the logic of forgeries. While a forged Vermeer painting is still a painting, it is not a Vermeer painting. Thus, it does not necessarily take on the cluster of attributions accorded to Vermeer paintings. Just this point lies behind Mark Sagoff's attempt to show that (for example) a Van Meegeren forgery and a true Vermeer "are not sufficiently the same sort of thing to be compared" in the way we might compare two Vermeer paintings.[15] This categorical differentiation applies whether or not Sagoff is correct that there are "radically different cognizable properties" between originals and forgeries.[16]

Wreen attempts to weaken the effects of the categorical differentiation between originals and forgeries in his effort to dismiss claims emergent from the institutional theory of art. Arthur Danto and George Dickie, in Wreen's account, claim that the discovery of a fake causes the object in question to lose its stature as an artwork insofar as being a fake is a defeating condition of being an artwork. For Danto and Dickie, "artwork" contains analytically the condition of being an "original," at least in the sense of having been done by an artist.[17] The radical and unacceptable result for Wreen is that a Van Meegeren painting fails to be a painting as a result of the denial that the forgery is an artwork.

As is typical of so much argumentation on forgery, Wreen carries his point only by importing to the institutional theory a Beardsleyesque theory of the aesthetic which guarantees that nearly all paintings (including forgeries) must be artworks. That a forgery be "intended to be capable of affording at least some measure of aesthetic gratification" satisfies Wreen's minimal requirement for it to be a painting and an artwork. However, the criterion not only imposes on Danto and Dickie a noninstitutional criterion of being an artwork, but as well makes housepainting (exterior or interior) the equal of any old master's work with respect to being an artwork.[18] The attributive nature of the charge of forgery does permit us to say with some assurance that comparing a forgery to works of the artist forged differs from comparing two works of the artist. We may also say that a comparison of a forgery on aesthetic grounds with a nonforgery presupposes that the forged work has acquired the status of an artwork on grounds other than those operative before the discovery of the forgery. However, nothing in the knowledge of forgery speaks to what grounds there might be (or might not be) for according artistic status to the forged work.

Forgery, Imitation, and Fakery

Forging in art differs from many other forms of imitation and fakery. Art forgery has classically included attempts to make deceptive copies of works, to misattribute works to better-known artists, to make composite works, and to produce properly aged works in the style of noted artists.[19] Art forgery does not include all forms of copy work, fakery, and imitation.[20] Additionally, we may distinguish among pirating, misrepresenting, counterfeiting, and forging. Forgery tends to involve the making or shaping of objects for fraudulent use. Piracy involves theft, even the theft of ideas, but—as Wreen has pointed out—for unauthorized use in the production or reproduction of a product, rights to which belong to another.[21] Counterfeiting and faking can involve objects, including natural ones, for which we do not ordinarily look for an author.[22] And, of course, without the attributions to other authors and the footnoting paraphernalia in this essay, everyone would know in what plagiarism consists.

Wreen, however, dismisses authorship in favor of the notion of "issuing from," thus recognizing that while reference to a source is inherent in a forgery (e.g., a forged Vermeer), the source (by current standards) need not always be a named individual. A parallel situation seems to apply to current standards of checking and forged checks.[23]

In both cases, however, the notion of presumable or identifiable authorship forms the paradigm against which forgery operates. Social extensions of the paradigm emerge from changing patterns of practice within various institutions. Magnetic check coding permits easy forgery of checks using any signature that is replicated on two identification cards (themselves also forgeries). Nothing similar accrues to art forgeries, except that some kind of extension is possible. But in art, the extension is to unsigned works replicating styles and materials of periods and places before the practice of signing works emerged. Thus the parallels Wreen sees between forging art and forging checks in their non-authorship aspects may be purely accidental.[24]

With equal disregard for what we can carry over from paradigms in one realm to those in another, Wreen thinks we can speak equally of forging a dollar bill and of forging a check or artwork, apparently because "we" also issue dollars.[25] However, while governments issue dollar bills, individuals paradigmatically issue checks and produce artworks, with corporate, school, and other sources of issuance as extensions. We must not lose sight of the varying nature of the authorship of forged works, whether they be checks, wills, bank loans, contracts, or art objects.

Similar considerations apply to the effort to expand forgery into the realm of performance, contrary to Goodman's autographic-allographic distinction among arts.[26] The expansion appears predicated upon an unwarranted extension of the notion of production coupled with modern technological means of converting performances into objects (audio and video discs and tapes, for example). Without the recording object, Dutton's worries over an electronically accelerated recording of a Liszt performance would evaporate. What gives plausibility to concerns over forging performances is the sense we give in art talk to performances having stylistic "signatures." However, Dutton's reduction of production (as in painting or sculpture) to performance forces us either to grow overly concerned with how (step-by-step) an artist like Monet got each dot of paint on the canvas or to empty the performing artist's activities of their artistry.[27] From focal (if not paradigmatic) concerns in forgery, we can remove neither the object nor the authorship.

Forgery and Victims

There is a rough correlation between the degree of victimization and our condemnation of practices that yield less than fully authentic art. Forgery depends upon detailed and sophisticated techniques of deception, usually involving authorship. The discovery of forgery usually casts doubts upon experts in the realm of art, thereby breaching the trust of ordinary viewers and supporters of art. Little wonder that forgery, over any other form of inauthentic art, has become the focus of aesthetic and philosophic discussion, even though music tape and record piracy is far more common and profitable.

To pirate is to copy without authorization whatever is copyable, e.g., recordings, texts, and the like. Despite Wreen's protests, we tend to link such efforts to theft more than to forgery or fraud. Piracy in music usually involves authentic performances, but unauthorized reproduction and distribution of the performance recording. Authorized reproductions of visual artworks usually employ other media than the original, e.g., photography, and they may not retain a work's original size. We consider them to have reputable purposes if one observes the laws governing control of reproduction by owners. By contrast, a counterfeit is a passable copy of a work in the general exchange within art's realm. Intended to deceive, it rarely touches the truly expert members of the realm. A copy passed as an original usually stings only the naive.

Each of these types of less than fully authentic art raises different issues. What they have in common is that none of the issues is simply or purely aesthetic. If Danto's notion of artworld—or as reformulated here, artrealm—has any utility, it is to call attention to this very fact.[28] Art does not exist in a vacuum. It arises and persists only because there is a complex social substructure that permits, encourages, and criticizes it, as well as buying and selling it. Forgery, therefore, is never a purely aesthetic issue. Perhaps it is not an aesthetic issue at all. Still, it is always a problem for artrealm.

In artrealm, we cannot separate readily, if at all, categorical, ethical, artistic, and aesthetic domains anymore than religion can separate ethical, theological, doctrinal, and reverential domains. This ultimate inseparability does not mean that we cannot focus upon one domain, excluding to the degree possible considerations from the others. However, to expect complete success in the separation is neither reasonable nor productive. Even Dutton's phrase, "artistic crimes," implies complex social, cultural, artistic, and aesthetic interrelationships, as well as relationships to social structures outside artrealm.[29] Van Meegeren was, after all, tried and convicted in a court of law and not a court of art.

Yet, the victims of forgery, more than those of most of the other fraudulent practices noted, tend to be members of artrealm rather than members of the general public. Experts, critics, art lovers, patrons, curators, and collectors fall prey to forgeries; the public—interested or not—tends to fill the role of innocent bystander. At stake are more than economic and legal concerns that define the evils of other inauthentic art. At stake are basic beliefs in art itself, not to mention careers based upon the health and integrity of all aspects of artrealm. Piracy, counterfeiting, and fraudulent sale of copies or reproductions affect at most the periphery of artrealm, its interface with the largely naive or ignorant public. Forgery threatens the heart of artrealm, the production of art itself.

The Forged and the Authentic

The opposite of the forged is the authentic. If we confuse many near synonyms with forgery, we equally take many wrong terms to be its opposite. The most common near synonyms are "original" and "genuine."[30] Neither of these vague terms equates more than conversationally—and then marginally—with the idea of authenticity that opposes forgery. Still the terms seem to answer to Margolis' search for a generic concept under which to subsume forgery ("the inauthentic or the ungenuine or something very much like it") and to Wreen's undeveloped claim that "forged" is logically parasitic on "genuine."[31]

Wreen equates authenticity and genuineness and defines a forged painting as "a painting that is not genuine with the intention to deceive."[32] Shortly thereafter, he speaks of a "genuine painting—not just a print," leaving us with the idea that being genuine may be no more than not being just a print. Genuine may often contrast with being a print, but prints are not forgeries. A poor-sighted, unschooled buyer might be fooled into purchasing a print thinking he had received a genuine painting, but forgery and authenticity would not enter into any serious talk here. Indeed, "genuine" may be a good term to avoid in any attempt to codify the language appropriate to forgeries, if the corruption of the term as applied to semiprecious and precious gemstones is any indication.

Likewise, originality fails to capture the contrast between the authentic and the forged. Most attempts to capture forgery in an opposition to originality lean upon the person of the artist. For Alfred Lessing, originality bespeaks "art viewed as a creative, not as a reproductive or technical activity," and the work viewed "as a great artistic achievement."[33] Dutton contrasts "forged" and "original" on the basis of the distinction between correctly represented and "misrepresented artistic performance."[34] What fails in these cases is the slant on originality. Not all or even many uncreative, lesser artistic achievements are forgeries. Contrarily, under a certain construal, a forgery might be a major creative achievement. To fill in convincingly a missing period in Vermeer's career is no small feat. Of course, not the painter's performance is a forgery, but his work. An A-work is forged if we discover the B did it in an attempt to deceive us, regardless of how B went about doing it.

It remains the case that we can definitionally say little about authenticity. This situation has a reason. Seldom are we called upon to say anything about the authenticity of authentic works. We presume things to be as presented, whether in statements or in objects set before us in the world's discourse. There are special (parasitic) contexts within which we expect otherwise, for example, magic shows, used car sales, and political campaigns. Apart from such contexts, we must have situationally or methodologically derived reasons for doubt. Like truth-telling in testimony or reportage, works of art carry a presumption of authenticity unless or until we have occasion and reason to challenge it.

It is in this way that forgery seems sometimes more fundamentally like lying than theft; not just, as Wreen would have it because forgery involves overt misrepresentation or is a species of fraud.[35] "Your love for me was a lie," complained the young lady when she confronted her (former) suitor arm-in-arm with another woman. In fact, the young man had made no protestations of love. But he had done other things, including giving the young lady many presents. They all looked different to her now, cheap and tawdry instead of bright and promising. Of course, it was only now that she realized that the presents had once looked bright and promising. In a similar manner, we challenge the presumption of authenticity whenever we encounter instances of artworks that suggest standards of authenticity by not meeting them.

Major challenges to artworks often invoke evidence that would defeat a claim of authenticity (had one been made). We know in detail (or can know, if we choose to study) the kinds of evidence and the techniques of discovery that falsify authenticity. We have learned to analyze styles, brush strokes, pigments, canvas, glazings, and frameworks using techniques that range from art scholarship to physics and chemistry. Some techniques, such as stylistic analysis, may only cast doubt upon a work; others, such as chemical analysis of materials, may be decisive. Any history of forgery detection provides a good catalog of criteria for defeating the presumption of authenticity. So long as authenticity remains a presumption, we shall always have great difficulty specifying criteria for attribution. Presumptive concepts often have few criteria for attribution except those derived from the defeat of challenges.

To fail a challenge to authenticity is not, however, yet to be a forgery—or anything else, for that matter. Challenges to authenticity go under virtually all the names of malevolent practices we have cited along the way, each with specific criteria that justify the label imposed. In contrast, authenticity functions predominantly as a presumption, acquiring content and criteria largely on a case-by-case basis by overcoming or negating particular challenges. We are thus unlikely to see fulfilled Margolis' plea for less attention to forgery and more to the "general question of authenticity."[36] Indeed, it is not unlikely that we shall come to understand the authentic largely, if not only, through meeting future innovative challenges to it.

Forgery and Individuals

The confusion of originality, genuineness, and authenticity that we saw in various accounts of forgery has a foundation. Briefly and inadequately put, the congruence of the three terms in artrealm is possible only under the influence of the idea of unique, individual authorship as a principal criterion of modern art. Dickie takes originality as a decisive criterion for the bestowal of the label "artwork."[37] Originality here entails origination of the work from essentially (but not absolutely) the creative efforts, the originality, of known individuals.

Attached implicitly is the idea of a work being fixed and finished upon conclusion of the artist's original efforts. Wilsmore has recently defended a "theory of identity for works of art which provides a rationale for their independent existence and which shows that our individuative practices are based in a humanist belief in the artist as creator of the aesthetic properties of the works of art which are essentially theirs."[38] Goodman's analysis of notation rests precisely upon a similar idea. A score written in a proper notation "has as a primary function the authoritative identification of a work," a function which is logically prior to any musical function.[39] In artrealm and in society at large, the work of art has taken on the aspect, first, of identifiable object and, second, of property, even if only in some cases "intellectual property." However, the philosophical question is not whether identifiable works are possible, but whether they are necessary to any artrealm whatsoever.

Before suggesting an answer to this question, we should distinguish between functional and committed levels of artwork identities, especially as we associate a work inseparably with its creator. Authoritative identification of a work can serve useful purposes that follow from the notion of identification without theoretical aesthetic additions. To identify a work as Klee's "Twittering Machine" allows us, among other things, to distinguish it from honestly signed student copies, to know where to go to find other works done in its style or at its level of competency, and to compare works done at a specific time, in a specific area, or by a specific person. Indeed, one interpretation of Goodman's notion of authoritative identification need lead us no farther than this.

However, functional identification often gives way to much more that follows only from the commitments to the operative presumptions of artrealm. Whether or not these presumptions stem from excesses (or their remnants) of periods of genius worship is a problem we may leave to historians of art theory. The introduction of creativity, originality, or similar attributes that are (debatable) functions of the individual artist reveals a prevailing set of assumptions underlying contemporary conceptions of art. That they serve as near synonyms within artrealm only tells us that paradigmatic art is creative, original, and a product of individuals.

The presence of these terms in discussions of forgery is suspect. A forgery remains a forgery, even if of an uninspired, dull school piece. If a university museum needed a school piece to fill out a certain historical collection, it would have to replace a discovered forgery in its collection with an authentic work. Upon learning that a work was a forgery, it would proceed virtually in the same way as with a forged Van Gogh. Only the level of excitement would be lower.

With respect to forgeries, authenticity requires the identity of a work's author or maker, not the evaluation of either the work or the author. If the operative paradigm calls for the author to be an individual, then works without individual makers cannot be forged. However, extensions of the paradigm may make it possible to forge or fake works from periods without known authors, for example medieval Madonna-and-childs, replete with gold leaf and plank foundations. Indeterminism over whether such productions deserve more the title of forgeries or more the label of fakes would reveal only the fact that at the frontiers of paradigm extensions, we lose the ability to be decisive for want of clear and clearly applicable criteria for decision.

The Limits of Individualism

The one thing we seem to learn about art from the study of known forgeries is that our current conception of art is inextricably linked to its production by individuals. This truism would require a treatise in itself to cover all its ramifications. We have seen that the notion makes all too easy a conflation of art theory with attempts to clarify the concept of forgery in art. The assumption that originality, genuineness, and authenticity all drove toward the same idea of individual identity of authorship led to unnecessary artistic requirements for the determination of forgeries.

Even a logically restrictive reading of Goodman's notion of authoritative identification places limits on artworks. Nowhere in the idea is there room for paradigmatic art being fluid, unfinished, evolving, and continuous in its creation. Current artrealm notions do not countenance, except as aberrations, exceptions, or derivations, continuous revision or improvisation. Foreign to modern artrealm is the idea of a neighborhood mural that represents a long-term journal. Each month or year, we might replace certain notable figures and portrayed events with others of more current note. A constant background might provide neighborhood "roots" against which the foreground might undergo complete change every four or five years.

Equally foreign would be the idea of music passed from generation to generation, evolving under the influence of both the current keeper and the life of the community in a changing world. More acceptable to artrealm since the beginning of the 19th century are the artificial terminations of these lines of progression by capturing the songs on tape or in a score. Just how many true lyrics to Scottish ballads were lost under the pen of Robert Burns we may never know. In any event, living songs freeze and die as they acquire permanence and the quality of correctness to a sample or a score.

In the imaginable world of fluid art, originality would take on a communal note, with emphasis upon continuing effort. Genuineness might come to suggest a freedom from artificiality and improper outside influence. And authenticity might become a matter more closely akin to Heideggerian notions than to legal notions. We might find a place for forgery in all this, but it would be quite different from the sort of thing upon which contemporary aesthetic debates have focused. Forgery might even return to its own roots more reflective of ways of making than of the propriety of making.

The imaginable world of fluid art does exist, of course, whatever the toll of our attempts to freeze it for display. Until frozen, it is not susceptible to being forged. Since we "capture" an improvisational jazz performance, we cannot forge one. Folk music lends itself to the process of periodic freezing and thawing perhaps more than most of the arts. Record labels declare a work traditional, with any royalties accruing to an arranger rather than to a songwriter. Such mechanisms to sort out questions of authenticity from property rights contribute to our ability to correctly track the history of a work. However, they may also occasion a loss, as future arrangers fail to look back to the source of the work and only examine the most recent arrangement. Self-taught musicians, disproportionately guitarists, tend now to learn their first licks from records rather than from live performances.

It is perhaps no accident that art's emphasis upon the individual creator coincides so closely with the intensification since the Renaissance of individualism throughout the spectrum of political and social rights. Artrealm is not a separate world, self-enclosed and self-determinate, Danto notwithstanding. Rather, artrealm carves a field of action out of the broader social realm and retains or imports standing concepts from that larger sphere. Forgery is one of them. It remains tied to property rights and their adjudication, whatever the aesthetic difficulties which a known forgery may present to those whose place of commitment is within artrealm.

Forgeries and Aesthetic Worth

We have noted in passing that forgery remains the paramount philosophical problem of fraud in art despite the greater prevalence and profitability of piracy both in music and in cinema and television. Yet, the analysis of forgery ultimately tells us little about the aesthetics of a forged work. We may compare two paintings, perhaps a known Van Meegeren forgery of a Vermeer and an original Vermeer. Let us suppose for the moment that we can do so on aesthetic grounds. To do so presupposes that we have bestowed upon the Van Meegeren work by whatever means turn out to be proper the status of artwork, not as a forgery of a Vermeer painting, but as a Van Meegeren painting. Within present strictures of the realm, it passes the basic test for being a worthy, original, genuine, and authentic Van Meegeren painting.

That we can compare the two on aesthetic grounds would entail that we can speak of each (and by extension strike attitudes toward each) in appropriate aesthetic terms. We can contemplate each, analyze each, evaluate each, interpret each, and even value each. Whether we should do any of these things for the Van Meegeren work is irrelevant; it suffices that we *can* do them.

The knowledge that the Van Meegeren work began its life as a forgery of Vermeer, as a work attributed to Vermeer and sufficiently like other Vermeer works that temporally enclosed the forgery to be accepted for a while as a Vermeer work, does not disappear from our considerations and contemplations. However, that knowledge does not prevent us from viewing the work as a Van Meegeren painting of sufficient aesthetic interest to merit contemplation and consideration.

For perceptual purists, there is a practical problem: can we set aside the painting's history and possible alienation well enough to receive and perceive it on its own? Within theories of immaculate perception, to a lesser degree and with other knowledge at stake, setting aside what we know is a problem for the reception and perception of all artworks. By way of contrast, Goodman and his ilk, who view perception as an active process, will find no such problem. They will only have some additional information and attitudes with which to approach the work. As with perceptual purists, there is a difference of degree rather than one of type. The matter of known forgeries ends as little more than a matter of what we can individually do with what we bring to an artwork.

Whether a forgery has aesthetic value, then, depends upon the theoretic commitment we bring to the work, the complex array of views on art, its value, its place in human life, and how we perceive it. Without much Holmesian deduction, we can fairly predict the aesthetic value an individual will see in a forgery by knowing the theory he or she brings to the work. It is the aesthetic theory, whether well-formed or ill-formed, whether presumed or explicit, that largely determines the aesthetic value of forgeries, and not the concept of forgery itself.

Yet, even those who let aesthetic value reside in the individual merits of a work without regard to the history of its production (e.g. Clark) presume something especially nasty about forgery, seeking to see of what the nastiness consists rather than whether it exists. As with "murder," but unlike piracy, we cannot by fiat expunge the attitude-directing aura from "forgery." Piracy does not threaten the authenticity or any of the artistic properties of the original work or the original performance. Consequently, it does not threaten the commitments, whether theoretical or perhaps even existential, of those who claim their place within artrealm as an expert, a critic, an art historian, a (not-for-profit) collector, a curator, a patron, or simply an art lover. The discovery of a forgery devastates in ways mere fraud, fakery,

Notes

1. Albert Lessing, "What is Wrong With a Forgery?" in *The Forger's Art: Forgery and the Philosophy of Art*, Denis Dutton, ed. (Berkeley: University of California Press, 1983), p. 58.

2. Leonard B. Meyer, "Forgery and the Anthropology of Art," in *The Forger's Art*, p. 78.

3. Nelson Goodman, *Languages of Art* (Indianapolis: Hackett Publishing Co., Inc., 1976), p. 104.

4. Jack W. Meiland, "Originals, Copies, and Aesthetic Value" in *The Forger's Art*, p. 116.

5. Mark Sagoff, "The Aesthetic Status of Forgeries" in *The Forger's Art*, p. 151.

6. Denis Dutton, "Artistic Crimes," in *The Forger's Art*, p. 183.

7. Michael Wreen, "Is, Madam? Nay, It Seems!" in *The Forger's Art*, p. 224.

8. Roger Clark, "Historical Context and the Aesthetic Evaluation of Forgeries," *The Southern Journal of Philosophy*, 22 (1984), 320.

9. David Goldblatt, "Remarks on the Ontology of Style," *The Southern Journal of Philosophy*, 24 (1986), 44.)

10. Dutton, p. 183.

11. *See,* for example, Joseph Margolis, "Art, Forgery, and Authenticity," in *The Forger's Art*, p. 161.

12. *See,* for example, Lessing's account of Van Meegeren's motives in "What is Wrong With a Forgery?" in *The Forger's Art*, p. 60.

13. Wreen, p. 194.

14. Wreen, p. 195.

15. Sagoff, p. 131.

16. Sagoff, pp. 146, 152.

17. *See* Arthur Danto, "The Artworld," *Journal of Philosophy*, 61 (1964), 571-584; "Artworks and Real Things," *Theoria* 39 (1973), 1-17; and "The End of Art," in *The Death of Art*, ed. B. Lang (New York: Haven Publications, 1984), as well as George Dickie, *Art and The Aesthetic—An Institutional Analysis* (Ithaca: Cornell University Press, 1974), pp. 46-48.

18. Wreen, p. 197; see also Monroe Beardsley, "Redefining Art," in *The Aesthetic Point of View* (Ithaca: Cornell University Press, 1983).

19. Lessing, p. 65.

20. *See,* for example, the pieces by Goodman, Meiland, Sagoff, and Dutton in *The Forger's Art*.

21. Michael Wreen, "Some remarks on Forgery, Plagiarism, and Piracy," *The Southern Journal of Philosophy*, 22 (1984), 134.

22. *See* Margolis, "Art, Forgery, and Authenticity," pp. 161-162.

23. Wreen, "Is, Madam? Nay, It Seems!" pp. 192-199.

24. Wreen, "Is, Madam? Nay, It Seems!" p. 193.

25. Wreen, "Is, Madam? Nay, It Seems!" p. 193.

26. Goodman, *Languages of Art*, pp. 113 ff.

27. Dutton, pp. 174-75.

28. *See* Danto, "Artworks and Real Things," 14-16.

29. Dutton, pp. 172-187.

30. *See* the articles by Meyer, Goodman, Meiland, Sagoff, Margolis, Wreen, and Beardsley in *The Forger's Art*.

31. Margolis, pp. 161, 170; and Wreen, "Is, Madam? Nay, It Seems!" pp. 194, 199.

32. Wreen, "Is, Madam? Nay, It Seems!" p. 189.

33. Lessing, pp. 68, 70.

34. Dutton, p. 186.

35. Wreen, "Is, Madam? Nay, It Seems!" p. 201.

36. Margolis, p. 171.

37. Dickie, p. 46.

38. S.J. Wilsmore, "A Humanist Theory of Identity for Works of Art," *The Journal of Value Inquiry*, 21 (1987), 43.)

39. Goodman, *Languages of Art*, p. 128. Cf. Margolis, p. 169.

40. See the suggestions, developed within the conceit of love, by Francis Sparshott, "The Disappointed Lover," in *The Forger's Art*, p. 246 ff.

No Dance Is a Fake

Kenton Harris

Elsewhere I have defined "dance-events" as events during which discrete objects present the opportunity for perceiving perceptual motion as patterned motion[1], leaving wholly untouched the question of what makes a dance-event an object of art. I believe that this definition can serve us in understanding why it is impossible to create a "dance fake." Despite the important but unanswered question of "arthood," I maintain that the above is an accurate definition of dance and that it is the nature of dance itself which prevents the existence of dance fakes and not dance's status as art.

In this paper I propose a basic ontological theory of dance-events as well as dance-as-performance-art-events in a way consistent with the above definition. After a review of some of the practical consequences this theory has for the practice of dance criticism and some ontological puzzles regarding dance, I shall draw my final conclusion, that dance is an art which can not be faked (but perhaps style can be).

I have limited the extent of my ontological speculations for obvious practical considerations (the topic seems sufficiently rich as to generate new puzzles endlessly). But I have a more respectable reason for curtailing discussion where I do. My intention in this paper is to give the fundamentals of an ontology and to defend it by showing it to be plausible and of practical value, yielding results which are, for the most part, in keeping with common sense. I am working with the assumption that most sentences about dance which ordinary language users have always assumed to be true are true, and most sentences

Kenton Harris wrote this paper for this collection. It is being published for the first time.

about dance that ordinary language users have always considered to be false are false. Therefore, where my theory differs from common wisdom, I attempt to provide non-question-begging reasons which account for this difference.

Given that the ontological status of a dance-event is exactly that of an event in which objects (usually physical) exhibit motion, presenting the opportunity for the perception of patterned motion as patterned motion, the next glaring problem of ontology for the philosopher of dance is, what, if anything, makes two dance-events instances of the *same* dance-event? My first response to this question is shallow but, I believe, accurate. No two events are instances of the same event if one means by that numerically identical. The very fact that they are known to be *two* events belies the fact that they are not the *same* event. But I recognize that this is a shallow response since the question may mean something else entirely. One may be asking, under what conditions is it proper to say that two distinct dance-events are instances of the same *kind* of dance-event.

I have a shallow response in mind once again. It all depends upon what one means by *kind*. One may mean under what conditions are two events both instances of dance-as-performance-art (DAPA) or under what conditions are two events both instances of jazz dance or both instances of *Swan Lake*. In the first case, I claim that two dances are both instances of the same *kind of dance* (DAPA) if the events conform to the definition that captures what the nature of a DAPA-event is, what its purpose is. For any two events to both be instances of DAPA, they must both be such as to have objective characteristics which satisfy the definition. In fact, for any large general sub-class of dance-events which can be specified by a definition, a similar response would answer the question what must an event be to be a member of the class in question.

The lattermost case deals with a more perplexing issue. What does it mean to say that two dance-events are instances of the same *work of dance*? Various DAPA-events can be labeled instances of the same type *work of dance*. What does one assert when one claims this? What conditions must be satisfied? I argue below that for two events to both be instances of a particular work of dance, they must adhere to certain reproduction rules that are implicit in the use of the name of the work of dance by the specified language community. I will explain this below.

The middle case is most curious and I will deal with that at the end of this paper. I take this question to be about sub-classes of DAPA-events, but not classes of specific works of dances. This is a question about "styles of dance" and presentations. What constitutes an instance of jazz dance can better be answered after the question of "work of dance" or dance identity is answered. Therefore I shall deal with the "work of dance" issue first.

But before I go into greater detail on the above, I wish first to stipulate a distinction between "same" and "identical" as they shall now be used for the remainder of this paper. By "identical" I shall mean numerical identity. I recognize that no two dance-events are identical so qualified. By "same" I shall mean two tokens of a type. I shall assume that it is often the case that two dance-events are the same.

Conditions for Sameness for two "Works of Dance"

The actual practice for ascribing sameness is a confusing affair. On the one hand any adequate criterion for *Swan Lake*, for instance, would have to be loose enough to allow for differences in sets, costumes, storyline, choreography, body types, dancing skills, budgets, contexts of presentation, artistic interpretations and even music that exist among the vast array of historical examples of *Swan Lake*. That is, the articulation of the identity criterion which people implicitly use must be loose enough to account for the various dissimilar events that critics (and others) have long held to be instances of a single work (other examples being perhaps *Coppelia*, *Giselle*, *The Nutcracker*, etc.). Since, as I stated, the point of these speculations is to discern this criterion, then we must look for one which explains how it is that two seemingly dissimilar events can both be instances of the same work (even if we restrict our examination to uncontentious claims of "sameness").

On the other hand, an adequate criterion would also be strict enough to account for the attention to detail the dance community pays to reproductions of other famous historical works (i.e. works of choreographers such as Duncan, Limon, Graham, Tutor, et al.) The puzzle seems to be that some of the time the criterion is very lax, other times it seems very tight. It may also be added that a good criterion would relate the dance-event in question to an historical predecessor yet be sufficiently pliant as to allow for furthering the aims of that historical work (continue its history, perhaps adding artistic merit).

To begin, let us re-examine what it is that DAPA-events have in common. An event is an instance of DAPA when it is a dance-event consisting of human performers who are dancing and presenting this patterned motion as an object of art. While this does tell us some of the objective characteristics which are shared by all DAPA-events, it is of little help in justifying our judgments that this DAPA-event is the same work of dance as some other. In as much as they are both DAPA-events, they are both tokens of a single type. But this is not the question raised. What is it to say that two DAPA-events are both *Swan Lake*?

Before I attempt to answer this question, I believe that it is worthwhile to say a few words about creating, naming and identifying dances. It has been my experience that the creation of a dance (both in choreography and in performance) is a much looser affair then one might think. Occasionally one has flashes of inspiration when an entire movement phrase is envisioned (or remembered for that matter), but more often it is the case that the making of a dance is a piecemeal thing that lurches unevenly forward, taking its impetus from what is going on at the moment. In choreography sometimes the only overriding concern is "How do I get her down-stage-left in 24 counts?" At times, the choreographer might know that this particular dancer turns well, but her body-type is ill-suited for impressive extensions. In such a case s/he might showcase the dancer's strengths and hide weaknesses. Since these decisions about the structure of the dance are contingent upon accidental features, they are readily changed given a different set of circumstances. In performance, should the audience respond a certain way, the dancer might augment or enhance a particular step. If a stage is fast or the performance area small, the dancer might change the choreography in order to give a better overall performance in this particular situation. This sort of thing goes on all the time in dance, yet choreographers, dancers, dance spectators, critics, etc., all make their way through this ephemeral world naming and identifying, usually with relative ease.

The point of these remarks is this. Dancers and choreographers, at least the ones with whom I have spoken, do not adhere to very strict identity criteria when recreating what they take to be same DAPA-events, at least, not all the time. Furthermore, the dance world does not seem to *require* very strict criteria. It has long been recognized that dance is one of the most transient of art forms. For the greater part of the history of dance, reviving a ballet meant simply finding someone who was in the original production and having him stage as much of the ballet as he could remember. After that, if there were blank spots, the choreographer would just have to fill them in as best he could. Works of dance lived only as long as dancers could remember them and were only as detailed as dancers could remember them.

This pliancy has been inherited by the dance community of today. Even with more sophisticated means of detailing dance performances we find that choreographers make only limited use of them. Choreographers almost universally criticize Laban and other notation systems as cumbersome and incapable of capturing the dance-type. Video and film, though more extensively used, suffer because they capture too much, specifics that are irrelevant or mistakes that need to be corrected, not repeated. But perhaps more to the point, the choreographers and persons who stage the dances have no problem with altering the specifics even when they are clearly documented by notation or film. If they think they can create a better production of some historical work they will.[2] And yet, all the time they maintain that theirs is but another in a series of tokens of a type.

Given the above, I think it unfruitful to search for strict prescriptions to determine what counts as two instances of the same "work of dance" when one is talking about historical works of dance. There is, as a matter of fact, much leeway in the ascription of type identity to a wide variety of tokens. When the very people responsible for creating and recreating the tokens adhere to no such strict rules (at least not all the time), it should not surprise us that such prescription cannot be found.

But now let us consider in a more rigorous way the limitations of a strict identity theory. To this end I wish to examine the curious case of *Swan Lake*. There would be little confusion if I told someone that I had seen *Swan Lake* last evening. They would assume that I saw a ballet consisting of many young women dressed in swan costumes, executing classical ballet movements to a musical score by Tchaikovsky, telling the story of a beautiful queen who suffered under the spell of an evil sorcerer, but who is saved by a valiant young prince. (They may make other assumptions about thirty-two fouettes in the third act, etc.) In the vast majority of cases they would probably be right. But do any of the above elements constitute a necessary condition for a DAPA-event being an instance of the *Swan Lake* type? It is difficult to see how they could. I shall argue that strict criteria of this kind do not work; they do not capture the actual practice of naming and identifying ballets. They do not reflect the pliancy the art form demands. And they are not necessary even for the purpose of identifying and categorizing types of DAPA-events. I shall argue for identity conditions that I believe to be more workable.

The Case Of *Swan Lake*

To start with, the original production of this work was mounted at the Bolshoi in 1877. (The premier was given on the evening of February 20 by the Julian reckoning that still persisted in Russia: according to the Gregorian calendar in effect elsewhere, the date was March 4.) Moscow Balletomanes could apparently buy their choice of at least two rather different *Swan Lake* scenarios even before the 1877 premiere. One version was known to be a "pirate" job, hastily run up by an unscrupulous publisher who had planted a spy at rehearsals. In retaliation the Bolshoi itself reportedly brought out an authorized edition *prior* to opening night. If so, then the official version, no less than any other, could not have reflected any last minute departures from the text. It is possible that there were no such revisions, but it is also highly improbable. Regardless, no eyewitness accounts of that first production have come down to us.

But there were various "modifications" even during the original season. After the ballet was finished, Tchaikovsky was asked to write a "Russian Dance" for the third act by the choreographer Reisinger. After the fifth performance he was asked by the ballerina Sobeshchanskaya to add another number for act two (a Pas de Deux in the form of variations).

Despite the above, many consider the history of this ballet to begin a full eighteen years later in 1895 with the celebrated Marius Petipa-Lev Ivanov revival at the Maryinsky in St. Petersburg (today the Kirov in St. Petersburg). Tradition has it that the original production was a flop and that it was not until the choreographic efforts of Petipa and Ivanov that *Swan Lake* enjoyed popular and aesthetic success.[3] This seems at best an overstatement, since each of the 33 performances given in the seasons of 1877-1883 was a sellout. By 1880 choreographer Olav Hansen was presenting an improved and embellished production in which he changed not only the choreography, but the musical score as well. During these later performances nearly a third of the score was cut, and substitutions were made of "more danceable" music by other composers.

After the Bolshoi's last 1883 performance, the ballet was never again shown in Russia during Tchaikovsky's lifetime. In 1894, after his death, the score underwent radical changes: four acts were reduced to three, several numbers were transposed, some were abridged, and three piano pieces were added. These modifications may or may not have been settled with the composer in the years prior to his death.

The official Soviet version, released in 1957, is drawn from the original 1876 score with the addition of the Russian dance for act III and the Pas De Deux from act II. This has been the score most used by contemporary productions of the *Swan Lake*. However even this general conceit does not assure uniformity in "music." In a televised performance of the Kirov's 1887 production from Wolftrap they did not use the *Andante Sostenuto* in the pas de trois in the first act and the tempos for the female variations were much slower than on the Soviet recording, so much so that the choreography for the Kirov could not possibly be danced to the Soviet recording, at least not without looking jerky and silly.)

Other discrepancies exist even among attempts to produce "Classical" performances in the Petipa-Ivanov tradition. In most western productions, at the climax of the ballet Siegfried and the Swan Queen Odette commit suicide together, ultimately breaking the sorcerer's evil hold on Odette. The lovers then are reunited in the afterlife. Marxist versions of the ballet, disdaining all things "other worldly," change the libretto slightly so that Siegfried kills the evil sorcerer, thus freeing Odette, and she and Siegfired emerge triumphant to enjoy their earthly existence together.

Greater variations can be found in productions of *Swan Lake* which do not seek to be reproductions after Petipa-Ivanov, as with Baryishnikov's reworking of the classic for American Ballet Theater. He rejected various choreographic conceits as well as traditional costuming. Another might be Eric Bruhn's version of *Swan Lake* for the National Ballet of Canada. This retains much of the choreography of Petipa, though adding some new passages. This production develops

a psychological picture of the prince. The evil Rothbarth is played by
a woman who resembles the prince's mother.[4]

For any given production of *Swan Lake* there has been a different
production that did not use the same music (for as we have seen there
have been many scores), nor the same set, costumes, choreographed
movements, librettos, etc. That is, for every property one can name of
a given *Swan Lake* one could cite some other *Swan Lake* which lacked
that property. (Even, "belonging to the tradition of Classical Ballet"
might not work, since there have been modern ballet versions and even
an ice skating version.) One might attempt to name a disjunctive
property such as "having three or more of the properties P1-P20," but
this would at best be an arbitrary stipulation. Objectors would be
justified in claiming that such unjustified disjunctive criteria would
simply be begging the question against them.

Swan Lake is not an isolated "hard case" which I mention just to
support an otherwise implausible point. Numerous other examples real
and imagined can demonstrate that a particular dance type can be
instantiated independently of various elements thought to be essential
to that dance type. Consider the following cases.

When the Bashiva Dance Company was on tour in Miami, the
buses transporting their costumes and sets were stolen. Hours before
the scheduled performance reporters asked the company director what
he planned to do. In the true spirit of show business he said the would
present the program as planned as much as possible (which they did).
Presumably he believed that he was still capable of presenting dances
that evening which were instances of the type the company had
previously performed. They were without the costumes and sets, of
course, but the dances were still the same, still dances of the type. It
would seem implausible to claim that it was some other dance that they
did that evening. Even if some of the steps were different owing to lack
of proper costume and set, the event was referred to by the same name
and understood to be the same dance program. The example again
strongly suggests that costumes and sets were not necessary for these
tokens to be tokens of a type previously instantiated by the company.
(It is also interesting to note that practical considerations encourage this
leniency with respect to the identity criterion.)

There are many examples of choreographers putting the "same
dance" to different music, thus showing that specific musical score is
insufficient to determine identity, even for pieces choreographed to

specific pieces of music. I shall note two examples, Balanchine and myself. Balanchine choreographed a piece to music by Stravinsky and later set it to music by Mozart.[5] He and critics saw no problem stating that it was the same dance but to different music, and each regarded it that way.

I have put the same dance to different music countless times. When I tell my dancers that I want them to dance the same dance, but to the other music they certainly behave as if they know what I mean. They execute the same pattern of movements, though sometimes to different tempos or even rhythm patterns. Their actions indicate that they understand the dance to be something which exists independently of the music which accompanies it.

I know of a case where, during the performance the sound system malfunctioned so that the dance had to be completed without musical accompaniment.[6] The dancers performed the piece through to its conclusion. No one claimed that they did not perform the specified dance. Actually, some said that it was the best performance of that dance they had seen. In a related case, a ballet company was giving a performance of the *Nutcracker* when the union musicians stopped playing because they were overtime. The company continued, as rehearsed, through to the coda (with some of them humming the melody).[7] Strange as this must have been, it was no doubt an instance of the *Nutcracker*.

It may be suggested that in these cases we have sameness without same music, costume, set, props, etc., because in each of these cases what remains the same are certain internal relations within the structure of the movement (i.e. so many steps, then turn), but I think it premature to assume that this "sameness of internal structure" is the necessary condition of sameness of DAPA-type. As noted earlier, some choreographers are forever reworking old classics or their own works. They sometimes change the ending or the beginning or something in the middle. Modern choreographer Merce Cunningham would deliberately include random elements so that no two instances of presumably the same piece were possessed of the same internal structure. Even other more traditional dance works leave room for solo variations. Joe Melchiona's "Cotton Club Stomp" lets passages of music open for the tap dancers to take their turn "jamming" within the specified counts. Despite the fact that the dancers do not recreate the same formal structures within the dance, this variation does not in itself prevent a performance from being an instantiation of "Cotton Club Stomp." As with Cunningham, it would seem that some deliberate variation by the dancers is required.

There are other practical considerations to be addressed. Different body types prohibit recreations of nuances, sometimes prevent the recreations of actual steps. While in some cases this matters, sometimes it does not.[8] Often in regional and non-professional ballet companies' productions, classical choreography is tailored to the abilities of the dancers who are available to dance the roles. This sometimes necessitates making turns less numerous, reducing the difficulty of leaps, lifts, partnering steps, and precision work by the corps. Further, some professional ballet companies will allow ballerinas to dance off-toe even when the choreography calls for pointe work, because of a slippery stage or previous injuries to the dancer. Some ballet companies do not present pointe work at all, maintaining that it is the equivalent of circus tricks. When they present classical works, the dancers dance in soft slippers only.

Let us review the points that have been made so far. We are seeking the sameness criterion for "works of dance." I have claimed that phenomenal identity is not necessary. Owing to the practical limitations on our ability to recreate previous performances with exactitude, this is a wildly impractical criterion. Given that not all dancers are clones of one another (and clones with exactly the same training and talent), it becomes a theoretical question only as to whether phenomenal identity is sufficient.[9] I contend that it is, but for reasons not yet specified. Thus far I have argued only that it is not necessary.

I have also discussed the possibility of phenomenal similarity as a criterion of sameness and dismissed it as neither necessary nor sufficient. First, it is a vague concept. Any formulation that would make it strict enough for *Jewels* would make it too strict for *Swan Lake*. It therefore cannot be necessary. Again, it may be sufficient in some cases. But even if we were to admit this, the real work would lie ahead of us in unpacking the notion of "similar" so as to capture just those cases that were similar enough and not those which were too dissimilar (consider bad performances which attempt to produce very similar dance-events, but fail to varying degrees).

Given what has been said before it would seem that neither same costumes nor sets nor music, libretto, nor even structure of movement can be said to be, across the board, a necessary property for sameness of the DAPA tokens. Perhaps then we are on the wrong track. Perhaps one calls a given DAPA-event the "such and such" dance more to tell history than to show identity. "Historical tie" seems to capture much of what we normally mean by ascriptions of sameness, but cannot on its own account for pieces with historical ties which fail to be instances of a type. Given faulty memories or inaccurate notating systems, how much of a tie need there be and to what? It seems that more than mere "inspiration" is required for something to count as a *legitimate* reproduction, but the criterion cannot be so strict so as to leave out revolutionary adaptations. Further, if we are willing to grant phenomenal identity as a criterion for sameness, then historical tie seems *unnecessary*, even for wellknown authored works.

Adherence to rule can capture the looseness and strictness of actual judgments of sameness

Allow me to digress for a moment. I believe that there is a similarity to "playing the same game" and reproducing the same dance. We call a wide variety of events "games of poker" in much the same way as we call a wide variety of DAPA-events *Swan Lake*. However, in neither case is one reproducing the identical item. I wish to study this analogy further.

What is it to say that two events are both instances of playing poker? At first, it seems that this is nothing other than to say that both events are events of agents acting in accord with certain rules. We can have two instances of the same game (instances of a type) not because of the physical specifics (cards, players, hands, bets), but because they adhere to the same rules. This is not a mere disjunctive account of a definition but an identity criterion which places the emphasis on the behavioral and participatory nature of the thing identified. It builds into the account room for difference and diversions and even allows for some variations of the rules themselves.[10]

Applied to DAPA-events this analogy can go a long way toward explaining the variations among dance-tokens of a type. It may be that every type carries with it certain rules for reproduction. Some of these types have very detailed and particular rules, while other of these types have rather general rules[11]. Producing one of these works would be, basically, adhering to the rules of reproduction. This could also explain why it is that a dance which adheres to the production rules of *Swan Lake* is *Swan Lake* even if it were historically independent of the tradition of *Swan Lake*.[12]

Imagine that we found a culture, isolated from others, which nevertheless developed a card game with identical rules to those of poker. The question then becomes: should we call it poker or a different game but just like poker? How we respond to this will be determined by whether or not we believed that calling the new-found game "poker" commits us to certain beliefs about its historical/causal origins, beliefs which in this case would be false.

Doubtless there are those that would wish to distinguish between them, refraining from calling one poker but not the other. However, I believe this to be a bad choice for practical reasons. As a consequence of deciding the matter this way, merely from witnessing the two events we would be unable to distinguish the legitimate poker from the isolated poker. They would be, on anti-geneticist grounds, the same, though fail to be tokens of a single type. When I saw some game going on I would have to say something like, "Those people over there are either playing poker or a game that is exactly like poker." This strikes me as strange.[13] Normally when I apprehend a game as poker I do not believe that I am committed to various historical beliefs about how the agents came to be playing this game. In fact, I really don't have any historical beliefs about the origins of poker, nor need I have them in order to identify it. Even if I have false historical beliefs about the origins of poker, I do not see how this would prevent me from knowing poker when I see it. It certainly is not explicit in the assertion, and I see little reason for considering it implicit in the assertion either.

A significant point turns on this issue. If one believes that causal/historical ties to the temporally first in the series of tokens are necessary for any later token to be considered a legitimate token of the type, then even a phenominally indistinguishable ballet could not legitimately claim to be Balanchine's ballet if it was not historically linked to him.[14] On the rules for reproduction account, any production which adhered to the relevant rules (intentionally or accidentally) would count as a token of the type. Since I have argued that no historical tie is necessary for two instances to be instances of the same dance, a "fake" *Swan Lake* becomes impossible. I shall explain this further below.

My general claim then is this; for two events to both be tokens of a single type work of dance, it is sufficient that they conform to the rules of reproduction that are implicit in the use of the name of the work of dance for the given community of language users. For any given type of a work of dance, if we judge a token as *failing* to be a token of the type, then the burden is on us to cite some rule which it violates. The sum of these rules constitutes the "rules of reproduction." A token reproduction may violate some of these rules, but not all (just as there may be some variation from the codified rules of poker for an individual poker game). And since this is the violation of a rule and not simply discarding one of a number of unneccesary disjunctive properties, this violation calls for justification (aesthetic, practical). What rules any given work has differs from work to work.

This is vague and relativistic, one might claim, and it does not adequately reflect the use of the names of works. I agree that we cannot leave the account at that. Judgments of sameness presuppose a means of justification, and if we make specific judgments we ought to be able to provide specific rules. But I am not claiming that there are no specific rules.

How specific the rules are or ought to be depends in part upon how specific the rules can be and on how specific we want them to be. As a general trend we seem to be getting more and more detailed with our rules for reproduction. This is due in part to the fact that we now *can* get more detailed, given the advances in dance notation and video recordings. We no longer must rely solely on the memories of dancers, and particular historical instances of choreographers' works can be preserved. More importantly, they are preserved as the works of particular choreographers, not merely as ballet with a certain story or to particular music, as with *Swan Lake*. This was not always the case. Before the advent of reliable systems of notations, the only credit that a choreographer could expect is for the program notes to say that the ballet was "after Petipa," or "after Ivanov."

Still, this seems to re-enforce my point. All that is meant in saying that a certain production of *Swan Lake* is "after Petipa and Ivanov" was that the production loosely adheres to the rules that were set down by Petipa and Ivanov when they staged the ballet. Conversely, when a new production is launched, as with Baryshnikov's staging of *Swan Lake* for American Ballet Theatre, it means that the production intentionally disregards those rules while at the same time staying within the broader set of rules which determines what counts as a production of *Swan Lake*. It would be a much more relaxed affair to reproduce "*Swan Lake*—after Petipa and Ivanov" then to produce Baryshnikov's *Swan Lake*. This is because "Baryshnikov's *Swan Lake*" means one is adhering to the very detailed rules now in effect which govern the use of the name.

We should not think that poor notation was the only thing that prevented strict rules for reproduction. Laban notations and videos have their problems, but beyond these, choreographers and people who stage ballets simply do not want and cannot function with those kinds of strictures.

As I stated earlier, the general trend seems to be greater details in the rules for reproduction, but this is not an inevitable trend. It could certainly reverse, and certainly would (does) reverse if the specifics of the situation demanded it.

Further, this new-found capacity for recording details leaves the important sameness questions unanswered. While videos allow greater detail and a system of notation allows somewhat less detail but greater room for "artistic interpretation," still neither solves the matter. Videos record too much of the particular details that even the most fanatic of purists would not wish to make necessary requirements (rules for reproduction). Consider the facial expressions, the carefree billowing of scarves and skirts, the random events of some post-modern works which, if necessarily brought about, would cease to be random. After all, the video captures only one token of the type. If I video one game of poker, I still have not captured what it is to be a game of poker; nor are we really that much closer to knowing how to determine poker tokens from non-poker tokens when we meet them.

Notation may fall victim to the same problem, but even if it escapes this difficulty, it is only because the decision has already been made as to what to notate. In other words, in the notation process one has already done the business (consciously or unconsciously) of deciding what rules to lay down as the reproduction rules. Not every detail of the performance or even of what the choreographer envisions is of equal value; nor is everything indispensable for sameness. Further, after the notated score is composed, the choreographer still may choose to adhere to every detail or not. There is still room for variations if practical considerations or aesthetic ones provide reason for the divergence.

Each is better understood as rules to follow, a recipe for a desired end, a recommendation for what ingredients to use, but with artistic freedom residing with the presently creating artists. One is free to change any of the particular ingredients one chooses. But depending on what one is cooking up, if s/he changes too much, people simply will not know what to call the end product. S/he may begin with the rules for Balanchine's *Jewels*, but end up with something that no one is willing to call *Jewels*. If s/he insists that it is a token of that type, people will assume that it is a very bad version. This would be so not because it lacks artistic merit, but because it purports to play by certain rules for reproduction and fails.

Who determines the rules is the person or persons using the name. Rules continue to be defined and redefined as the history of the piece unfolds. It is always fair for someone to alter the rules to some degree so long as everyone knows that the person is doing it and they all agree. I might say this is *Swan Lake*, but on ice skates instead of in ballet slippers. If the community agrees, then the token in question is admitted as counting as an instance of *Swan Lake*. We rightfully ask the choreographer why s/he staged the ballet on ice skates and require a justification. This is so not because the rule can never be broken but because the rule should only be broken with justification. What we are really asking is why we should call this dance-event *Swan Lake*. Ultimately, the community may object, saying that this constitutes too wide a variation[15] from the rules and so reject the token in question as belonging to the type. When this occurs, there is no "fake" because being legitimate *is being accepted* as legitimate.

To use the poker analogy once again, we do allow variation within the rules of producing a poker game. If, for example, I lost the king of spades of the only available deck of cards, we might remove all the kings and play without them, or we might redefine the function and value of a king in the game. In either case we would have altered the rules significantly, but the resulting games would still be tokens of the poker type. Conversely, if I altered the rules in certain other ways (perhaps so that I could win more easily), I would be open to the charge that I simply was not playing the game. This is not to say that no deviation from the rules is tolerated, but that the deviation must be justified and acceptable to all concerned and justified by reasons acceptible to everyone[16].

The theory is helpful in explaining the phenomena with which we have been concerned. In short there are instances of very loose reproduction rules (*Swan Lake*) and very strict ones (*Jewels*) for a better codified piece. However, even with the advent of notation mechanisms, detail is not always wanted.

The objection must now be considered, "What if the whole community of language users decided to change the rules?" Could it ever be the case that any old thing could count as an instance of Balanchine's *Jewels* so long as everyone in the imagined community agreed? A negative response would seem to indicate that there is some essential nature to *Jewels* such that, even if the whole world should deny it, a *Jewels* is simply not a *Jewels* without it. I wish to deny this. I believe that the history of dance as a performing art will not support a theory which posits essential natures. Still I agree that it would be strange indeed if, as a result of my theory, any old thing could count as an instance of Balanchine's *Jewels*. I shall attempt to answer the objection in a way consistent with the foregoing account.

If my account is correct, to call something *Jewels* means no more than to say that the thing adheres to the rules that language users agree govern the use of the name. Again, on my account, these rules are not mind-independent (though independent of any individual mind) and do not capture the essence of the thing specified. I admit that one might plausibly claim that it could never be the case that any old thing could count as an instance of *Jewels*. But let us look at the case more in depth. What reason could there be for the entire community of language users to adopt so strange a set of rules that "any old thing" could count as an instance of *Jewels*?

Since using the name of a work of dance is a purposeful act on the part of language users, that is, they use names in order to do things (refer, distinguish, tell a bit of history, etc.), changing the rules by which these names have the capacity to refer and distinguish, etc., must itself be a reasoned affair. It defeats the purpose of name-use to change the rules of the names willy-nilly. Changing rules is generally not a capricious act. Experience suggests that communal agreement is precipitated by some practical (perhaps aesthetic) reason. This is what accounts for the uniformity in poker in particular and language generally.

When I call a game poker, I am trying to say something about the phenomenon in question. This is also true when one attempts to call an event *Jewels* or *Swan Lake*, etc. While it might make sense to change some amount of *Jewels* in order to effect a better performance, or to tailor it to the abilities of the available dancers, it would make no sense to change it *too* much. This is not because there is some essential feature of *Jewels* without which it ceases to be that which it is, but rather, there would be no point in calling it *Jewels* if too much of it is altered. Again it would simply be counter to the aims of naming it in the first place. How much change is "too much" is an empirical question to be answered in practice and not a priori. However, we may generalize a bit here. For any given proposed rule change, its acceptability will depend to a great extent on the strength of its reason. A practical reason or even aesthetic reason will be weighed against the value of keeping the rule. If the proposed rule change is such as to undermine the whole point of using the name, then it is unclear what compelling reason could be given for adopting the rule in question. "Why not simply call it something else?" one would ask. Since it seems that one of the points of calling some dance event *Jewels* is to attribute responsibility for the internal structure to a great extent to Balanchine (though clearly others are responsible as well, most notably those mentioned in the program), changing the internal structure to a like great extent undermines the point of the name. So long as telling the bit of history remains a point of calling some performance *Jewels*, no compelling reason can be given for adopting rules which would license great changes.

In the case of famous well-documented historical works by revered choreographers, then, it seems clear that the point of using the same name (not merely the same word) to refer to the dance is to attribute the work to that choreographer. That is, by calling something *Jewels* or *The Moor's Pavane* or "Paul Taylor's *Duet*," one is either telling a history of how a certain pattern of movement came to be constructed, or asserting that the work in question resembles very much paradigmatic work of a certain class, so much so as to be admitted to that class[17]. If the work in question does not resemble paradigmatic works in the class, the only point of calling it by a certain name is to tell its history and authorship. Now if the work does not even have the purported history, then there remains no reason to call the work by the name at all.

Concepts such as "great extent," "enough," or "too much" are admittedly vague. I would prefer to tighten these, but I admit at present not to have enough empirical evidence to justify a specific principle. Suffice it to say that, in the cases of historical works of dance attributed to a particular choreographer, one could not get reason for changing everything. One could not even get reason to change a lot. Some purists among us would say that we must change nothing at all, but this is unhelpful, for as I have already said, on at least one interpretation this would literally mean that only the original cast during the first run could produce the authentic *Jewels* (and then perhaps only on opening night).

We may say this, that only those changes that Balanchine himself would have consented to are allowable, and any others are too much. As a conceptual model this may be of practical use, but as far as rigorous precision goes, I am afraid we are no further along. After all, God only knows what changes Balanchine would have admitted. If he had run into Gelsey Kirkland before Marie Talchief, who knows what "Firebird" would have looked like? He would occasionally restructure ballets for particular dancers (as I mention choreographers are given to this), but it would undermine the historical information giving function of a name if we allowed subsequent generations to likewise alter the ballets, even if Balanchine himself would have approved.

Given the problems inherent in any theories of universals presently available, I would have preferred to stay mute on this subject. We may wish to consider these rules as mind-dependent, ultimately arbitrary means of classifying human artifacts, or we may wish to posit absolute rules which are as yet unknown, but which we approximate. These approximations are tested throughout the history of the inferior approximations giving way to the better ones.[18] But I do seem committed in my theory to the following metaphysical claims. Works of dance are not the same in virtue of sharing common essences. They are the same in virtue of adhering to certain rules for reproduction, and these rules do not constitute timeless and unchanging universals but a language dependent practical means of lumping certain DAPA-events together for purposes determined by the needs and desires of the community.

For the ordinary dance spectator or dance critic not much turns on this issue. I would prefer to refrain from making contentious claims if they are not necessary, and the contentious metaphysical claims of the preceding paragraph I believe to be unnecessary for most thinking (even critical thinking) about dance. However, they do follow from a careful examination of the practice of naming and the theory of sameness that justifies it.

So then the identity criterion for a work of dance is that it adheres to the rules of production which are implicit in the use of the name of the work of dance. The work may be phenomenal identical to the paradigmatic examples of the historical series, but not part of the causal/historical chain itself, or it might be produced by persons with the intention to adhere to the rules of reproduction, but be significantly dissimilar from previous historical examples of the same work. If the latter, but the intention is thoroughly frustrated, then we might wish to refuse to admit the token in question as a token of that type.[19]

Classes of Dance Styles

What remains to be discussed are the various classes of dance styles such as ballet, Jazz, tap, modern etc. This question identifies classes of dance phenomena that stand midway between the class of performance dance generally, which has a specific definition, and specific works of dance which are incapable of that kind of definition. Dance styles do seem to have some identifiable essence. They can be captured by definition and these definitions are not, as a matter of fact, subject to the kind of revision which rules for reproduction can undergo. Conversely, "ballet" for example, has undergone significant revision since it was originally codified by Beauchamps. Further, there exist differences in schools of ballet technique (i.e. the French, Russian, Italian, American, and Danish schools) which not only include different steps as part of their classical technique, but differ in approach and execution of certain steps.[20] To describe the phenomenon one would say that there are certain unchanging facts about ballet, characteristics without which it would cease to be ballet, and there is also room for revision and evolution. What must be accounted for is why and how it is that styles of dance are more codified than works of dance.

I believe that answer is two fold. Taking ballet as an example, we see that it has certain stylistic objectives, qualities of movement that define it as the style that it is. Ballet resists gravity and seeks to present motion with the appearance of lightness, agility, and elegant grace. This is not an exhaustive account of the stylistic objectives of ballet, but I believe that it cites the most central.[21] These objectives and others define the ballet style and constitute its essence.

Further, throughout the history of ballet a system of codifying and identifying steps as well as a detailed system of training dancers has developed. Given the movement objective and the constant of the human body, a system of training and vocabulary of movements evolved which serve as the best means to the desired end of the style. Even with the variation which exists in ballet, there are some things which are universally recognized. The plie, the releve, the five feet positions, the eleven body positions, the two classical poses; arabesque and attitude. These rules for ballet production are more fixed; the words have meanings of their own. Calling one step by another name can, in some cases, be seen as a logical contradiction. Unlike the names of works of dance (where Balanchine's *Jewels* may not necessarily mean the ballet choreographed by Balanchine; for perhaps, unknown to us, someone else choreographed it) a pirouette en de dans on the right *means* a spin on the right leg to the right. In the ballet style of dance, the working leg is held in one of several positions (passe, arabesque, attitude, etc.) and little variation is tolerated. I can not call something else a pirouette en de dans on the right. The name is at once a name and a description.

Ballet is a style defined by certain movement objectives and a certain vocabulary of steps. It is composed, at least in part, by those movements specified in the ballet dictionary and executed in keeping with specified technique. There is room for growth; new steps can be invented. And there is room for deviation. I may alter the technique of a particular performed movement sequence, alter it to a degree that it is no longer "ballet" as defined, however, this could not be ballet itself unless these movements are performed within a larger setting of a ballet proper. Unless they are surrounded by the traditional ballet, they can not even count as part of a ballet performance.

Modern dance has evolved in much the same way. First there is a movement objective and the evolution of a technique to achieve and communicate it. This naturally requires a terminology. Since the terms used to refer to steps are partly descriptive, their meanings can not be readily altered and only those movements which satisfy the description can *be* the movements designated by the terms. Since an evolved style is partly constructed by such a fixed vocabulary of movements, it is difficult, if not impossible, to change the movement objectives of the style. If one desired to achieve a different objective, it would make little sense for him to avail himself of a fixed vocabulary and technique which was antithetical to his aims. I contend that this is why, while there is room for growth and development within a style, refining objectives etc., one can not radically change the style itself from within. The essence of the style, if we wish to call it that, is a practical consequence of having to work with a fixed vocabulary of movement and a fixed technique. However, this essence is practical in nature, for if one could work with the designated technique and vocabulary, but nevertheless, alter the objective of the style itself, we would continue to have the original style, but it would perhaps be radically different.

That Works of Dance Cannot Be Forged

To present a fake of Balanchine's *Jewels* one would have to present something that was not *Jewels* as *Jewels*. But if it were relevantly similar (that it if it adhered to enough of the reproduction rules to count as *Jewels*) then it would not be a fake because it would be a legitimate instance of *Jewels*. Further if it had the some historical tie (after Balanchine) but failed to be importantly similar as determined by the critical community then it would either be a legitimate *Jewels* but a very bad one, or it wouldn't be *Jewels* at all. In either case no one is deceived. If an unscrupulous choreographer presents some dance and tells an uninformed audience that it is *Jewels* though it is not similar enough to count as an instance of the work, then he has deceived some people but he has not produced a fake. It would be analogous to my painting a sad clown and telling an uninformed spectator that it was the Mona Lisa. They might be deceived but that is not enough to make my work a fake. Since it is the critical population's pronouncement that makes a legitimate instance of a dance work a legitimate instance of a dance work, they cannot be "fooled." Convincing them *is* the test of sameness.

I wish to conclude with a few remarks about choreographer style. I believe that some choreographers exhibit a distinctive style. I do not believe that it is as well-defined or systematically generated as dance style, nevertheless I believe that as a practical consequence of training and aesthetic sensibility and artistic concerns, many choreographers exhibit recognizable patterns of characteristics in their choreography that allow critical observers to recognize their style, sometimes independently of program notes, etc. Since these objective movement characteristics can be mimicked, the choreographer's style can be implemented by other choreographers. This means that, theoretically one could present something that resembles Balanchine's work, indeed *was* Balanchine's style but was not created by Balanchine. Further, one could attribute such a work to Balanchine and in so doing present a fake of sorts. While it would not be a fake of a particular work of dance, it would be a fake nonetheless. This is because it would not be trying to imitate a particular work but rather only a style. In this attempt it would succeed, but the work is also falsely attributed to Balanchine. The deception comes not from claiming that this is an example of Balanchine's style (for it is) but in claiming that this is Balanchine's work (for it isn't). As such it constitutes a fake. The above scenario, while theoretically possible, is highly unlikely since dance by its very nature is a public matter. Unlike painting, there are no unproduced Balanchine ballets left in a closet somewhere. However, should it become the case that choreographers begin to choreograph using written notational score, or computer generated images, then the possibility for these kind of fakes becomes more conceivable. Still, fakes of specific works of dance would remain unaffected.

Notes

1. Hither-to unpublished papers on the nature of dance.

2. This is so mostly for historic works such as the Grand Story Ballets or with their own works. It is not the case for reproductions of well-documented works of famous choreographers. Here they seem to adhere to stricter identity criteria than they would impose on their own works.

3. " . . . as recently as 1969 the Soviet Commentator Daniel Zhitomirsky proclaimed the clear superiority of the 1895 Swan Lake, which he described as the first. . . worthy of Tchaikovsky's Score. . . . opinion was unanimous that the (1877) production was very mediocre, mostly due to the lack of creativity of the choreographer (Julius Reisinger)" [James Lyons, Editor, The American Record Guild. From accompanying notes to the Moscow Radio Symphony Orchestra Recording, USSR Melodiya/Angel recordings].

4. I should note that these are all *intentional* departures from known aspects of the Petipa-Ivanov productions. I have not even considered the details that were simply forgotten.

5. It may be claimed that in performance these were two different dances. I believe that this is a confusion. First, certainly these constitute two distinct objects of criticism, but again that is not our present topic. Second, there seems to be a confusion of reference, referring to the dance by the name of the music to which it might be performed. If there were some neutral way to refer to the dance, say "the 40th dance that Balanchine ever choreographed" then the confusion would be cleared up. Both dances, even in performance, were token of this type.

6. June Dance Recital, Heidi and Joe Melchiona Dance Center, 1986. The ballet piece was entitled Maple Leaf Rag, taking its name from the music which, as a matter of fact, did not accompany it.

7. Ballet Theater of Miami 1990 dressed rehearsal for their annual production of the Nutcracker. While this was a dressed rehearsal, it was also a free performance for Dade County school children.

8. One might claim at this point that some works, as a condition of sameness, call for sameness of internal structure while others do not. With this I heartily agree, and I will develop this point in greater detail later in the paper.

9. If aliens came down from space and reproduced a ballet that was exactly like George Balanchine's *Jewels* would it in fact *be* George Balanchine's *Jewels?* I believe it would be if it were *exactly* like *Jewels* but then the interesting questions becomes, what does it mean to be exactly like *Jewels?* The question presupposes we know what that means, but that is precisely what we are trying to find out. Suffice it to say that if what the aliens did was phenomenally indistinguishable from some previous historical

production of *Jewels* then it would be considered a member of the class. Still left unanswered is "by virtue of what is the historical production of *Jewels* a production of *Jewels*."

10. In poker one is allowed to define the specific rules for any given hand. One may even redefine existing rules or add innovative new ones. When one cheats at poker, one might still be considered "playing the game," but one is defying the rules. Morality questions arise if one is attempting to deceive his fellow poker players into believing that he is playing by the agreed upon rules when in fact he is not.

11. Consider the pliancy granted "Poker" as compared with the relative constancy of "Bridge."

12. Some might argue that what I have in mind here would be better understood as a complex disjunction of properties. Rather than adhering to rules, such a position would hold that something is a production of Swan Lake if it adheres to some minimum set of a large number of conditions.

The reason I have not opted for a disjunctive-property account is mainly because on such a view there need be no justification for neglecting any particular property so long as one is recreated with the minimum of the other property. But it is characteristic of the dance community to insist on some justification for a departure from the standard versions. The community tolerates changes but only with practical or artistic justification.

This is captured by the notion of rule adherence but not by a simple disjunctive set of properties. Further, it is not clear to me that any one non-arbitrary set of properties could be specified which could not be altered in the future for practical or aesthetic reasons.

13. I can image a host of problematic cases arising from the move. I shall mention two here. You see four foreigners playing poker-esque. They get up and leave and four of your explorer buddies pick up the cards and "continue the game." Are they now playing poker or poker-esque? Then two of the natives come back and resume their hands. Are they now playing poker or poker-esque? Wouldn't it be much easier to say that they all were and are playing poker?

14. There is of course a difference between a revival or contemporary production and a reproduction of an historical piece. One presents an historical piece and calls it a historical piece for certain reasons. This perhaps requires a historical tie. But I deal with this in greater length later.

15. On what ground might the community see the variation as 'too wide'. As partial answer I submit that a variation would be too wide if admitting the candidate as a token of the work in question would serve no useful (practical, aesthetic or artistic) purpose and would undermine the very point of naming and grouping DAPA events together.

16. For instance, agreeing to call something Jewels despite the fact it ignores many of the rules simply because you have been hypnotized would not count.

17. Note that I have argued so far that these form a disjunctive criterion, one or the other is necessary, either is sufficient and neither is individually necessary.

18. I recognize that if we think that some rule formulations are objectively better than others, this presupposes a standard of evaluation, and for that reason we might wish to posit the rule absolutes. But an alternate way of viewing the matter is to say that the rule decisions are made on the basis of the immediate practical considerations of the moment as well as the function of the name in the given community. Here, some decisions may be more justified than others, but not because they are closer approximations to the absolute.

19. If something was intended to be a particular work of dance but failed in all or nearly all of its attempts, is it proper to say that it was not an instance of the work or merely a very bad instance of the work? I believe that this sort of thing occurs very infrequently. More frequently it happens that a work succeeds in many of its attempts but fails in other crucial areas. We ought not confuse the two separate types of cases.

In the former case my account commits one to saying that it is not an example of the work at all, intentions not withstanding. I don't believe that this is counter intuitive, at least not in the cases I can imagine. Consider this. If I have the intention to produce a knife but produce an object which is so poor an example of a knife as not to be an example of a knife at all, then it is well said that this object can be a knife in name only. This, I take it, is an admission that the thing does not deserve the name.

20. For instance, the classical position 'attitude' is held very high and retracted in the French school, somewhat longer and lower in the Italian school, and at a compromised length and height in Russian technique.

21. Martha Graham built her distinctive style on contraction and release, Doris Humphry on fall and recovery, Jose Limon on breathing. Spanish dance seems built upon the polyrhythms and rhythm-layerings accomplished with percussive foot movements.

III

Artistic Property

Why Artworks Have No Right to Have Rights

Francis Sparshott

Philosophers and others worry more than they used to about the dangers inherent in moralities of a Kantian or Aristotelian stamp. A moralist preoccupied with the idea of a community of autonomous beings whose primary obligations are to each other may become dangerously insouciant about whatever lies outside that community. He may even be negligent about what is only doubtfully or presumptively included in the community, such as children or future generations. The rest of us, concerned on behalf of whatever may be suffering from maltreatment or insufficient cherishing, especially when we feel that the neglect stems from the preemptive character of moral considerations, may be moved to express our concern by asking: What about the unborn? What about the trees? Don't they have any rights? But many philosophers hold that the concept of a right is only rhetorically suitable to the demands made on it in such appeals, and that the concern expressed would be more intelligibly formulated in other terms. The present essay reflects the conviction that no one with anything definite to say and any capacity to say what he meant would express himself in such language. Rather than risk having this prejudice painfully confirmed or shamingly refuted by looking to see what if anything has been written about the alleged rights of artworks, the author has chosen

Francis Sparshott presented this essay at the conference of Art, Law, and Society, sponsored by Temple University, June 3 and 4, 1982. It was first printed in the *Journal of Aesthetics and Art Criticism* 42 (1), Fall 1983, pp. 5-15. It is reprinted here by permission of the publisher, the American Society for Aesthetics, and the author.

to reflect on why he might himself be tempted to ascribe rights to artworks, and why he would resist that temptation. In doing so, he has made no attempt to collect and analyze the great variety of legal provisions by which the treatment of artworks has been hedged about in various jurisdictions.

Most of what follows makes no distinction between two very different contentions. Given that artworks at present do not as such have any legal rights, one may argue, first, that it is in some respects as if they did, and we ought to give some theoretical recognition to this fact; or one may argue, second, that we ought to acknowledge moral or axiological rights of artworks, and wherever we acknowledge such a right we necessarily open the question of the feasibility and propriety of giving those rights some expression in positive law.[1] These two positions are run together here because it is not clear that they do not come to the same thing. To say that it is as if there were a legal right is to say that the law is as it would be if it were shaped by the sense that there is a moral right. It will be time to make fine distinctions when it is clear what the underlying issues are.

If I could be moved to ascribe rights to artworks, it would be by two things. First, there certainly are legal and moral obligations not to mishandle artworks in various ways. Some of these are obligations to the artist. The artist has certain rights, basically his copyright. And these, it may be said, are not simply property rights affecting his sales and royalties, but extend to considerations affecting his integrity and that of his work. Other obligations are obligations to the owner of an artwork as a physical object. Here too the obligations may go beyond the straightforward right of an owner not to have his property stolen, damaged, or destroyed, and may extend to restraints on unauthorized reproduction and on irresponsible denials of authenticity, though it seems likely that these additional rights of the owner will all have to do with the value of his property as property. A third class of obligations is less clearly directed, as when a celebrated artwork is regarded as part of the national heritage and it is accordingly forbidden to deface or export it. Since all these diverse inhibitions and obligations have to do with ways in which artworks may not be interfered with, it might be thought advantageous for some theoretical purposes, even if for no practical purposes, to bring them together under a single head, and the most appropriate and pithiest heading for the collection might well be "the rights of artworks." In using that heading one would not necessarily be doing anything more than using a perspicuous metaphor than which no other was more readily intelligible or more evidently appropriate, without suggesting that one's maneuver should be enshrined in law or that this viewpoint should displace or override other viewpoints.

The second thing that would tempt me to speak of the rights of artworks is this. Not only is it the case that our obligations to accord artworks proper treatment are not all owed to the same person or group, but the person or persons injured by a violation is not necessarily the actual bearer, or someone who could easily be made the bearer, of any legally recognized right. In fact, the heart of the matter is that it is above all the legal owner of the artwork against whom the work must be protected. The owner of a sculpture may feel that he has a perfect right to remove a layer of paint from his property; the owner of an elegant but uncomfortable house may feel that he has a perfect right to remodel or rebuild his own home; someone presented with an unflattering portrait of himself may feel justified in burning it and thus preventing himself from becoming an object of mockery to posterity. If these property rights are to be overcome it can only be by some countervailing and preemptive right.

The alleged rights of an artwork against its proprietor might be illustrated by the position of a slave under Roman law.[2] A slave is his owner's property, and the owner can do as he wills with his own. The slave, as mere property and without civil standing, can have no rights against him. Nonetheless, slaves are human, and it is unthinkable that there should be no recognized restrictions on what may be done to them. His owner will have the right to protect his slaves against all others; but how is a slave to be protected against his owner? The Roman solution was to assign to a senior magistrate, the Praetor, the duty of taking the slave's part whenever the permissible bounds were transgressed; and in theory, though doubtless not in practice, the duty to respond to a slave's appeal for protection took precedence over the Praetor's other activities. The slave cannot be a legal person and cannot be a bearer of rights. But it must be as if he has rights. And if we speak of the rights of a slave under Roman law we shall not be misunderstood: we will be speaking of those cases in which the Praetor, if appealed to, will intervene not out of a feeling of humanity but as a matter of duty. To ask whether slaves have any "rights" in this sense is to ask whether there are any cases in which the Praetor has a clear duty to hear the appeal and, having heard it, to act on it.

The case of artworks merely pushes the analogy one stage further. If there are cases involving threatened or actual harm to artworks in which there could be some official representative like a praetor, and something corresponding to the slave's appeal, and in which the praetor-like person would have a clear duty, it makes sense to speak of the rights of artworks, and the more those conditions come closer to being actually fulfilled the more sense it makes to speak of rights. And perhaps such an appeal to a set of admittedly metaphorical rights will be illuminating as well as fulfilling a sort of moral craving, for it may usefully focus our minds, when we are considering the violation of art, on four separate questions: Whence is the appeal? What is the enforcing authority? When and why does a duty arise? And, if we belong to that school of thought which holds that there is no right where there is no sanction, what is the sanction for infringing the alleged right?

The two things that would tempt me to attribute rights to artworks, then, would be the desirability of theoretically consolidating the heterogeneous obligations surrounding the sacrosanctity of art, and the need to protect that sacrosanctity against the property rights of the owner—and perhaps even against the copyright of the artist. Before we move on, something more should be said about the latter of these two factors. Copyright is vested in the artist or the registered promoter of the work or their heirs and assigns; obligations stemming from the status of a masterpiece as cultural heritage are presumably owed to the representatives of the people whose heritage it is supposed to be. Neither of these is necessarily the same as the owner of the physical work. It is not uncommon for an artifact to be owned by one person and the copyright by another, while an interest is declared on behalf of the community by government. But none of these rights and duties pertain to works of art as such. Copyright pertains to any intellectual work having a recognizable and repeatable embodiment, and much of this has no artistic interest. Again, a work may be assigned to the cultural heritage because it is part of the artistic glory of the nation, but the reason is just as likely to be historical association or religious significance. And the owner's right in his art collection is of course no different from his property right in his other chattels. The point relevant here is that, when we are dealing with artworks, the significance of copyright, of owner's right, and of heritage right may each take on an extra dimension. The artist's right in his work may have something to do with the enormity of violating his artistic integrity and sullying the fountain of inspiration. It may be that that part of the national heritage that is esteemed specifically as art is an object of admiration and veneration importantly different from the nostalgic or pious attitude appropriate to birthplaces and deathplaces. And it may even be that an art collection is one's own in a different way from that in which either heirlooms or useful purchases are. To the extent that that is the case, the notion of the rights of artworks will consolidate and draw together, not the totality of these three kinds of interest and inhibition, but an aesthetic or artistic component that is common to all of them.

The phrase "aesthetic or artistic" component has just been used as though the artistic and the aesthetic were for all present purposes the same. But perhaps they are not. And that possibility introduces a new consideration which may be decisive.

In addition to the three sets of obligations specified so far, there may be, and there is often recognized to be, another set of obligations, legal as well as moral, the focus of which is essentially aesthetic. Beauty is not to be wantonly destroyed; amenities are to be preserved. This is roughly the ill-defined realm of environmental values, and has nothing to do with art as such. We may then wish to separate off within this area of obligation, or to discriminate as overlapping but not identical with it, the obligations relating specifically to those things of beauty that are artworks, or to those things that are to be treated as though they were beautiful in the relevant sense because they are artworks and, as such, proper objects of an analogous esteem. Our reason for wishing to speak of the rights of artworks will now be more complex. It will be the desirability of separating out and consolidating what is specific to art in the obligations surrounding those artifacts and creations that are artworks and at the same time distinguishing that from whatever general obligations the existence of recognized aesthetic value might generate. If we refuse to speak of the rights of artworks, it may prove hard to effect the dual separation conveniently. If it is still objected that the metaphor of "rights" is too strong, we may reply that the imperatives in question are to override recognized rights, specifically property rights, and that a large part of the point of establishing rights in any context is to establish a preemptive claim. Property rights accordingly can be overridden only by other rights; and in this case, though the right to override is vested in the overriding agency, its justification must, as in the case of the Praetor and the slave, rest on something like a right vested in that on behalf of which the overriding is exercised. Something more than naked authority is necessary to trump the proprietor's ace, and the metaphor of the rights of artworks is the handiest way to show what this is.

To all of the foregoing it may be replied that metaphors are fool's gold. It is a notorious error to suppose that because we recognize an obligation to treat some thing or person in a certain way we must therefore be recognizing an obligation *to* that thing or person that corresponds to a right on its part. What has here been called a handy metaphor is in fact an attempt to hallow an elementary blunder. In this case, my duty to do right by art, however clear and strong it is, may equally be a duty owed to the muses or some other handy deity, or to mankind, or even to myself. If metaphor and personification are necessary, the metaphor of a duty to oneself and the personification of the arts as a gaggle of goddesses are not obviously less useful or more misleading than the fiction that artworks can be bearers of rights. In fact, they are less misleading, because the temptation to take them literally is less strong.

If we are unwilling to speak of the rights of artworks but still wish to acknowledge that the obligations surrounding artworks must involve rights or something very like rights, we have to face the question who or what the bearer of these rights or quasi-rights must be.

A possible answer may be approached as follows. The point of conceptually consolidating the obligations surrounding artworks was that we clearly have some sort of obligation to cherish, or at least not to destroy or deface, and perhaps even not to demean, at least some artworks, as such. But which artworks, and why? The only plausible answer, if we are to speak of clear obligations, is that it is at least some and perhaps all of those that are *established as* cherishable, or perhaps only as eminently cherishable. The obligations presumably arise because the eminent cherishability of some artworks as such is an established fact, and they may be extended insofar as other artworks or presumed artworks are comparably cherishable or may become so. The relevant notion will be of the general sort that George Dickie was working out a few years ago, according to which to be an artwork is to be established as a candidate for a sort of status, with associated attitude and treatment, modeled on that accorded to artworks already recognized.[3]

If the open-ended obligation to cherish or to respect actual and potential cherishability is owed to anyone and establishes a corresponding right, the only plausible bearer of the right is the notional community of present and future cherishers—in fact, of art lovers and art worshippers. The associated right can only be a sort of diffuse right of such persons not to have the object of their love or worship violated. But then one has to ask why this right should be recognized, and why and in what circumstances it should be granted any privilege over other less diffuse rights. The appropriate analogy here seems to be with that equally diffuse and obscure right not to have one's way of life flouted, for which Patrick Devlin argued some years ago.[4] At least, the claim may give rise to the same sympathy and the same unease. What could be more important than to have an environment in which the moral ethos is secure, or in which art is not imperiled? Who would not wish to have his deepest values safeguarded from blasphemers, smut merchants, philistines and vandals? But, on the other hand, one does not see by what right the alleged upholders of community standards claim to represent the community more truly than those members of the community whose way of life they deplore, or why a mere taste for denunciation should be thought a sign of moral superiority; and, in the matter of art, when we substitute the rights of art lovers for the rights of works, we may wonder whether we can or should differentiate between worthy and unworthy loves, and whether and how the lovers and worshippers are to be differentiated in practice from the dealers, the snobs, and the mere traffickers in reputation and display. The bearers of the alleged right can only be those who declare an interest or those on whose behalf an interest is declared, and it will be a hard matter to give moral or legal effect to appropriate decisions as to the legitimacy, the good faith, and the relevance of such declarations.

In the light of the foregoing considerations, we may wish to retreat once more from the rights of art lovers to the rights of the works themselves, which at least are innocent of cupidity and corruption. Besides, the bearer of a right must surely be identifiable. We cannot admit the right of just *anyone* who might claim *any* sort of aesthetic interest to have that interest practically entrenched; and it was the inescapable crux of Dickie's position that anyone might declare such an interest in anything. Our starting point must rather be the *relevantly established* status of being an artwork, and hence presumptively cherishable; the original judgment of cherishability is merely inferred from that present status. The presumed art lovers are only a projection of the lovability assigned to the work. It is only

because there is an art lovers' interest that the question of the rights of
artworks can arise; but what we are sure of, what grounds our action
in any particular case, is that the work in question is an appropriate
object of such an interest.

This brings us to the most fundamental objection to converting the
rights of artworks into the rights of art lovers: namely, that the
aesthetes have done nothing to deserve it. The merits we recognize, if
merits there be, are those of the work and not of its public. This
objection, though fundamental, is very weak. The bearer of a right has
to be appropriately qualified to bear it, but there is no reason for this
qualification to be merit or desert in any independently recognizable
form. The heir to a fortune or a throne has a right to his inheritance
that does not significantly depend on his personal merits. But to this
conclusive rebuttal we may rejoin that since we are, admittedly and
necessarily, working in the field of fiction and metaphor, discussing not
what rights there are or could be but what rights we may usefully
pretend there are or wish there might be, the fiction we adopt should
be one that reflects not the way things are but the way things should
be, embodying the impulse that led us to embark on the fiction in the
first place. And then we may follow the Aristotelian principle of
distributive justice, that rights should be assigned according to
appropriate merit.

If an artwork is to have rights, whether moral or legal or
metaphorical, someone is going to have to decide what is or is not an
artwork. The appropriate status is going to have to be conferred on it.
Even if we say that artworks are all and only those things produced by
artists in the way of business, someone is going to have to decide who
is an artist and how one is to distinguish between his product and his
garbage. How, and by whom, are these decisions to be made? On one
level, it seems there is no problem. Tax and customs authorities and
insurance companies have developed ways of dealing with these matters
that obviously work well enough. The famous court case in which it
was disputed whether Brancusi's *Bird in Flight* was an undutiable
artwork or not illustrates, not the difficulty, but the ease of deciding
such matters. Despite the disputes raging between conservative and
advanced elements in the American art community, and the starkly
opposed testimony presented to the court, it proved possible to establish
grounds on which the status of radically innovative work could be
decided.[5] Policemen and law courts have no difficulty in devising

procedures for settling insoluble problems such as what is obscene and what is art, and there is no compelling reason not to accept the rough justice they do, so long as we concede that it is rough and install procedures to smooth it out at a higher level when necessary. As in all other legal and moral matters, we must not expect that all cases will be easy to decide or that all decisions will be uncontroversial when made, or even that there will not be some decisions which in the fullness of time will be unanimously agreed to have been wrong. But such considerations never stand in our way when the need for making decisions is sufficiently strong. The case of art is no different.

We might, indeed, object that although existing insurance and fiscal procedures suffice for tax purposes, they do not meet the needs of those who wish artworks to have recognized rights. For we have just seen that the appropriate ground for those rights would be merit; and the customs make no attempt to distinguish art from kitsch. Their concern is with existing valuations and actual processes of manufacture and marketing. Similarly, a dealer who certifies an object as an original work of art for export purposes is not making an aesthetic judgment but testifying to appropriate context and provenance, even if the ultimate ground of that appropriateness is putative aesthetic value. And in the other direction, it would go against the weight of the thinking that leads to this talk of rights for artworks if we decreed that nothing could be an artwork that was not distributed through the established channels of the art industry. Present official ways of identifying works of artwork well enough for present purposes because the prima facie criteria employed at the routine level are relevant to those purposes, so that only a small proportion of cases is appealed; but if the status of artwork is to be a matter of merit it is easy to see that the application of existing criteria could leave a proportion of appealable decisions that would clog the courts.

If, however, the status of artwork is not to be assigned on prima facie but defeasible grounds that any experienced bureaucrat can apply, how is it to be assigned? Once again, the only recent attempt to answer precisely this question in terms that might meet our concerns is George Dickie's "institutional" theory. On this theory, the status of artwork is conferred, as it were, by an unreal institution, the "artworld," that consists of the relevant operations of all institutions and persons involved in the production, packaging, marketing, distribution, possession and appreciation of artworks of all kinds; and, just because this institution is unreal, the status is in fact bestowed by anyone who chooses to confer the status of artwork on any artifact "on behalf of" that institution. That is, the conferring person commits himself to treating the candidate as other artworks are treated and so acts as to convey his presumption that others will do likewise. But this model, the only available one, is useless for our present purposes, because it designedly leaves it unascertainable whether anything is an artwork or not. Anyone at all may have done something about any artifact that may be construed as claiming for it the status in question. Despite this, we may well feel that no model less nebulous than Dickie's can be relied on to do what we want, because no other model establishes the exactly appropriate link between the right-bearing work and those whose interest grounds the right. We are thus left with an unwelcome choice. Either our criterion of being an artwork is too open to ground anything so concrete as a right, or else our criterion risks being found the wrong one in many cases because what it is based on is questionably relevant.

The same point may be put in a slightly different way. If the artwork is to be a bearer of rights, it will have to be constituted a fictitious or artificial person. Its being so will result from some process like incorporation. Now, setting up a corporation is easy. A group of people fill out the appropriate form, file it with the appropriate fee in the appropriate office, and become or appoint the officers of the corporation. If the procedure is correctly followed, a charter will be granted in due course, and behold, with the aid of the law the group of people have created a person. Their right to do so, as well as the procedure for doing so, is prescribed by law: there will be a statute on the books containing the words "Any three persons normally resident in the State of . . . ," or whatever it may be. But what about the right to become an artwork? The right to be a part of the national heritage is appropriately bestowed by a commission appointed by the nation's elected representatives; the right to be intellectual property is appropriately set up by creation or publication. But what of the right to be an artwork? Who is appropriately authorized and by what jurisdiction, to create that person? It cannot be the art world, for they are even more grossly fictitious than the work itself, and require a prior act of authorization of a sort which no one in his senses would contemplate.

To put a sharper point on the matter consider for a moment Arthur Danto's contention that the status of artwork is bestowed by interpretation: that all and only those artifacts are artworks to which the "is of artistic identity" properly applies, and that whatever loses its susceptibility to interpretation loses its status as art.[6] On that view, the right to be an artwork is the right to be interpreted, and the right to remain one is the right to continue to be interpreted. The right to constitute something an artwork will either be the right to interpret artifacts, or the right to have one's interpretations accepted—that is, the right to be a critic or the right to be an accepted critic. It is hard to see how any such right could be recognized; but it may well be that no more sharply defined criterion could relevantly ground the rights of artworks *as artworks* in any sense that the advocates of such rights would want to recognize.

The qualms expressed in the preceding paragraphs may, however, be unjustified. They arise from the supposition that if artworks are to have recognized rights there must be procedures for identifying the entities that are to have the rights, procedures either for conferring and abrogating those rights or for recognizing and denying recognition, and comparable procedures for identifying and regulating the real individuals who from time to time are to pull the strings that animate these artificial persons. But, in reality, governments are used to dealing with the arts. Procedures for establishing commissions who in turn consult experts or professional bodies are thoroughly familiar, as are the abuses of bias and patronage and the risks of conservatism and gullibility to which they are inevitably subject. The risks and abuses are not such as need stand in our way if we wished to safeguard rights of artworks to the best of our power. We might of course decide that the best job we could be sure of doing was not good enough to be worth doing at all; but that would be a prudential decision rather than one of principle.

Hitherto we have been considering rather specific reasons for and against recognizing rights of artworks. It is time to look briefly at some broader issues. The general practice of talking about rights of entities not hitherto thought of as possible right bearers can be justified as reflecting the principle that all values should be respected: that value should be treated as value.[7] One could argue that the created value of art is a value that especially commands respect because it combines aesthetic value, which in itself is universally recognized, with a special value derived from its symbolization of humanity and life itself. And the principle that all value should be respected can be thought of as grounded in an overriding requirement of fittingness, the recognition of which is a necessary condition of civilization whether or not it is formally recognized by the technical philosophy of the day.

On this way of thinking, the supposed rights of artworks might be thought of on the analogy of the natural rights, the inalienable rights of man, postulated in old-fashioned political philosophies. Such a natural right was a ground of claim that could be argued *against* any legal system. The ground was a rational one. Any workable legal system must be worked up from a system of claims and obligations that must be justified somehow—it cannot be confessedly arbitrary. The argument for natural rights was that all justifications of all legal systems, if subjected to a rational critique, converged on a set of considerations that was thus the ground of all law and thereby the ultimate ground of the claims and obligations of positive law. But if that is the case it makes sense to invoke these grounding considerations directly against provisions of positive law, and to speak of natural rights and natural duties which need not be enacted in positive law, and are not necessarily such that they should be so embodied, but are such that if they cannot be intelligibly or defensibly invoked positive law is unintelligible or indefensible.[8]

On this showing, then, to speak of the rights of artworks is to say that the reasons for appropriately recognizing the value of artworks as such and acting on that recognition are such that if they are denied the whole system of our political and legal values is undercut. The right of an artwork to be suitably cherished can then be invoked against any formally recognized legal right, and any properly articulated system of jurisprudence will take account of this possibility somehow; and the question whether rights for artworks should be incorporated in positive law, even if it is always answered in the negative, is a question that must always remain open.

We may, however, grant that what lies behind talk of the rights of artworks is a sound principle and still urge that the metaphor of rights is the wrong metaphor, or that the concept of a right should not be stretched in this direction. To do so might undermine some specific good more significant than the good we would promote. One might, for instance, urge that the primary reason for recognizing rights as such is to preserve a space for freedom, to guarantee a range of autonomy within which individuals can act.[9] And it is quite reasonable to argue that the autonomy of persons takes precedence over all other values. Only freedom has a right to limit freedom; only free agents can have rights. The clarity and purity of this principle are not to be compromised by introducing other considerations, however important, such as that the weak must be protected and value must be respected. Those considerations should be argued for on a different basis, protected by a different set of strategies, spoken of in a different language. Unless we observe such distinctions we will not be able to think clearly about what should take precedence over what, about what principles should be followed in reconciling and adjudicating heterogeneous claims.

The point is an important one; but it is not decisive. The ability to observe a distinction never depends on and is never guaranteed by the availability of a terminology. And, if the language of rights is not necessarily the most suitable language for the brokerage of the most radically divergent claims, it is not necessarily *not* the most suitable language.

The alleged basis of the extension of rights to artworks and other unlikely objects was that it is a fundamental principle that value is to be respected. The implication is that it is the respect for value, and not the preservation of autonomy, that is the ultimate ground of the attribution of rights. It is hard to see how such a dispute could be adjudicated. But one could argue that the preemptive nature of rights is such that to ascribe any limited basis to rights is effectively to disfranchise all other claims. And then it is easier to see how autonomy could be one supremely important value than to see how values could be forms of autonomy. However, if we extend rights in this way we may be setting up a category of axiological rights alongside the legal and moral rights we already recognize. It is useless to say that this is after all only a metaphor, and the best metaphor we have; we will in effect be calling for a profound conceptual shift, involving the rejection of our entrenched system of normative thought. If so, this loose and irresponsible-seeming talk about rights of artworks is a straw in a big wind.

So much for philosophy. But the mental confusion or conceptual revisionism involved in attributing rights to artworks is less worrying than the immediate impulse from which it seems to spring. The misgivings now to be expressed may be unwarranted, and are certainly rather nebulous, but the treatment of the topic would be incomplete without them.

The fundamental reason why we attribute rights to people is that we recognize that "the poorest he that is in the world hath a life to live as the greatest he."[10] All the rights we recognize stem from, and are a variation on, a basic right to live some sort of human life.

This is not quite the same as the claim of value to be valued, or the need of autonomy for a space to be exercised in; it is rather what Hobbes recognized in his claim that in a state of nature every person has a right to everything.[11] To be human is to steer a course from cradle to grave, and the rights we recognize reflect what we take to be the minimum conditions, or the minimum acceptable conditions, or the proper conditions, in which that can be done. We can be generous with such recognition for the same reason that makes it urgently necessary for us to exercise it: that to the best of our knowledge each of us has only one life to live, and that our generosity with rights will in the end be revoked by death, which eventually overcomes even testamentary dispositions. It is sad when someone dies, especially when that someone is loved, and even when that someone is full of years, and we can mourn without restraint; but we can do so only because mortality is universal and certain. Deploring the loss of those we love is a luxury we can allow ourselves only because the loss cannot be averted or reversed. If it were not for death the old would clutter the earth. That is why the excesses of geriatric medicine (culminating in the conversion of moribund heads of state into mere pumping stations to be kept in circulation until the succession is secured) are so disturbing and demoralizing: in threatening the terminability of life they undermine the idea of a finite lifetime and thus tend to weaken the whole structure of love and law that is built upon that. The intolerance of mortality seems to bespeak a fine sensitivity until it threatens to become effective. Then we learn that we must let go with the hands, even if we will not let go with the heart.

The rights of man, then, stand for the feeling that human beings are infinitely precious. This feeling is one we treasure, but we can indulge it only because of the fragility of life. Perhaps the ascription of rights to artworks reflects the attribution of an unlimited value to art. But artworks *as such* suffer no natural mortality. Whatever rights we assign to artworks are likely to involve, and to be centered on, the right not to be destroyed, not to be damaged, not to have their artistic integrity impaired or infringed. But this is not the right to live an artistic life under the shadow of inevitable death. It is the right to be preserved from destruction.

Two things are wrong with the insistence that works of art are not to be destroyed. One is that it converts art into the object of curatorship. "Of eminent men," said Thucydides, "the whole world is the memorial;" and the curatorial obsession that underpins talk of the rights of artworks threatens to convert the world into a necropolis for dead masterpieces.[12] In some regions of the artworld it has seemed that even new works have "nowhere to go except to the museum," as though a premature infant were to be hustled straight from the incubator into the oxygen tent of the geriatric ward.[13] Let me illustrate. Some sixty years ago, the benefactor who endowed the student union at my university, himself a friend and supporter of contemporary artists, thought it would be a good thing for young people to be surrounded by the living art of their place and time. He therefore provided for a fund from which the students could buy works of local artists and hang them on the walls. All went well, and the students now go about their business surrounded by a varied collection of paintings many of which are both interesting and valuable. But recently people have started objecting. What are these aesthetically precious monuments doing out there where people can get at them? They may get dirty, or dry; they may even be touched, or dropped and damaged. They should be taken away and stored in a proper gallery, where the climate can be controlled and they will not be threatened by the contaminating presence of human life. Art is not for living with, not to share our fragility and mortality; it is for storing where it can be properly tended by salaried curators.

One sees the point, of course. We can easily work ourselves into a despondent mood by reflecting that we shall never see the Parthenon whole, never see Leonardo's Last Supper unfaded, never see Phidias's Olympian Zeus at all. If only our forefathers had been more careful! But we can as easily console ourselves by reflecting that there is more art left than we have time to see, and that we have time to see more art than we take the trouble to visit. There is at least enough art left. If anything, there is too much, as a visit to any museum will persuade you.

That brings us to the second thing that is wrong with the insistence that works of art are not to be allowed to perish. Like old people in an age of geriatric incontinence, they might clutter up the place. Rights of artworks must in the first instance be rights of extant artworks. Preservation threatens creation. By all means let the value of the old be respected, but not to the point where it leaves no place for the new to live. That art is to be cherished, that value is to be valued, are fine principles. But saying that artworks have rights is not a good way to express our adherence to those principles.[14] By translating the will to cherish into a duty to preserve, it drains our relation to artworks of the best part of its meaning.

Notes

1. This is not to say that there is no jurisdiction in which any object that is an artwork has a recognized right, or in which some law is in place that can be loosely construed as conferring rights on some classes of artworks. But it would be surprising if any jurisdiction purported to confer rights upon artworks *as such*.

2. The following account of the Roman law about slaves reflects memories of distant schooldays, not current research. But the merits of the illustration as an illustration are not affected by any historical errors there may be.

3. *See* George Dickie, *Art and the Aesthetic* (Cornell University Press, 1974), Chapter 1. The versions of this position presented in the text are interpretations with which Dickie might not agree.

4. *See* Patrick Devlin, *The Enforcement of Morals* (Oxford University Press, 1965). Devlin's own development of his position does not depend on the concept of a right.

5. The progress of the case is related by Carola Giedion-Welcker in *Constantin Brancusi* (Basel, 1958), pp. 213-18.

6. *See* Arthur C. Danto, *The Transformation of the Commonplace* (Harvard University Press, 1981), especially Chapter 5. The phrase "the is of artistic identification" is from Danto's earlier article, "The Artworld," reprinted from the *Journal of Philosophy* (1964) in George Dickie and Richard J. Sclafani, eds., *Aesthetics: A Critical Anthology* (New York, 1977), pp. 22-35.

7. The argument here is indebted to Robert Nozick, *Philosophical Explanations* (Harvard University Press, 1981), Chapter 5.

8. This argument is derived from Ronald Dworkin, *Taking Rights Seriously* (Harvard University Press, 1978), Chapter 2.

9. *See* Nozick, *Philosophical Explanations*, p. 501.

10. Thomas Rainborowe said this about England in 1647, according to the dictionaries of quotations, but it seems to hold for the world just as well as it does for that part of it.

11. Thomas Hobbes, *Leviathan*, Part I, Chapter 14.

12. Thucydides, *History*, II xliv 3.

13. The quoted phrase was applied to Marcel Duchamp by Hilton Kramer, *The Age of the Avant-Garde* (New York, 1973), p. 18.

14. This essay nowhere defines what it means by a "right." It is assumed that the meaning of the term is not more obscure than the meanings of any terms by which it might be defined. The sense intended is captured by S. I. Benn's article on "rights" in Edwards' *Encyclopedia of Philosophy*. Roughly, a right is a specific interest capable of prevailing against considerations of

public policy—different sorts of right correspond to different senses in which, different communities (real or ideal) within which, different circumstances and arenas in which, and different degrees of strength with which, the interest may prevail. Dworkin in *Taking Rights Seriously*, p. 91, offers a more precise definition, in which "a political right is an individuated political aim," a political aim being any "generic political justification": thus A has a right to X if it counts in favor of a decision that it promotes a state of affairs in which A has X. This is a very weak definition, perhaps designedly so in view of the strategic role Dworkin assigns to rights in his general theory of jurisprudence: it misses what others take to be the distinguishing feature of rights, that they are not just favorable factors but factors establishing some kind of claim that overrides considerations of general welfare. Dworkin conducts his argument as though he had established this feature, but it is not clear how he has done so.

Also unclear in the present essay is the relationship implied between what is law and what is not law—what sort of consideration could warrant enshrining a right in law, and how judges assign rights in the absence of determinate rules. One defensible view is of the following sort.

(1) It is a necessary condition of any society that its members refrain from interfering with each other's actions and the necessary conditions of those actions. It is also a necessary condition of society that its members stand by agreements they have made with each other.

(2) Courts and equivalent institutions exist to ensure that these conditions are fulfilled and to provide remedies when they are not fulfilled. That is, they are in the first instance courts of justice.

(3) Rules may be elaborated (are elaborated in most societies) to specify what non-interference amounts to, what counts as an agreement or as the violation of an agreement, and so on. Courts may elaborate these or accept them as elaborated by other authorities. In either case, the effect will be to mold or generate a climate of expectation, a general sense of what can be demanded and what is to be expected.

(4) Difficult cases in law will be properly decided, as Dworkin says, not by caprice or the judge's free decision, not by mysteriously underlying rules that are somehow implicit in formally stated rules, and not by considerations of general policy, but by determining the rights of the parties in accordance with principles. But we can state what the relevant principles are. They are the basic conditions stated in (1) above, which are the conditions the court exists to secure and further (as in (2)). And, since these conditions are almost empty of precise content (for one person's right to uninhibited action may intersect another person's right not to be interfered with at almost any point), the principles will take effectual form in accordance with the climate of expectation, as in (3) above, generated by the existing elaborations of specific rules.

(5) The individual cannot but have rights against the state. Both the purpose the courts exist to serve and the climate of expectation (sense of justice) generated by the existence of courts are perfectly general in scope. Rights against the state may have no legal effect; but that is only to say that injustice may be institutionalized.

(6) Different conditions of society may call for different sorts of restrictions, as Patrick Devlin argued. Dworkin's assumption to the contrary rests on the assumption that a society is a freely-entered association between individuals whose interests and characters could be formed and can be understood in isolation. But no society is entirely that (even the first settlers of America arrived by boatloads); there is no reason to think that that is the only way that societies can be analyzed and understood—since it is a blatant fiction, we cannot suppose it is a necessarily necessary fiction; and the reasons for thinking it is the best way are not beyond controversion. The first necessary condition of any society (as in (1) above) may be subject to a restriction on the initial scope of action for the members of a society, and it is notorious that it often is.

(7) The popular notion that law is the ideological instrument of the ruling class, and that the courts of law are instruments of state power, is simply wrong: it is based on a consideration of how certain restricted sets of rights are handled. No legal system anywhere has its scope restricted to such issues. Again, the scope of law and of expectations of justice is perfectly general; courts are inevitably called on to decide cases in which class interests and state power are not involved, even if it is true that the rules they decide by are biased in favor of wealth and strength and authority *whenever* such a bias is applicable.

(8) As indicated in the text, moral rights can always be invoked against the letter of the law, because one can appeal to the underlying function of legal institutions against their specific procedures. No one can be supposed to be a member (that is, a free participant) of any society otherwise than on the basis of some supposition about rights, as Hobbes argued. But what that supposition is will vary according to the style of the society. None of the foregoing remarks are intended to contribute to an understanding of their subject; they are intended merely to indicate the general character of the position from which this essay is written, in matters not directly relevant to the argument presented.

A Defense of Colorization

James O. Young

In the mid-1980s a new technology made it possible to convert black and white motion pictures into color films. The process of transformation, known as "color conversion" or "colorization," has been, perhaps, more reviled than any other development affecting the arts since the Visigoths and Vandals sacked Rome. Many questions have been asked about the aesthetic merits of colorization, and the use of the process has also raised a number of moral issues. Both philosophers and several distinguished directors have denounced the (unauthorized) use of colorization.[1] Legislation to control the use of the process has been introduced in the U.S. Congress (although it was not passed). The source of much of the controversy is the suggestion that the unauthorized use of colorization is a violation of a director's rights as an artist. Many writers have argued that no one may colorize a film (without its director's permission) without unjustifiably interfering with an artist's freedom of expression. In this essay I argue that colorization does not unjustifiably interfere with artists' prerogatives. Indeed, restraints on the use of color conversion can impose counter-productive and unjustifiable limitations on artistic freedom. There are no moral objections to color conversion.

Saying that the colorization of films is not immoral is not equivalent to recommending that the process be carried out for every black and white film. On the contrary, there are many good artistic reasons why (at least some) films should not be colorized. Directors

James O. Young's article first appeared in the *British Journal of Aesthetics* 28 (4), Autumn 1988, pp. 368-372. This revision is printed here by permission of the publisher, Oxford University Press, and the author.

often take advantage of black and white photography to achieve particular effects. Colorization may very well obscure what a director wished to express without adding any new expressiveness. Woody Allen uses one of his own films as an example of one whose expressive properties would be altered by colorization. If *Manhattan* were colorized, the feeling of nostalgia would be lost and the film would cease to express what Allen intended. No doubt there are many similar cases where colorization would be artistically unsuccessful. Moreover, we should be under no illusions as to why color conversion is being undertaken. Colorizers have monetary and not artistic motives. Still, even if there are artistic reasons why some films should not be colorized, color conversion might still be perfectly moral.

Questions about colorization are quite distinct from questions raised by restoration. Few would deny that it is (at least sometimes) unobjectionable to restore a work of art. There are differences of opinion about the sort of steps restorers may take, but most people think that steps may be taken to ensure the preservation of artworks as created by the original artists. Sometimes such restoration is impossible. We know that ancient Greek statues were originally painted. The "re-colorization" of these statues would be controversial (at least in part) because restorers do not know how to preserve the intentions of the original artists. The colorization of films is controversial for another reason. It is controversial just because the process involves the deliberate departure from what artists have intended. There is no question of simply preserving what artists have expressed.

A very strong intuition underlies the argument for the immorality of colorization. It seems wrong to tamper with works of art without the permission of the artists who created them. Suppose the privatization of public resources continues and I were able to buy from the Smithsonian Institute Leonardo da Vinci's *Portrait of Ginevra de' Benci*. Even if the painting were my property, most people's intuitions suggest that it would be wrong for me to draw a moustache on it. Or suppose I discovered a previously unknown novel by Jane Austen. I would act wrongly if I rewrote some chapters, destroyed the manuscript and published the revised version. My acts would still be wrong even if I improved the novel or if many people thought the portrait looked better with a moustache. In both cases I would have unjustifiably interfered with an artist's freedom of expression. My act would be like preventing someone from speaking, or like falsely reporting what someone said in a speech. And this is surely wrong.

The opponents of colorization suggest that the unauthorized use of this process is exactly parallel to the cases just considered. Their argument could be formulated as follows. Artists express themselves in works of art. It is wrong to limit a person's freedom of artistic expression. Altering a work of art always limits an artist's freedom of expression. Colorization involves altering a work of art. Therefore, colorization is a limitation of a director's freedom of artistic expression. Therefore, colorization is wrong. This is a valid and plausible argument, but unsound since its third premise is false. Altering a work of art does not always limit an artist's freedom of expression.

In order to see why altering a work of art is not always objectionable it is necessary to distinguish between two sorts of artwork. This distinction can be drawn without entering into any of the debates about what works of art are. There is a distinction between artworks embodied in a single artifact and works instantiated in more than one object. Into the first class of works fall many paintings, sculptures and works of architecture. Perhaps not all such works fall into this class. Two statues cast from the same mould perhaps instantiate the same work of art. But the *Portrait of Genevra de' Benci* clearly either is, or is instantiated in (depending on one's ontology), a single artifact. The second class consists of artworks such as novels, poems, musical compositions and ballets of which more than one copy exists. Not all novels and so on fall into the second class. Most novels, for example, have at one time existed in only one copy. At this time, they belong to the first class. *Pride and Prejudice*, however, is instantiated in many different artifacts and clearly belongs to the second class.

Only altering artworks with a single instantiation is objectionable. Only tampering with the first sort of artwork constitutes an infringement on freedom of artistic expression. Once works in the first class have been modified, they are no longer able to express what their creators intended. Not even all altering of the first sort of artwork is always objectionable. The cathedrals of the Middle Ages were constantly altered. Each generation would modify and add to the efforts of earlier generations. There was nothing objectionable in these alterations. Indeed, much of the beauty of mediaeval cathedrals is due to the fact that they are the cumulative work of an era. Still, there can be no doubt that it would be wrong for us to tamper with the cathedrals. To do so would be to prevent an era, and not just an individual, from expressing itself. And it is equally clear that, in general, where some artists' ability to express themselves depends on the continued integrity of one artifact, it is wrong to tamper with it.

There is nothing wrong with modifying works of art of the second sort. At any rate, there is nothing wrong with such modification so long as at least some unmodified instantiations of the work survive. Not only is the modification of art unobjectionable, but it is done every day. Musicians perform compositions on instruments other than the ones composers intended. Compositions are arranged, transcribed or borrowed from. Poems are translated into different languages or set to music. Novels are adapted for the stage and screen. Even films are constantly subject to alteration. Subtitles are added or their sound tracks are dubbed. Many of these modifications affect a work's capacity to express what its creator wished to express. But they do not restrict artists' freedom of expression since artifacts still exist which embody what they wished to express.

Now the question to be asked is whether films belong to the first or second class of artworks. They are not, perhaps, such paradigms of the second class of works as are published musical compositions. There can be no doubt, however, that films are artworks of the second sort. Typically there are many prints of a film and more can be made. Furthermore, the color conversion of a film does not destroy any instantiations of an artwork. After a film has been colorized just as many black and white prints of the film exist. These black and white prints continue to express what the director intended. Since films belong to the second class of artwork, and since the modification of such works is unobjectionable, there is nothing wrong with colorization. If there were only one print of a film and colorization modified its original state, then color conversion would be objectionable. But this is not what happens.

Not only is there nothing wrong with colorization, but there is also a strong case to be made against forbidding the use of the process. To forbid the unauthorized use of color conversion would limit artistic freedom. Virtually all colorization is without aesthetic justification. There is, however, good reason to suppose that the creative use of colorization could result in new works of art. These would be different works of art than the original artists created. After all, by the admission of the opponents of colorization, it would express something different than does the original black and white film. A prohibition against unauthorized colorization would be, in effect, a ban on creating certain new works of art. Perhaps some directors do not or, because of death, cannot consent to the colorization of their films. Their cases are no different than those of dramatists, novelists or musicians whose works have been adapted. Jane Austen cannot, and likely would not, consent to the dramatization of her novels for television. Handel would probably be outraged by one of his operas performed on modern instruments and by singers in space suits. But such alteration of works of art cannot be forbidden without limiting artistic freedom of expression.

An insistence of the inviolability of films would not only limit artistic freedom. It might deny the world important works of art. Not all modification of artworks is bowdlerization. Some of the greatest artists of the past thrived on the modification of their predecessors' works. Bach, Handel and, indeed, most baroque composers modified the works of other musicians. Even Beethoven was not above borrowing. Shakespeare, of course, regularly modified the works of other artists. The result was great art. It is possible that an artist will create important works of art by colorizing or otherwise modifying films. Consequently, a ban on colorization might deprive the world of valuable art. (A surrealist reading of *Casablanca*, for example, in which Rick appears in a variety of jackets, each a different, rather striking fluorescent hue, might be quite interesting.) I can only endorse a remark by R.G. Collingwood, who wrote "that this fooling about personal property must cease. Let painters and writers and musicians [and filmmakers] steal with both hands whatever they can use, wherever they can find it."[2]

Opposition to colorization is motivated, in part, by a mistaken view of art and artists. Underlying arguments against color conversion is the assumption that artists are heroic individuals who create works of art in isolation. In fact, however, works of art are, in an important sense, social products. They always owe much to a tradition, even if they are reactions against it. Even the solitary novelist had teachers, read other works, and has editors and readers. Films are, of course, paradigms of socially produced artworks. They are the result of the co-operative efforts of many individuals. If artworks were the work of single individuals, it might make some sense to allow individuals

complete control over their fate. But artworks are not produced by
isolated individuals. At the very least we should recognize that actors,
screenplay writers, cinematographers and camera operators should be
consulted about the alteration of a film. But it is better to recognize that
an artwork is produced by and becomes the property of a community
of artists. Just as mediaeval artists could continue to work on
cathedrals, modern filmmakers can modify the works of their
predecessors. Members of an artistic community may do what they like
with artworks, so long as they do not prevent others from expressing
themselves.

It is easy to sympathize with directors who see their films being
colorized against their wills. Even if the choice of color film was not
available to them, they directed their films in a way that, in their view,
best exploited the medium. The fact that most colorization is often done
for mercenary reasons and without aesthetic justification must be
particularly galling. Some directors may be in a legal position to stop
unauthorized color conversion. There are, however, no moral reasons
why it cannot be undertaken, even against a director's wishes.
Moreover, there are good artistic reasons why some alteration of
artworks should be permitted to proceed unfettered.[3]

Notes

1. Woody Allen writes that it is "sinful" to colorize a film against the wishes of its director. He holds that no one should ever be able to tamper with any artist's work in any medium against the artist's will. To do so is, he says, morally "atrocious." See *New York Review of Books*, Vol. 34, No. 13 (13 August 1987), p. 38. The late John Huston is another director who opposed colorization of films on moral grounds. For the views of philosophers, see, John Fisher, Editorial, *Journal of Aesthetics and Art Criticism*, 45 (1987), 227-28; Jerrold Levinson, "Colourization Ill-Defended," *British Journal of Aesthetics*, 30 (1990), 62-67; Flo Leibowitz, "Movie Colorization and the Expression of Mood," *Journal of Aesthetics and Art Criticism*, 49 (1991), 363-65. The essays by Levinson and Leibowitz are responses to the original version of this essay. My rejoinder to Levinson and Leibowitz is found in "Still More in Defense of Colorization," *Journal of Aesthetics and Art Criticism*, 50 (1992), 245-48.

2. Collingwood, *Principles of Art* (Oxford: Oxford University Press, 1958), p. 320.

3. The original version of this essay was written while I was a research fellow at Melbourne University. In the course of writing it I profited from the comments of Christopher Cordner, Stephen Davies and Barry Taylor.

tions are dominated not only by the Machine but also by the total aesthetic[2] environment be it ugly or beautiful. This environment comprises the products of fine artists, commercial artists, and the entertainment industry, including art reproductions, objets d'art, motion pictures, and broadcast programs. It also consists of the surrounding architecture; music and Muzak;[3] advertising art in the form of neon, photography, and graphics; the aesthetic[4] design components of mass-produced commodities developed to appeal to the consumer and to express the commercial identity of the producer; and all of the man-made shapes, sounds, colours, and even tastes and smells[5] which permeate the experiences of millions of people.

In this environment there are scarcely any manufactured articles not designed for some aesthetic appeal.[6] Another remarkable aspect of this aesthetic domain is that it is cluttered with mass-produced commodities whose market values are largely determined by aesthetic considerations. The exchange values of motor vehicles, furniture, buildings, eating utensils, and all the accoutrements of everyday life are enhanced just as much by better aesthetic design as by increased utility.[7]

The second concomitant development is the expansion of intellectual property laws[8] to embrace almost all products of intellectual labor, including the aesthetic components of mass-produced commodities. Just as patents, once limited to machines, engines, devices, manufactures and and useful arts[9] were extended to genetically engineered life forms,[10] copyrights, originally granted only for books and charts,[11] now protect all "original works of authorship[12] fixed in any tangible medium of expression, now known or later developed."[13]

It is extraordinary that almost all man-made objects in this aesthetic environment are actually or potentially subject to intellectual property laws, including copyright, trademark, unfair competition, and patent laws. Even a creative work with minimal artistic form and content, if a *work of authorship*,[14] may be protected by copyright laws from the moment of its fixation[15] in tangible form. The shapes and configurations of goods or the containers in which they are sold, and the design features which distinguish the goods of one party from those of another, may be protectible under trademark[16] and unfair competition laws[17] from the moment the goods are circulated in commerce.[18] Many two- and three-dimensional patterns, configurations, and shapes which are applied to mass-produced articles are eligible for design patent protection.[19] Thus, the surrounding world of objects is subject to the hidden residual rights of other persons so that, in relative terms, the effect of law on art is almost as pervasive as the impact of art on society.

Property

But what are these copyrights, design patents, and trademark rights in the surrounding world of objects? How are these rights deemed *property* rights? Before we can determine what is intellectual property, we must first determine what we mean by *property*.

We start with the fact that the modern world is characterized by complex property relations, exemplified by the hidden residual rights held by people in the surrounding world of objects.[20] In this environment the notion of "property" as a *thing* which one owns is only an illusion, at least relatively speaking. This illusion is fostered by patterns of thought, language, and behaviour originating at a time when one could actually have *fee simple*,[21] i.e., relatively complete, ownership in land and similar ownership of personalty.[22] It is true that the ancient owner of land may have been subject to water rights and easements owned by other individuals,[23] but such interests could not have rivaled in quantity or quality the divisions of ownership characterized by trust deeds and time-sharing interests, and other rights now possessed by persons other than the principal owner.[24] Today, "property," even real estate, is seldom owned outright by the named owner. For instance, real estate is subject to laws on eminent domain; mineral, aviation, and riparian rights; community property laws; zoning laws; laws on security interests; restrictions imposed by nuisance, tort, and pollution laws; and numerous other legal incursions, such as easements, licenses, and rights acquired by prescription.

Therefore, it might be more in keeping with the times to describe *property*, ultimately derived from the Latin adjective "proprius," meaning "one's own,"[25] in terms of the legal relations between the *owner* and all other persons concerning the *use, enjoyment,* and *disposition* of a tangible *thing*.[26] This new mode of thought regarding property is appropriate for our relational universe which has replaced a Newtonian and Cartesian world of separate objects moved around by independently motivated egos. Ownership in a preindustrial society more often may have connoted discrete "bundles" of exclusive rights,[27] but in the post-industrial age of greatly expanded productive forces and intricate relations of production, the web of legal relationships delineating one's property rights is too complex and tangled to maintain the concept of property as a "thing" and not a set of relationships.[28]

What do we mean when we say that one's property is a set of legal relations between the *owner* and all *other persons* with regard to the *use, enjoyment*, and *disposition* of a *thing*? This set of legal relations reflects numerous variegated relationships between the owner and other persons in many dimensions of social intercourse. By definition, the *owner* is a living being or else a juristic entity[29] controlled by living beings,[30] but not necessarily a rational being since animals and incompetent human beings[31] may own and inherit property. The *other persons* with whom the owner is related may be either natural persons or juristic entities, but, generally speaking, rational beings[32] or else represented by rational beings since property rights may only be effectively enforced against rational beings.[33]

By the term *use* we refer to the employment of the thing to achieve a specified end or ends, i.e., actual behaviour of the owner in physically exploiting the thing.[34] The term *enjoyment*, in contrast, refers to the relatively passive pleasure derived from the thing.[35] By *disposition* we mean the alienation of the thing from the owner by destruction, dismantling, lending, transferring, bequeathing, or otherwise disposing of the thing.[36] Together, *use, enjoyment*, and *disposition* exhaust the possible benefits to be derived from material objects.

The *thing* itself must have a material existence, that is, it must be tangible and sufficiently stable so that, using the language of the Copyright Act, it should be capable of being "perceived, reproduced, or otherwise communicated for a period of more than transitory duration."[37] The *thing* may actually be a group or concatenation of things which are used or enjoyed collectively or in a coordinated fashion by the owner.[38]

Because of human ingenuity and the ever-increasing complexity of the means of production, distribution, and provision of goods and services, property relations have become correspondingly complex.[39] After all, this is the age of time-sharing, trust deeds, and futures. The complexity is manifested in a number of dimensions—in time, in space, and in matter. Some examples may suffice.

The previously mentioned encroachments on property rights in land illustrate how many persons are involved and how the physical material is affected in different ways, e.g., by mineral, aviation, and riparian rights of other persons.

Not only may one thing be affected in many ways, but several things may coalesce in one transaction conferring ownership. The purchase of a condo, for example, gives the new owner the right to use and enjoy several physical amenities offered by the condominium complex.

An even more complex set of property relations illustrating the role of several persons in relation to several objects is share ownership in a corporation. The owner of a share theoretically owns an undivided fractional interest in all of the assets of the corporation, mediated by the control of the officers and directors over the assets.

Time and space variables are perhaps best exemplified by ticket ownership which, although describable as a species of contract rights, may also be described as a minor variety of property rights, i.e., as a license or leasehold. The theatre patron who owns a ticket to a performance does not rely on ownership of that ticket but on what it represents, that is, the right to exclude all others from a specific seat in the theatre during a specific interval and, affirmatively, the right to enjoy the artistic production presented to the occupants of the theatre seats.

In other words, these variables—the number and nature of the objects; time; space; the nature of the use, enjoyment, and disposition; the degree of exclusivity; and the number of the persons—dictate what property is. These are the same types of variables employed in analyzing the relationship between a principal and an agent. In some sense, an owner of property is only society's appointed agent to use, enjoy, and dispose of its tangible assets. The titles "owner," "lessee," "licensee," and the terms "ownership," "possession," and "custody" only denote points or regions along the spectrum of property relations and also the degree to which the agent is appointed to "own" the property.

This appointment, this exclusivity, really means that property rights constitute only artificial monopolies created by law on the use, enjoyment, and disposition of tangible assets. Land ownership is just as artificial as and no less a monopoly than a patent or franchise. These monopolies secure for their owners a certain degree of freedom, leisure, predictability, and security; but more importantly they encourage productivity with the rewards of exclusivity. Moreover, such artificial monopolies are delimited by the demands of social utility. For each of the variables defining property relations concerning a thing—time, space, use, enjoyment, disposition, persons, etc.—where the marginal benefits of expanding property rights equal the marginal costs of expansion (i.e., the costs of monopoly) the cutoff point is reached at which the property rights should be restricted.[40] Thus, the monopoly granted on the use of a natural or man-made resource is often delimited to ensure maximum social benefits.

Intellectual Property

What, then, is this special type of property, *intellectual property*? What are the things which are subject to the use, enjoyment, and disposition of the owner?

Almost all man-made goods are potentially the product of three types of labour, both mental and physical: the labour of the scientist or engineer, the labour of the craftsman or workman, and the labour of the artist or other aesthetic designer, which respectively correspond to inventorship, workmanship, and authorship. The scientific or engineering labour, often largely mental, gives the product its utilitarian characteristics so that the product functions, has stability, and serves its intended purpose. The labour of the craftsman or workman, largely physical, is employed to give the product its physical form and content and its "workmanship." Finally, the labour of the artist or other aesthetic designer is used to make the product appeal to the eye of the beholder or express the personality of the creator. All three types of labour embodied in a product were often performed by one person, for example, by the medieval guildsman who designed, crafted, and ornamented his products. Furthermore, each of these types of labour may be embodied in the work to varying degrees. Certain works of "fine art," especially contemporary art, embody little or no craftsmanship or scientific labour, whereas most mass-produced articles incorporate significant investments of each type of labour to give the product its full value to the consumer.[41]

Intellectual property rights, which represent special types of monopolies, were developed to promote investment in these three types of labour.[42] No one will be encouraged to hire an inventor or invest in research if protection is not granted for the resultant products in the form of *letters patent*.[43] Neither will a publisher be likely to publish an author's manuscript unless security is afforded by a copyright. Nor, for that matter, will one necessarily invest in producing high quality products unless they can be sold with a trademark or trade name which can be identified by the public to indicate the source of the products, and unless the trademark or trade name can be monopolized by its first user.[44]

Since this article concerns aesthetic creations[46] which are primarily governed by the law of copyright, we shall examine copyright law to discover the nature of intellectual property as it applies to aesthetic creations. Therefore, we ask, In what does the copyright subsist?

A copyright is a conglomeration of rights in relation to a work of authorship. For instance, as defined by Section 106 of the Copyright Revision Act of 1976, a copyright may be composed of as many as five exclusive rights including the rights to (1) reproduce, (2) adapt, (3) publicly distribute copies of, (4) publicly perform, and (5) publicly display the protected work. Actually, these five types of rights exhaust the means by which a work may be commercially exploited.[47]

As mentioned above,[48] the subject matter of copyright is original works of authorship fixed in tangible media of expression. Of course, this definition set forth at Section 102 of the Act[49] *ipso facto* infers that the "work of authorship" is *not* a tangible thing,[50] as does Section 202 which confirms that:

> Ownership of a copyright, or of any of the
> exclusive rights under a copyright, is distinct from
> ownership of any material object in which the work
> is embodied.

The work of authorship, thus, may only be a mental creation, the melody or poem in the mind, the ballad or epic poem passed from generation to generation for centuries by oral tradition, or in certain cases may comprise both the conception and the labour involved in fixing it in a tangible medium of expression. Insofar as the work represents the labour of fixation, it reflects the bodily experience of that labour, or, in Collingwood's words, "an imaginary experience of total activity."[51]

The copyright does not cover all works of authorship, only works that are fixed. This does not mean, of course, that property rights may not apply to unfixed works if capable of being described and identified;[52] it only means that fixation adds a desired measure of certainty in delineating protection for the work.[53]

The copyright owner, then, has certain legal rights in relation to other persons, but—and this is the principal question—in connection with what *thing*? In connection with the original copy of the work, the template, mould, or manuscript? Certainly not, because other persons affected by the copyright may be affected in relation to other things, for example, other copies.[54] The original copy, and perhaps even all copies, may cease to exist without impairing the copyright or the continued existence of the work of art.[55] Copyright infringers, in fact, may never actually experience the original fixed version, nor are they necessarily using, enjoying, or disposing of such a copy or any other copy, physically or otherwise, when they create a reproduction or derivative work in the same or other medium of expression.[56] At least there may not be any physical use of the original copy or any other copy manufactured by the owner. Even if copying an object were considered a use of it, what of the copyist who copies indirectly by employing a reproduction as his or her model?[57]

It should also be noted that the original copy is not the fixed and stable thing it is imagined to be. Land that one owns is subject to constant accretion, erosion, and change caused by plant and animal life and the elements. In the same manner, the original copy of the work of art is subject to deterioration and continual molecular change. And, of course, where there is statutory protection other than copyright for unfixed, intangible works of authorship,[58] no theory can be based upon the existence of any copy.

Another alternative, consistent with present day legal terminology, is the notion that there is property in intangibles;[59] thus, in owning a work of authorship one has legal relations with others concerning the use, enjoyment, and disposition of an intangible which may or may not be notated in tangible form. This alternative is inconsistent with the hypothesis that property represents legal relations between people concerning the use, enjoyment, and disposition of tangible things. Moreover, we might ask, how does one use, enjoy, or dispose of an intangible when it is almost contradictory to say that an intangible can be used, enjoyed, or disposed of? Perhaps one can argue that it is possible to use and enjoy an intangible work of art which exists only in the imagination. However, how does one dispose of an intangible by gift, device, or destruction? In addition to this objection, there are still other difficulties in claiming intangibles as property.

Works of authorship, the subject matter of copyright, have been analyzed in terms of three components: *ideas*, their *patterning*, and the ultimate *expression* of the ideas and patterning.[60] By *ideas* we refer to motifs, subject matter, concepts, emotions, lessons, feelings, and principles that are conveyed by the work. By *patterning*, especially with a literary work, we mean the direction, development, and structure of the ideas in terms of plot, character, and composition. The ultimate *expression*, of course, is reflected by the notation and rendering of the work which colours in all of the details and gives flesh, sinew, and blood to the skeletal structure already devised.

If the owner lays claim to the work of authorship, his or her title or relations with others usually does not extend to the use, enjoyment, and disposition of the ideas alone since property rights in ideas have seldom been recognized.[61] Perhaps one reason is that the law cannot countenance a monopoly on a literary idea, for to do so would impinge upon the rights of expression of others without compensatory benefits.[62] Additionally, ideas in themselves often have little creative or aesthetic content. As the cases show, protection begins at the level of patterning and certainly extends to expression.[63]

However, as soon as one considers infringement, this model for intellectual property, based on special relations with others concerning the intangible pattern or expression, runs into problems. The owner of a "pattern expression" may be confronted with a competing work of authorship characterized by an expression which is totally different but having a pattern sufficiently similar to justify further inquiry. In this case, without direct proof of copying, the copyright law will generally look to "substantial similarity" judged by the ordinary reasonable observer.[64] As Judge Learned Hand said, to find infringement the plaintiff must show that "the ordinary observer, unless he set out to detect the disparities [between the two works], would be disposed to overlook them, and regard their aesthetic appeal as the same."[65] Nevertheless, the owner's argument that s/he "owns" his or her pattern is open to attack. This is because the alleged infringer may contend that s/he never used, enjoyed, or disposed of the owner's pattern and because his or her pattern is slightly different. Then, the owner will be forced to claim that his or her ownership of the pattern expression may be used to prevent construction of a similar pattern expression. But property rights are not defined or delimited by the original pattern; there is no legal relationship regarding the use, enjoyment, or disposition of a pattern which can prevent the use of a different but similar pattern. What the owner really should be saying is that "your pattern expression produces the same type of imaginative experience in an audience as does mine even though the pattern and the expression are different."

But now, of course, one is going around in circles because the scope of ownership rights in the pattern expression is measured in conceptual and perceptual terms. There can never be a fixed physical aspect of a work, even the notation, which measures the scope of property protection.[66] It would make better sense if one could say that his or her ownership was directed at one defined physical entity, an approach which would mimic the change from geocentricity to heliocentricity.

A Suggested View

A better view is that the thing which is used, enjoyed, and disposed of is not any particular copy, embodiment, or discernable pattern of ideas, but the entire *terra firma* or material universe. In other words, the property rights of a copyright owner, or his legal relations with others, pertain not just to one isolated object or even class of objects, but to all matter which may be formed to simulate the work of authorship. Or expressed in another fashion, the owner controls the earth's use, enjoyment, and disposition in a very limited way.

Therefore, copyrights and related rights in aesthetic creations reflect legal relations regulating the shaping of the world in aesthetic forms. The owner of a copyright in a sculpture, for instance, may prevent others who have seen the work[67] from shaping any part of the universe, using any materials, to simulate the sculpture.[68] The use, enjoyment, and disposition subject to legal rules is the use, enjoyment, and disposition of all matter.

This outlook is better illustrated with patents.[69] The patentee (who receives open letters, *literae patentes*,[70] from the sovereign granting exclusive rights to use natural and man-made resources in certain ways) is given a monopoly on the making, use, and sale of certain processes, articles of manufacture, machines, and compositions of matter, now including life forms.[71] In essence, the monopoly extends to use of the material universe. With a patent for a composition of matter, the patentee can prevent others from combining the same elements regardless of location. The original patents issued by the Crown in England before the Statute of Monopolies 1624,[72] i.e., the exclusive rights to quarry metals, manufacture foodstuffs, and practice inventions, clearly show how property rights in intellectual creations, including processes, can be monopolies on the management of natural resources.

This theory with its overtones of universality is well-suited to the world of today. For example, with international treaties establishing patent,[73] copyright,[74] and trademark[75] rights for owners in almost all countries,[76] these rights are almost universally applied and affect the whole planet. Thus, a plagiarist without authorization may not be entitled to copy a copyrighted work in a treaty country regardless of the source of materials used for making the copy.[77]

This paradigm for intellectual property as a monopoly on shaping the physical universe also fits in with new developments in art and the rapid development of the aesthetic environment. In an age of mass-replication when certain aesthetic designs and works of art are experienced by millions of people worldwide,[78] and when large environmental works[79] and urban redevelopment projects with aesthetic pretensions are undertaken, the creator of the work is really changing the social environment worldwide or shaping a portion of the world's material surroundings.

With works of visual art this new outlook, as simple as a change from phlogiston to oxygen,[80] is immediately viable. The copyright owner of a sculpture prevents the use of matter by others to duplicate or simulate his or her work. But what if the shaped matter does not by itself mimic the protected shape, for instance, holographic plates which, when projected, depict the sculpture three-dimensionally? The copyright still holds and the unauthorized maker of the plates is an infringer, with the assumption that copyright covers both substance and appearance. Another example is suggested by Professor Goodman's analysis of representation in art.[81] Even though the painting does not reproduce the optics of the scene depicted or of other types of representations of the scene (e.g., photographic),[82] the copyright is infringed by different types of representations, including the *tableaux vivant*, which create the impression of the original. Really, the copyright regulates the shaping of the material universe so that the works of others do not give the perception of mimicking the protected shape, or more correctly, do not create the same or similar types of imaginary experiences in the minds of the audience.

As an aside, it should be noted that what may constitute an infringement at one time, at one location, or in one culture may not amount to an infringement in another. After all, the fixed physical aspects of a copy of a work have different meanings and effects at different times, at different locations, and in different cultures.[83]

Some Illustrations

Some cases are actually elucidated by this approach. In *White-Smith Music Publishing Co. v. Apollo Co.*,[84] the unauthorized manufacture and sale of piano rolls did not constitute copyright infringement of sheet music since one could not visually perceive that the music was reproduced on the piano rolls; so the rolls were not considered "copies" within the meaning of the copyright law. (This result was later repealed by statute.)

Obviously, the pattern of the music was not directly inscribed on the rolls. The rolls plus the machine resulted in the infringing sounds only when the rolls were played. The emphasis on the fact that the owner only had an interest in a pattern of notes, which were not explicitly reproduced on the piano rolls, gave rise to the unfortunate result. Had the law adopted the notion that copyright controls the shaping of the material world to give the impression of the work to the senses, the result might have been different.

The same is true with cases involving computer games, which have confused the courts. These cases arise when the copyright owner registers the software program which generates the image on the screen. The owner is more interested in protecting the screen images than the software despite the fact that the images are fluctuating and evanescent and may not constitute a fixed work of authorship. With the older outlook that protection is for the pattern, the registration of the computer program protects only the pattern or literary content embodied in the program, the copyright in which may not be infringed when a totally different program produces a similar screen image on other machines. Under the new model the property rights pertain to shaping the material universe to give the conception and perception of the protected work, i.e., the visual work. Infringement occurs even when the shaping instrumentality is totally different from the copyrighted work.[85]

Of course, it could be said that the pattern is protected when one registers the computer program. The true work arguably is in the program and is only revealed by the machine or device that finally translates it into screen images. However, there are some problems with this argument. First, there may be many machines or devices involved. For example, the computer program may be mediated by many processes and devices before it is finally translated into screen images. Theoretically, the program could generate different screen images if used in connection with different processes and devices. To support the "pattern" theory one would have to argue that the registration covers the computer program used only in connection with specific devices and processes. The screen image constitutes the pattern notated only by a computer program which must be used in connection with a specified set of devices and processes. As a practical matter, nonetheless, when submitting the computer program the registrant never specifies the devices and processes with which it is employed. In any case, the language of Section 102(a) of the Copyright Act does not support the pattern theory because it reads:

> Copyright protection subsists, in accordance with this title, in original works of authorship fixed in any tangible medium of expression, now known or later developed, from which they can be perceived, reproduced, or otherwise communicated, either directly, or *with the aid of a machine or device*. (emphasis added)

In *Gross v. Seligman*,[86] the defendant infringed a copyright in a photograph which his assignor, the photographer, had sold, rights and all, to the plaintiffs. The first photo posed by the photographer showed a nude woman and was entitled "Grace of Youth"; the second infringing photo, entitled "Cherry Ripe," showed the same woman two years later posed the same way by the same photographer, this time with a smile and a cherry stem between her teeth. Clearly, the first photo was not exactly copied. The infringement resulted from reshaping the world in basically the same configuration as before. The copyright in the first photograph was infringed not only when the second photograph was developed, but arguably when the photographer posed the nude for the second photograph. As the court correctly pointed out in *Burrow Giles Lithographing Co. v. Sarony*,[87] it was the arrangement of Oscar Wilde with the background props that made the photograph copyrightable. The defendant had argued that photography was not really an art since the photographer did very little to achieve his result; and perhaps the court would have been sympathetic with this argument had the photograph merely constituted a snapshot. The protectible matter was derived from shaping the material universe in the form of props just as much as from the selective focusing of the photographer.

Literary Works

The new approach may apply to the visual arts, including painting, sculpture, and drawing,[88] and even to the performing arts, such as dance, silent film, and mime[89] where the physical expression of the work appears without notation. But with works embodying mostly literary content,[90] in written or oral form, problems emerge. Such works in their full splendour are often much more complex than statuary or inventions.

With literary works the *materia universa* is not regulated by controlling its shaping in the form of notation, e.g., inked letters, because the literary work's aesthetic content does not lie primarily in its sounds or lettering.[91] At most the sounds and letters denote an imaginary shaping of the world by the author.

If the literary work is to be protected by the owner, s/he must prevent others from shaping the material universe so that the patterning of ideas, the expression of visual, auditory and other sensual experiences, and the dialogue and narration are not duplicated or mimicked. Thus, the would-be infringer is barred from shaping the real world in the form of notation or performance which duplicates the patterning of ideas and the world depicted in the protected work. But is the prospective infringer shaping the world by fixing a new work in the form of notation? Yes, because, after all, most fictional literary works, except certain forms of poetry, are dramatic works played on a planetary stage without the spatial, temporal, and other practical restraints imposed upon the playwright.[92]

However, protection is usually limited to patterning and expression and is not often extended to ideas alone. The idea will only be protected if readily identifiable, sufficiently elaborate, and aesthetically significant. That is, the articulation and elaboration of the idea must reach a certain point where quantity changes quality, and where it is detailed enough to have its own pattern and sufficient creative or aesthetic content.[93]

The best expression of legal reasoning with regard to literary works and infringement is the opinion of Judge Learned Hand in *Nichols v. Universal Pictures*, a case which concerned two similar dramatic works.

Upon any work, and especially upon a play, a great number of patterns of increasing generality will fit equally well, as more and more of the incident is left out. The last may perhaps be no more than the most general statement of what the play is about, and at times may consist only of its title; but there is a point in this series of abstractions where they are not protected, since otherwise the playwright could prevent use of his "ideas" to which, apart from their expression, his property is never extended. But nobody has ever been able to fix that boundary, and nobody ever can. In some cases the question has been treated as though it were analogous to lifting a portion out of the copyrighted work, but the analogy is not a good one, because, though the skeleton is part of the body, it pervades and supports the whole. In such cases we are rather concerned with the line between expression and what is expressed. As respects plays, the controversy chiefly centers upon the characters and the sequence of incidents, these being the substance.[94]

A test suggested by Judge Hand is to take the most detailed pattern common to the works of owner and plagiarist and to see whether this pattern is so old, common, bloodless, and emaciated that it should belong in the public domain.[95] Of course, Hand was chiefly concerned with maintaining free access to ideas and restricting unnecessary and pernicious monopolies. However, another rationale is that ideas alone usually have little creative or aesthetic content worthy of protection. Only when ideas are patterned by the development of characters and the weaving of plot is there protectible creative or aesthetic content. Thus, although intellectual property law could provide protection for any identifiable idea,[96] in the literary realm it waits until the idea is clothed with some creative or aesthetic content. For example, a brief sketch of the plot of *Hamlet* will not protect the idea, nor will the copyright in the completed play protect the idea for a tragedy about a Danish prince who seeks to avenge the murder of his father. More is needed than Orestes in Danish garb.

Poetry represents a most intriguing example because the aesthetic content is expressed in it purest form, for as Hegel argued, in some sense poetry is the pure essence of all art.[97] Poetry is rife with metaphor and metonym; it transforms the exterior world into aesthetic relations. A line of poetry generally conveys more aesthetic meaning than a line of prose in a novel or short story, which itself is only a constituent part of a patterning process that is completed after the passage of pages of text. Thus, there is literary property and even copyright in haiku even though words and short phrases are not ordinarily protectible because they reflect minimal creativity and labour.[98]

With poetry, especially lyric in contrast to epic, the ideas and feelings themselves have aesthetic content. The copyright in the poem usually can only be infringed by another poem having almost the same words. (The paraphrased copy almost surely would fail unless it were a parody.) The author's rights pertain to the use of the material world to shape it in the form of sounds and letters so that the experience of the poem is recreated in the imagination.

Conclusion

Our final conclusion is that property rights in an aesthetic creation enable the owner to restrain plagiarists from using the material world to recreate in the audience the imaginative experiences first created by the protected work.

The author doesn't own the work of authorship per se but has legal relations to others regarding the use of the material world to copy the work. The rights conferred on the owner are not plenary but only sufficient to prevent others from commercially exploiting the real world with reference to the work.

This notion that property rights in aesthetic creations involve shaping the entire material universe is consonant with the underlying reality that art pervades the whole environment and that certain mass-produced aesthetic creations pervade the experiences of millions of people around the world. The seamless universe which has been delicately carved up into discrete objects is returned to its full plasticity.

In the world of the near future we can anticipate, for better or for worse, hidden residual rights not only in the flora and fauna surrounding us but also in the shaping of the whole environment. It will not be as important to own tangible things as to control how the planet will be shaped in our own images.

Art, then will be perceived in its true form, the shaping of the exterior world to reflect man's inner nature.

Notes

1. *Cf.* Peter Karlen, "What is Art? A Sketch for Legal Definition," *Law Quarterly Review*, 94 (1978), 383; Peter Karlen, "Legal Aesthetics," *British Journal of Aesthetics*, 19 (1979), 195.

2. Notwithstanding *Berman v. Parker*, 348 *United States Supreme Court Reports* 26 (1954) and its progeny, which have sustained "aesthetic" zoning in the interest of pleasing and beautiful surroundings, by *aesthetic*, legally speaking, one does not necessarily refer to that which is beautiful or pleasing. *See* Uddo, "Land Use Controls: Aesthetics, Past and Future," *Loyola Law Review*, 21 (1951), 851. The urban environment, in any case, is not always attractive or pleasing. Instead, *aesthetic* refers to that which has artistic qualities or that which relates to perception by the senses, at least insofar as the perception is an artistic one. As Professor Collingwood noted: "Aesthetic theory is the theory not of beauty but of art." Robin Collingwood, *Principles of Art* (New York, 1958), p. 22. *See also* Peter Karlen, "What is Art? A Sketch for a Legal Definition," *Law Quarterly Review*, 94 (1978), 383, 396.

3. Muzak is innocuous music which creates an aesthetic environment to suit the needs of business and commerce. *See Public Utilities Commission v. Pollak*, 343 *United States Supreme Court Reports* 451 (1952) (Muzak piped into streetcars offended sensibilities of unwilling listeners).

4. The aesthetic design components of an article of manufacture are the non-utilitarian elements of the product which have aesthetic or ornamental value and which may or may not be inseparable from the utilitarian aspects of the article. *Compare* the definition of "pictorial, graphic, and sculptural works" at Section 101 of the Copyright Revision Act of 1976 which talks about artistic elements of such works which may or may not be inseparable from utilitarian characteristics.

5. One cannot doubt after reading J. Huysmans, *Against Nature* (R. Baldrick trans. 1959) that the senses of taste and smell as well as those of sight, hearing, and touch are the concern of aesthetic experience. *See* Quinet, "Food as Art: The Problem of Function," *British Journal of Aesthetics*, 21 (1981), 159; Fretter, "Is Wine an Aesthetic Object?" *Journal of Aesthetics and Art Criticism*, 30 (1971), 97. *Contra* M. Beardsley, *Aesthetics: Problems in the Philosophy of Criticism* (1958), pp. 98-99 (denying role of taste in olfactory senses informing works of art).

6. In other words, it is very difficult to pick any man-made object in our surroundings which does not have an aesthetic component. Even purely utilitarian devices including cookingware and computers are designed not only for utility but also for appearance.

7. *See* Peter Karlen, "Moral Rights in California," *San Diego Law Review*, 19 (1982), 675-77. The price of almost any practical household device, for instance, is largely dictated by aesthetic design. As an example, well-designed eating utensils sold in connection with a designer name may command a much greater price than other eating utensils which serve the exact same function but less gracefully. The same is true of clothing.

8. Intellectual property laws are those laws designed to create property interests in products of intellectual labor such as inventions and works of authorship.

9. Act of April 10, 1790, ch. 7, 1 Stat. 109-10.

10. *Diamond v. Chakrabarty*, 447 *United States Supreme Court Reports* 303 (1970) (microorganisms held patentable).

11. Act of May 31, 1790.

12. A *work of authorship* is a creative work, usually having significant aesthetic content, and usually being a product of the arts. According to Section 102(a) of the Copyright Revision Act of 1976, works of authorship include "literary works; musical works, including any accompanying words; dramatic works, including any accompanying music; pantomimes and choreographic works; pictorial, graphic, and sculptural works; motion pictures and other audiovisual works; and sound recordings."

13. Title 17, United States Code, embodying the Copyright Act Section 102(a).

14. *See* note 12, *supra*.

15. A work is deemed "fixed" in a tangible medium of expression, according to Section 101 of the Copyright Act:

> When its embodiment in a copy or phonorecord, by or under the authority of the author, is sufficiently permanent or stable to permit it to be perceived, reproduced, or otherwise communicated for a period of more than transitory duration. . . .

16. A trademark, according to Section 45 of the Lanham Trademark Act of 1946 (15 United States Code, Section 1127):

> Includes any word, name, symbol, or device or any combination thereof adopted and used by a manufacturer or merchant to identify his goods and distinguish them from those manufactured or sold by others. Such marks include words, phrases, logos, shapes and configurations, signatures, and any other distinctive devices which can be used as commercial symbols.

17. The law of unfair competition concerns itself with maintaining proper competitive practices within the free market economy and, in particular, is concerned with preventing merchants and manufacturers from passing off their

products as those of other merchants or manufacturers by, for example, using misleading advertising and similar techniques which create a likelihood of public confusion as to source or origin of goods or services. (Rudolf Callahan, *Unfair Competition, Trademarks, and Monopolies* (4th ed., 1981) Section 109.)

18. The Lanham Trademark Act of 1946 permits federal trademark registrations for devices which distinguish products after the "first use of the mark in commerce." Title 15, United States Code, Section 1051. According to Section 45 of the Lanham Trademark Act of 1946 (15 United States Code, Section 1127):

> A mark shall be deemed to be used in commerce
> (a) on goods when it is placed in any manner on
> the goods or their containers or the displays
> associated therewith or on the tags or labels affixed
> thereto and the goods are sold or transported in
> commerce and (b) on services when it is used or
> displayed in the sale or advertising of services and
> the services are rendered in commerce, or the
> services are rendered in more than one State or in
> a foreign country and the person rendering the
> service is engaged in commerce in connection
> therewith.

For purposes of determining what is "commerce," the same statute says that the term "means all commerce which may be lawfully regulated by Congress," which, in turn, means interstate and foreign commerce.

19. Design patent protection is allowed by Title 35, United States Code, Section 171, which says:

> Whoever invents any new, original, and ornamental
> design for an article of manufacture may obtain a
> patent therefore, subject to the conditions and
> requirements of this title. . . .

The purpose of design patent protection is to grant protection for industrial designs that are aesthetically pleasing but not otherwise protectible by copyright law which does not extend protection for aesthetic components of products which are inseparably linked to the utilitarian features of the product. *See* Section 101 of the Copyright Act (17 United States Code Section 101) on the copyright protection for utilitarian articles.

20. These residual rights not only include intellectual property rights in terms of patents, trademarks, and copyrights but also other property rights in realty and personalty. *See* text following note 24, *infra*.

21. A fee simple estate in land is:

> The estate which a man has where lands are given
> to him and to his heirs absolutely without any end

or limit put to his estate. 2 *Blackstone's Commentaries* 106.

Black's Law Dictionary (5th ed. 1979), p. 554.

22. *Personalty* is personal property; movable property; chattels. *Ibid.* at p. 1030.

23. [*See Maitland*].

24. *See* Charles Reich "The New Property," *Yale Law Journal*, 73 (1964), 733.

25. E. Drone, *A Treatise on the Law of Property and Intellectual Productions in Great Britain and the United States* (1879), p. 6. *See also Funk & Wagnalls Standard Dictionary of the English Language, International Edition* (New York, 1960), p. 1011 (definition of *property* with origins).

26. Felix Cohen.

27. *See* R. Brown, *The Law of Personal Property* (3rd ed. 1975), Section 1.5 (ownership connotes collection or bundle of rights). [*See* Powell, U.S.D. article, note 46.] Ownership often consisted of a predictable grouping of rights purchased or possessed with respect to any particular piece of property within that class of property. One owns rights not things. And, of course, the jural correlate of "right" is the "duty" of others not to infringe upon the right, implying that there is always a relationship between an owner and a third party concerning the thing. [*See* Hohfeld, U.S.D. article, notes 45-46]

28. The full use of one's property, especially real property, is restricted by the rights of others and often confined to that which does not offend the sensibilities of others. Today it is difficult to convert one's house for use as a bawdy house or a funeral parlour. *See* W. Prosser, *Handbook of the Law of Torts*, 592 nn. 28-29 (4th ed. 1971). Nor can one burn down own's own house. *See* R. Perkins, *Perkins on Criminal Law* (2d ed. 1969) 228. Indeed, one cannot necessarily build a house in a certain fashion or let it deteriorate. *See generally* Noel, "Unaesthetic Signs as Nuisances," *Cornell Law Quarterly*, 25 (1939), 1. Even to hang one's clothes on a clothesline in order to create an eyesore may be subject to prosecution. *See People v. Stover*, 12 *New York Reports* 2d Series 462, 191 *Northeastern Reporter* 2d Series 272 (1963), *appeal dismissed*, 375 *United States Supreme Court Reports* 42 (1963).

29. The most common juristic entities are trusts, corporations, associations, and partnerships. Incompetent human beings may include infants, the insane, or the disabled. *See Black's Law Dictionary* (5th ed. 1979), p. 477 (definition of *entity*).

30. See above.

31. Of course, it is arguable that the animal really doesn't own the property. Rather, the property is owned by a trustee for the benefit of the animal. Almost the same relationship is present with an incompetent person whose estate is managed by a conservator.

32. A rational, sane individual is one who is capable of understanding the rules of law which must govern his conduct and of conforming his behavior to the requirements of law. [*See* insanity rules.]

33. See above.

34. The use of property is its employment, occupation, exercise or practice. *See Black's Law Dictionary* (5th ed. 1979), p. 1382 *citing Central Surety and Insurance Corporation v. Anderson,* 446 *Southwestern Reporter* 2d Series 897, 903.

35. *Black's Law Dictionary* (5th ed. 1979), p. 475 refers to *enjoyment* as "comfort, consolation, contentment, ease, happiness, pleasure and satisfaction."

36. *Black's Law Dictionary, ibid.* at p. 423 refers to *disposition* as "act of disposing; transferring to the care or possession of another. The parting with, alienation of, or giving up property."

37. This is the definition for "fixed" at Section 101 of the Copyright Act. *See* note 15, *supra.*

38. The owner of a condominium owns more than just the real property constituting the living space; in addition, s/he owns rights to use other facilities in the condominium complex.

39. *See* Richard Powell, *Powell on Real Property* I (1977), Section 13 on the development of "new" property rights. *Cf.* Charles Reich, *supra,* note 24 ("new" property rights in governmental largesse, i.e., franchises, licenses, and monopolies).

40. *Cf.* Richard Posner, *Economic Analysis of Law* (Chicago, 1972), pp. 10-40 (discussion of the economics of property rights).

41. For notes on craft, art, and the division of labour, *See* Osborne, "The Aesthetic Concept of Craftsmanship," *British Journal of Aesthetics*, 17 (1977), 138 (*designer, workman,* and *engineer*); Fethe, "Craft and Art: A Phenomenological Distinction," *British Journal of Aesthetics*, 17 (1977), 129; Martland, "Art and Craft: The Distinction," *British Journal of Aesthetics*, 14 (1974), 231; Dufrenne, "The Aesthetic Object and the Technical Object," *Journal of Aesthetics & Art Criticism*, 23 (1964), 113. As Plato said in "Politicus," quoted in *Esquire, Inc. v. Ringer*, 414 Federal Supplement 939, 941 (District Court, District of Columbia 1976):

> All the handicrafts possess a scientific content which has grown up along with them and is embodied in their practice. The manufactured article is the joint product of the science and the practice [technique] which are combined in the handicraft.

42. Article I, Section 8, clause 8 of the United States Constitution granted the right to the federal government:

> To promote the Progress of Science and useful
> Arts, by securing for limited Times to Authors and

Inventors the exclusive Right to their Writings and
Discoveries.

In other words, the copyright or patent is not granted to reward the author or inventor but rather to promote the sciences and arts by promoting investments in monopolies.

43. The Latin term is *literae patentes*. *See Black's Law Dictionary* (5th ed. 1979), p. 841. The original patents were open letters to the realm written by the sovereign, usually to inform the public that exclusive rights to manufacture certain articles of commerce and to use certain inventions had been granted to particular persons. The patent of today is "open" because letters or disclosures in the form of the issued patent are made available throughout the jurisdiction in which the patent issues, so that during the term of the patent the public is informed about the scope of the patent, and thereafter the public will know about how to make, use, and sell the patentable device or process.

44. *See* note 16, *supra*, on definition of *trademark*.

45. A trademark is more than an indication of source or origin, it is also an indication of quality. Under Section 5 of the Lanham Trademark Act of 1946 (15 United States Code Section 1055), for example, the registrant may take advantage of the use of the mark by a related or licensed company provided that the mark is not used so that its use deceives the public, i.e., by using it with substandard goods. In the case of a certification mark, under Section 14 of the Act (15 United States Code Section 1064), the registration for the mark may be cancelled if the owner does not control or is not able to legitimately exercise control over the use of the mark, that is, by permitting the mark to be used in connection with substandard goods.

46. By *aesthetic creations* we mean works of authorship as defined at note 16, *supra*, although not every work of authorship is an aesthetic creation because some works of authorship, like computer programs, have very little or no aesthetic content. In copyright cases, the courts will not assess artistic or aesthetic merit. *See* Melville Nimmer, *Nimmer on Copyright* (1983) Section 2.01[B].

47. There are no other means of commercial exploitation, especially since the adaptation right is so broad. The right to adapt a work includes the right to prepare "derivative works." A derivative work is:

> A work based upon one or more pre-existing
> works, such as a translation, musical arrangement,
> dramatization, fictionalization, motion picture
> version, sound recording, art reproduction,
> abridgement, condensation, or any other form in
> which a work may be recast, transformed, or
> adapted. . . .

17 United States Code Section 101.

48. *See* text accompanying note 13, *supra*.
49. 17 United States Code Section 102(a).
50. Professor Nimmer says succinctly:

> As used in the Copyright Act, a "literary work" is a work of authorship, but a "book" is not. A "book" is merely a material object which may embody, and hence constitute, a copy of a given literary work.

Melville Nimmer, *Nimmer on Copyright* (New York, 1983) Section 2.03[C].

51. Robin Collingwood, *Principles of Art* (New York, 1958), p. 151.
52. *See, e.g.*, California Civil Code Sections 980-82, which refer to "original works of authorship not fixed in any tangible medium of expression." The present Copyright Act at Section 102(a) is confined to works of authorship fixed in tangible media of expression and preempts all state laws which cover the same subject matter with the same exclusive rights. (*See* Section 301.) Thus, the source of law for protection of unfixed works must be the states, although it is conceivable that Congress could even preempt state laws with federal legislation concerning unfixed works since the constitutional provision at Article I, Section 8, Clause 8 refers to *Writings* which arguably may be fixed or unfixed. *See* note 42, *supra* for the constitutional clause.

53. When the work is fixed, by definition it is reproducible, perceivable, or communicable for more than a period of transitory duration (*see* note 15, *supra*), and there is less confusion about what constitutes an infringement than if the work were to remain unfixed and merely subject to oral descriptions.

54. For instance, the plagiarist who wrongfully copies a literary work rarely has access to the original manuscript but rather uses copies of the original.

55. Section 101 of the Copyright Act requires only that the work be fixed in a tangible medium of expression. It does not on its face require permanent fixation. If it did, then someone could destroy the author's copyright in a work of authorship, such as a painting, merely by destroying all copies. In the case of a work appearing in only one copy or a few copies, this result makes no sense. Moreover, this type of rule might mean that mutilation of a work appearing only in one copy would change the scope of the copyright to cover only the changed version of the work.

56. For instance, one who unlawfully copies a musical composition may only have heard its performance and may never have had access to a physical copy of the musical notation or recorded performance.

57. *Cf. Grove Press, Inc. v. Greenleaf Pub. Co.*, 247 Federal Supplement 518 (Eastern District New York, 1965). In this case, Jean Genet's book *Thief's Journal*, originally in French, was translated with authorization into English. The English version fell into the public domain. The defendant copied the public domain English version and was sued for copyright

infringement based upon the original copyright of the French edition. The plaintiff prevailed.

58. *See* note 52, *supra*.

59. *Black's Law Dictionary* (5th ed. 1979), p. 726 defines *intangibles* as:
>   Property that is a 'right' rather than a physical
>   object. Examples would be patents, stocks, bonds,
>   goodwill, trademarks, franchise, and copyrights.

Black's Law Dictionary, *ibid.*, p. 726, refers to an *intangible asset* as:
>   A non-physical, non-current asset which exists only
>   in connection with something else, as the goodwill
>   of a business.

60. *See* Gorman, "Copyright Protection for the Collection and Representation of Facts," *Harvard Law Review*, 76 (1963), 1569.

61. Section 102(b) of the Copyright Act explicitly rules out protection of ideas. *See Baker v. Selden*, 101 *United States Supreme Court Reports* 99 (1879) (bookkeeping system is not protected by copyright of literary work containing bookkeeping forms).

62. Comparatively speaking, a literary idea not fully developed by a complete expression in the form of words has very little social value. In other words, the vague idea of a plot for a play is of little value compared to the completely written play. Given the fact that basic dramatic plots are restricted in number of terms of their essential components but the expression of such plots is unlimited, it makes no sense to grant a monopoly for any particular plot or plot idea.

63. *See, e.g., Nichols v. Universal Pictures Co.*, 45 *Federal Reporter* 2d Series 119 (1930) (copyright infringement case involving two plays having somewhat similar characters and theme, "Abie's Irish Rose" and "The Cohens and the Kellys").

64. Melville Nimmer, *Nimmer on Copyright* (New York, 1983) Section 13.03 [A] (substantial similarity); *ibid.*, Section 13.03[E] (average reasonable man).

65. *Peter Pan Fabrics, Inc. v. Martin Weiner Corp.*, 274 *Federal Reporter* 2d Series 487, 489 (2d Circuit 1960) (copyright infringement case involving similar fabric designs for women's dresses).

66. *Cf.* text accompanying note 94 *infra* (opinion of Judge Learned Hand, which indicated that no one can fix the boundary at which the expression of an idea is no longer merely an unprotectible idea but is a protected expression). It should be noted that Section 106(2) of the Copyright Act gives the copyright owner the exclusive right to prepare derivative works. According to Section 101 of the Copyright Act, in the literary field, derivative works include not only translations, abridgements, condensations, but also dramatizations, fictionalizations, motion picture versions, or "any other form in which a work may be recast, transformed, or adapted." Once again, using the language of

Judge Hand, 'no one can objectively fix the boundary between that which is an infringing derivative work and that which represents a new work of authorship.' As mentioned above, *supra* note 64, infringement is determined by "substantial similarity" judged by "the ordinary reasonable observer."

67. It is not a copyright infringement to recreate the protected work if such recreation is an independent creation. (*See* Melville Nimmer, *Nimmer on Copyright* (New York, 1983) Section 2.01[A], n. 13.) In fact, the independently created work which is identical or similar to the protected work enjoys its own copyright protection. The requirement for copyright protection is originality (17 United States Code Section 102(a)), whereas for patent protection one must establish novelty in addition to originality (Title 35 United States Code Section 101). In other words, patentable subject matter must be entirely new, but copyrightable subject matter need only be original with the author, that is, the author need only establish that the work was not copied from the material of others. The reason for the difference between copyright and patent law is simple. The odds of independently creating an identical or substantially identical work of authorship are extremely small, whereas, because of the continuing progress of science and engineering, simultaneous or near simultaneous developments of the same invention are quite commonplace so that protection must be given to the first inventor.

68. I use the word *simulate* rather than *reproduce* to indicate that the creation of the plagiarist must subjectively give the appearance of the copyrighted work rather than objectively reproduce it. *See* text accompanying notes 81, 82, *infra*.

69. Of course, with patents there is not the same element of subjectivity. As mentioned above, in the text accompanying note 67, *supra*, patentable subject matter must be novel rather than merely original. A patent infringement takes place where the new subject matter substantially performs the same functions in substantially the same manner as the patented subject matter to obtain the same result. (*See Sanitary Refrigerator Company v. Winters*, 280 *United States Supreme Court Reports* 30, 42.) This form and function test is much more objective than the test for copyright infringement which depends upon substantial similarity judged by the ordinary observer.

70. *See* note 43, *supra*.

71. *See* Title 35, United States Code Section 101 on the scope of patent protection. In *Diamond v. Chakrabarty*, 447 *United States Supreme Court Reports* 303 (1980), the Supreme Court extended patent protection to microorganisms.

72. 21 Jac. 2, c. 3.

73. *See, e.g.*, Paris Convention for the Protection of Industrial Property.

74. Universal Copyright Convention; Berne Convention for the Protection of Literary and Artistic Works.

75. Paris Convention for the Protection of Industrial Property.

76. *E.g.*, the Paris Convention for the Protection of Industrial Property, the Patent Cooperation Treaty, the Universal Copyright Convention, and the Berne Convention for the Protection of Literary and Artistic Works.

77. Universal Copyright Convention, Article II.

78. In the fine arts the Mona Lisas, Guernicas, and Davids have long since become household images; in the performing arts, the mass replication of audio and audiovisual works conveys the same experiences throughout the world.

79. *E.g.*, works of Christo, such as "Wrapped Bay" in Little Bay, Australia; "Valley Curtain" in Rifle, Colorado; and "Running Fence" in Sonoma County, California.

80. *See* T. Kuhn, *The Nature of Scientific Revolutions* (University of Chicago, 1954) for an excellent discussion of the evolution and birth of new scientific outlook, and, in particular, the decline of the phlogiston theory. Phlogiston was an imaginary element, believed in the eighteenth century to separate from every combustible body in burning. The presence of phlogiston explained why certain materials became heavier after burning, i.e., because the light phlogiston element escaped, whereas, in fact, the material had combined with oxygen and became heavier.

81. *See* Nelson Goodman, *Languages of Art* (Indianapolis, 1976), pp. 34-39.

82. *Ibid.* at pp. 10-18.

83. *Compare* the Supreme Court opinion in *Miller v. California*, 413 *United States Supreme Court Reports* 15 (1973) in which obscenity is judged by the eye of the beholder so that local standards for obscene materials replace national standards. In other words, obscenity is to be judged by the standards of each local community. *Cf.* note 66, *supra*.

84. 209 *United States Supreme Court Reports* 1 (1908).

85. *See* Melville Nimmer, *Nimmer on Copyright* (New York, 1983) Section 2.03[B][1] citing cases and statutory authority overruling the doctrine of *White-Smith Music Publishing Company v. Appollo*, 209 *United States Supreme Court Reports* 1 (1908).

86. 212 *Federal Reporter* 930 (1914).

87. 111 *United States Supreme Court Reports* 53 (1884).

88. These are visual arts according to the Copyright Office classifications, and are registered under a Form VA distributed by the Copyright Office. *See* Copyright Office Regulations promulgated under the Copyright Act of 1976, Section 202.3(a)(3)(iii) appearing at 37 *Code of Federal Regulations*, Chapter 2.

89. These are considered performing arts and are registered as such under Form PA with the Copyright Office. *See* Copyright Office Regulations promulgated under the Copyright Act of 1976, Section 202.3(a)(3)(i) appearing at 37 *Code of Federal Regulations*, Chapter 2.

90. Non-dramatic literary works are a separate category registered on a Form TX with the Copyright Office. *See* Copyright Office Regulations promulgated under the Copyright Act of 1976, Section 202.3(a)(3)(ii) appearing at 37 *Code of Federal Regulations*, Chapter 2.

91. *Compare* Richard Shusterman, "Aesthetic Blindness to Textual Visuality," *American Journal of Aesthetics and Art Criticism*, 41 (1982) p. 87.

92. The modern novel, especially the modern historical novel, is characterized by its unrestrained travels through time and space.

93. *See* Melville Nimmer, *Nimmer on Copyright* (New York, 1983) Section 1.10[B][2].

94. 45 *Federal Reporter* 2d Series 119 (2d Circuit 1930), cited at Note 63, *supra*.

95. *Ibid.* at p. 122, following *Dymow v. Bolton*, 11 *Federal Reporter* 2d Series 690 (2d Circuit 1926), opinion of Hough, Judge.

96. Ideas are protected but not as property. Rather, the sanctity of certain interpersonal relationships is respected so that a breach thereof, involving a theft of an idea, may be remedied. For instance, a contractual relationship whereby one party promises not to disclose an idea may allow protection for an idea via a breach of contract action. If there is a confidential relationship between the parties, such as a relationship between attorney and client, physician and patient, or penitent and preacher, the wrongful disclosure constitutes an actionable breach of the relationship, thus indirectly protecting the idea. *See* Melville Nimmer, *Nimmer on Copyrights* (New York, 1983) Ch. 16.

97. As Hegel says:

> Thus the genuine mode of poetic representation is the inner perception and the poetic imagination itself. And since all types of art share in this mode, poetry runs through them all, and develops itself independently in each. Poetry, then, is the universal art of the spirit which has attained inner freedom, and which does not depend for its realization upon external sensuous matter, but expatiates only in the inner space in the inner time of the ideas and feelings.

Georg Hegel, Preface to Vorlesungen uber die Aesthetik (J. Loewenberg, translator) in *Hegel Selections* (J. Loewenberg, editor) (New York, 1957), 336.

98. *See* Melville Nimmer, *Nimmer on Copyright* (New York, 1983) Section 2.16.

IV

The Sponsorship of Art

Can Government Funding of the Arts Be Justified Theoretically?

Noël Carroll

The purpose of this article is to explore various avenues for justifying arts funding. Our results are mixed. Some grounds for government arts funding are found, but it is noted that in embracing these justifications untoward consequences may be incurred. Thus, it is urged that we refrain from government funding of the arts because the effects of such funding, when guided by the kinds of justifications available, would be deleterious to the art world. However, the conclusions of this article are provisional; there is no reason to believe that someone may not construct better justifications for government arts funding than those examined here.

The question of whether there are theoretical grounds for government arts funding is unwieldy and needs trimming. First, what does "funding" refer to? Funding can be either direct or indirect. One might say that there was government arts funding in this country before 1965 but that it took indirect forms, including land grants, tax exemptions to educational and cultural institutions such as museums, and tax advantages for private donations of art to the public.[1] Concern here is not with indirect funding but with the justification of direct state funding of the arts.

But still the scope is too broad to be manageable, because there are so many different kinds of arts-related activities with which direct state funding may be involved. Much government funding is aimed at

Noël Carroll's article first appeared in the *Journal of Aesthetic Education* 21 (1), Spring 1987, pp. 21-35. It is reprinted here by permission of the publisher, University of Illinois Press, and the author.

what might be thought of as the preservation of culture intact. Other objectives of government funding target community art centers, regional theaters, and school programs. And funding may also be directed to professional artists for the purpose of enabling them to produce new works of art. This latter type of funding is the sort with which this article is concerned. Whereas funding of museums looks to the past of our culture, funding artists is prospective. It is not a matter of preserving culture but of creating culture. The preservation of culture, of course, is involved with education, which appears to be the legitimate realm of state activity. And, furthermore, though even more vaguely, art preservation keeps us aware of who we have been, which knowledge is relevant to us in our practical decision about who we shall become. But it is not so easy to see the way in which prospective funding—i.e., support for the production of contemporary art—can be defended as educational in terms of the state's responsibilities in this arena in the way that preservation might be. Bluntly, contemporary art is not our heritage yet, nor is it clear how much of it will be. So even if funding for the purpose of preservation falls within the state's educational responsibilities, prospective arts funding calls for some other kind of theoretical justification, that is, a justification in terms of the way in which prospective arts funding can be seen as implementing one or more of the proper functions of the state.

Clearly, commissioning arts to design stamps and government buildings is a legitimate government activity. So our question is whether state funding of the production of new art that is not connected to state projects is also legitimate. Admittedly, the great bulk of governmental funding of the arts is not directed to artists. But the question is how even this admittedly small expenditure is to be funded. (Hereafter, "arts funding" refers only to this issue.)

Before proceeding, a word or two about the use of "state" in this discussion is appropriate. Though certain issues particular to the United States will be canvassed, in general our question concerns whether there are theoretical justifications for prospective arts funding in what we broadly think of as modern, pluralistic, democratic states. We should not have in mind the sort of Marxian utopia where we all fish in the morning and write art criticism in the afternoon. That state of affairs would not be blighted by a scarcity of resources or by differences of opinion and, anyway, would not, one presumes, need arts funding (or a state, for that matter). Nor do we have totalitarian regimes in mind; they have no need for justifications. Rather, our question is addressed to pluralistic, democratic states which have fundamental commitments to protecting their citizens from harm—both foreign and domestic—and to securing the welfare of those within their boundaries, i.e., to providing some manner of generally economic assistance to individuals in need, where such needs are connected to the individuals' capacity to maintain a livelihood.[2] Such states are also committed to the protection of the civil institutions upon which democracy rests.

It is important to stress that the viewpoint of this essay is not based on opposition to the idea that states have responsibilities to the welfare of all persons within their borders. For example, the state has responsibilities to the victims of structural unemployment. When someone, through no fault of his or her own, loses the means to a livelihood, the state upholds a system of property distribution that restrains that person from walking onto a local farm and taking whatever she and her family need to live. Since the state thus contributes to the cause of that person's need, it has a responsibility to her.[3] Full acceptance of the principle that the state, in our conception of it, has welfare obligations needs to be emphasized here just because in discussions of arts funding it is often assumed that if one has any doubts about the propriety of arts funding, one must also be skeptical about welfare. Welfare is a legitimate arena of state activity, but it is not clear that all prospective arts funding is.

What does this talk of legitimate arenas of state activity come to? Maybe we can approach this by reviewing one of the more popular defenses of arts funding that recurs in contemporary debates. The point is stated succinctly by Sir William Rees-Mogg, chairman of the Arts Council of Great Britain. He writes, "The Arts Council grant is equal to the interest on the interest on the capital cost of the Trident programme. That is the relative priority the state gives to the enhancement of the human spirit. I am a firm supporter of national defense policies, but just look at the state's priorities—the capital on defense but not even the interest on the interest on the arts."[4]

Many supporters of prospective arts funding will not be so temperate as Rees-Mogg. Appalled at our defense expenditures, many Americans will say it is a scandal that so much is spent on defense and so little on art or that art should not suffer so that defense spending may flourish. Perhaps they will urge that greater bounties for art should be carved out of the gargantuan defense budget. But these remarks miss the point in assuming that defense spending and arts funding are somehow linked. They are not.

Defense is a legitimate function of any state. It is not clear that prospective arts funding is, nor if it is, that it is such a crucial function that it makes sense to tie its destiny in any way to that of so central a function as defense. Undoubtedly our defense spending is extravagant. But it is perfectly compatible to be opposed to the present level of defense spending while also wondering if prospective arts funding is appropriate. For *some* defense spending is recognized as legitimate by nearly everyone, save pacifists and certain types of anarchists, whereas it is not yet apparent that any prospective arts funding is legitimate. The defense spending argument may be politically persuasive, especially for those opposed to the current defense budgeting, but it is not a theoretical justification, for it does not show that prospective arts funding is a proper function of government, whereas defense is.

The discussion of proper state functions may suggest an avenue of justification for prospective arts funding, viz., welfare. If one agrees that the state has a responsibility to secure the welfare of its citizens, then one may be tempted to say that prospective arts funding is a means by which the state secures the welfare of those within its borders. But "welfare," as it applies to state activity, refers to assistance to individuals in need of the basic goods that comprise a livelihood. Is it plausible to suppose that prospective arts funding provides some such goods?

A conclusive answer would require a full theory of needs, which unfortunately we lack. But perhaps we can at least determine whether the products of prospective arts funding sound like the things we ordinarily think of as needs. On one reading, to say that someone needs Z is to say that if she lacks it she will suffer injury, sickness, madness, hunger, or avoidable death.[5] Does the production of contemporary artworks assist individuals in needful situations such as these? Would anyone be harmed, in any literal sense of the term, if prospective arts funding were discontinued? Am I harmed if painter X does not execute the series she would have created had she received a state grant?

Of course, defining basic needs in terms of harms has limitations. But suppose we define welfare needs in terms of the amount of goods and services sufficient to raise an individual from his present state to somewhere above the poverty line.[6] If this is how we conceive of the welfare jurisdiction of the state, then it is difficult to see how prospective arts funding has anything to do with welfare.

Undoubtedly, the picture presented thus far involves thinking of the welfare of nonartists. Our rhetorical questions really ask, "What nonartists will be harmed, in a basic, literal sense, if they do not have the opportunity to see so-and-so's planned series due to a lack of government funding?" Or, even more ridiculously, "What nonartist will fail to be raised above the poverty line should so-and-so's proposed series not be funded?" It may be charged that the case has been rigged. Haven't we forgotten about the welfare responsibilities of the state to artist so-and-so? Isn't it possible that artist so-and-so will fail to rise above the poverty line without funding?

The problem with these new questions, however, is that if artist so-and-so has a legitimate welfare need, then the state will have the responsibility to assist her. That is, if a state is meeting its basic welfare responsibilities to everyone, then there is no reason to propose prospective arts funding as a further aspect of the state's welfare function. Of course, this raises issues about the relation of welfare to the active promotion of employment by the state, and we will come back to that matter.

Some writers who attempt to connect state arts support to the state's welfare function introduce a concept of "aesthetic welfare." Aesthetic welfare, in turn, is defined as "all the aesthetic levels of the experience of members of the society at a given time."[7] It is then suggested that there is a prima facie government duty to preserve the aesthetic wealth of society where that wealth—pictures, plays, and so forth—is what gives rise to aesthetic welfare. It is not certain, however, that this particular notion of aesthetic welfare helps the case for prospective arts funding since it may be that, if there were such a prima facie duty, retrospective arts funding might suffice to discharge it.

Also, one must question whether the connection between "aesthetic welfare" and the concept of welfare relevant to government activity is really unequivocal. First, "aesthetic welfare" doesn't correlate with definable needs, especially basic needs; nor does being below the poverty line imply being aesthetically disadvantaged. And clearly promoting individuals' aesthetic welfare will not raise them over the poverty line. Moreover, the state's welfare responsibility under this conception of aesthetic welfare doesn't seem to be directly connected to individuals but is a matter of ensuring that there will be a large number of aesthetic objects around so that people can have aesthetic experiences if they want them. The state is to ensure the permanent possibility of high levels of what is called aesthetic welfare but might better be called aesthetic well-being. This well-being is to be secured for society at large, construed additively, whereas the state's welfare responsibilities are discharged toward particular persons, viz., anyone in need. Thus the notion of "aesthetic welfare" appears not to refer to welfare of the kind that defines the state's proper domain of activity; it is merely a homonymous term that, though sounding like the concept employed in the discussion of the state's welfare responsibilities, is actually quite separate. Of course, we have not adequately dealt with the notion of aesthetic needs but will turn to it shortly.

In the discussion of welfare, it may be objected that our perspective is too narrow. By speaking of basic needs and poverty lines, we have restricted the compass of the welfare activities of the state to aid in desperate situations and to matters of life support. But must the state's welfare jurisdiction be so constrained? It might be argued that apart from assisting those in need, the state's welfare function also includes benefiting the populace, supplying human goods even to people above the poverty line, thus enabling people to flourish. Were this the case, the defender of prospective arts funding could argue that such a practice would be justified in virtue of the state's responsibilities to benefit the populace, to promote as much good as possible.

First, if the state does have a responsibility to promote human goods over and above the responsibility to prevent harms, it is not obvious that this is best conceived of as part of its welfare responsibility. Perhaps it is rather an obligation to beneficence. Whether the state has such an obligation is an important question which we cannot answer now. Some might argue that the state has such obligations but only after it has discharged all its welfare obligations— no money for paintings until all the needy are assisted. Personally, I find this viewpoint compelling in our present circumstances. There are, however, other arguments against state obligations to beneficence that also bear serious consideration. In pluralist societies—such as we envision modern democracies to be—that which constitutes human goods over and above welfare goods is essentially contested. If the state, given conditions of scarce resources, promotes some goods rather than others, it is unjustifiably favoring the proponents of one good over the proponents of a rival good who may, in fact, deny that the good so favored is a good at all. Of course, the problem disappears if we think that the state's obligation to beneficence extends to promoting every human good, every kind of benefit that facilitates human flourishing or that is believed to contribute to human flourishing. But this seems implausible. Even if the state has legitimate obligations of beneficence, there remain questions of the extent of these obligations even where scarce resources are not at issue. Assuming an obligation of beneficence, we may still argue that the state is not obligated to administer every human benefit to its populace. Consider love and affection. These are things that contribute to the flourishing of human life. But we do not think that the state should intervene in human relations to redistribute affection within society so that each receives his fair share. We would not countenance the formation of a new state agency, the Department of Love, whose duty it would be to assist anyone who has fallen below some putative affection line, construed on the model of a poverty line.

The state, even supposing a legitimate function of beneficence, will not be expected to deliver every possible benefit to its citizenry. This observation, of course, is relevant to the question of prospective arts funding, because if the proponent of such funding invokes beneficiaries in defense of it, we shall still want some demonstration that art is the kind of benefit the state has a duty to supply. Is prospective arts funding more analogous to discharging a welfare obligation or to assisting the lovelorn? For a number of reasons, including the degree to which personal preference is involved with both art and love, one suspects that prospective arts funding is more analogous to the imagined administration of affection than it is to the administration of welfare. But that suggests that prospective arts funding cannot be grounded in a putative state responsibility of beneficence.[8]

Of course, the preceding discussion of benefit will dissatisfy those who feel that art is not merely a benefit to human life, but that it satisfies a human need, call it an aesthetic need. Often this belief is advanced through environmentalist metaphors. In the first annual report of the NEA, it was proclaimed that "we need to make our open spaces beautiful again. We must create an environment in which our youth will be encouraged to pursue the discipline and craft of the arts. We must not only support our artistic institutions, both national and local, but we must also make the arts part of our daily life so that they become an essential part of our existence."[9]

The underlying spirit of this plan seems to suggest that just as the government has an obligation to forestall the deterioration of our ecosystem, so there is an obligation to reverse the deterioration of the aesthetic environment. Human animals have aesthetic needs; environments replete with aesthetic and expressive qualities satisfy them. Perhaps it will be argued that environments bereft of such qualities, or possessing them in minuscule degrees, result in some sort of psychic tension, ranging from irritation to alienation. Miles of service stations, fast-food restaurants, used car lots, body shops—the strip phenomenon—present an impoverished aesthetic habitat that has unsettling psychic consequences. Similarly, the private sphere, flooded with tawdry, mass-produced consumer goods, is aesthetically deprived in a way that is psychically unnerving. Vigorous arts funding is urged as a countermeasure, including prospective arts funding, which presumably will provide some of the objects we need to restore or perhaps to create the kind of aesthetic environment that promotes our psychic health. Thus, prospective arts funding would be warranted on the grounds that it implements that state's obligations in regard to the health of its citizens.

This argument is not implausible. Of course, it requires "fleshing out." Before it can be accepted, research would have to be undertaken to show that we do indeed have aesthetic needs whose frustration results in some form of psychic discomfort. And if this could not be demonstrated, this particular argument would falter.

But suppose it is the case that there are such aesthetic needs. What would that suggest about prospective arts funding? It would imply that we should do further research in order to determine the kinds of art that satisfy whatever aesthetic needs the earlier research identified. We might then go on to fund the kind of programs and the kind of art that satisfies those needs. But note that this will not imply support for any kind of art whatsoever. It only grounds support for those projects which function to alleviate aesthetic needs or which we predict are probable to alleviate aesthetic needs. Not all art will have this causal capacity. For example, Duchamp's *In Advance of a Broken Arm* as well as much Punk Art will not have this capacity, nor will films like Bunuel's *The Andalusian Dog*. Thus, prospective arts funding of works such as these will not be justified by an aesthetic need argument.

The problem here, of course, involves what is meant by "aesthetic." It is not synonymous with "art." Generally, it is associated with the beautiful and the sublime, or it is associated with the qualitative appearance of things. An aesthetic need, under this reading, would be a need for experiences of the beautiful, the sublime, or for the experience of objects and environments with marked expressive qualities such as warmth, friendliness, or joyfulness. Much art, including, significantly, much contemporary art, is not dedicated to producing aesthetic experience. Indeed, much contemporary art is even avowedly antiaesthetic. If an artist makes a junkyard piece to portray modern life, it seems curious that he should expect funding on the basis of alleviating aesthetic privations. Nor is it obvious that every expressive quality projectable by a work of art will have the equilibrating effect presumed by the aesthetic need argument. Works marked by turmoil, horror, anguish, and so on are not prima facie defensible under the aesthetic need argument. The point is that even if the aesthetic need argument is acceptable, it will not support prospective arts funding as we know it. It will only support funding of those prospective artworks with high probability of bringing about equilibrating aesthetic experiences. Nonaesthetic, antiaesthetic, reflexive, and certain darkly expressive artworks will not be defensible in the name of aesthetic experience.

If the aesthetic need argument gives us the means for justifying prospective arts funding, it also seems to have the unfortunate consequence that it only warrants the funding of certain kinds of art—the art of the beautiful, the sublime, and that expressive of psychically equilibrating qualities. If no further justification can be found, the consequence of this is that the state can only fund a certain type of art. Artists pursuing certain nonaesthetic aims cannot be funded by the state. But proponents of art funding, lovers of art, and artists with nonaesthetic projects should be disturbed by this. For if the government places large investments behind one type of art, the evolution of the art world will undoubtedly be affected. Whole avenues of artistic development will appear less viable than the production of aesthetic art. And from the contemporary art world's point of view, this kind of prospective arts funding might be regarded as having a regressive effect overall.

At this point, it may be claimed that the relevant need to consider is not an aesthetic need but a need for art. All societies, it might be said, have artlike practices—i.e., symbolizing practices of some sort—which suggests that art of some type answers a human need. Next, the idea will be advanced that in modern industrial societies, art will disappear if the government does not support it. Thus, without government support the conditions necessary for satisfying our need for art cannot be sustained. Perhaps prospective arts funding can be endorsed as a corollary to this via the claim that the need for art includes a need for new art. And if the state does not fund new art, no one else will.

Of course, this is an empirical claim and a dubious one at that. The arts flourished in democratic societies before the advent of direct public funding; there is no reason to suppose that they will disappear without the direct government funding of new artworks. Where people are interested in art, there will still be an audience to support new work. Were there no audience whatsoever, it would be difficult to determine on what basis the government would justify funding new art. Moreover, in advanced capitalist societies at least, big businesses are attracted to arts patronage because projecting the kind of upwardly mobile profile associated with interest in the arts attracts upwardly mobile investors. One could go on elaborating considerations that count against the disappearance-of-art thesis. But perhaps what is most important to say about it is that, at best, it is not worried about the disappearance of art per se but only of certain types of art, viz., what for want of a better label we call high art. Popular art—movies, TV, pop music—will not disappear if prospective arts funding is discontinued. So it is not the case that our society will be deprived of art, including new art, without prospective arts funding. Hence, if there is a need for art, it will not be frustrated. On the other hand, it is unlikely that there is a human need for our kind of high art. But, in any event, it is also unlikely that our kind of high art is about to disappear if prospective arts funding is halted, though the assumption that it will seems implicit in too many of the arguments of proponents of such funding. Of course, sans funding, high art might be produced at a diminished rate. But here the burden of proof rests with the proponent of funding to show what social evil results from a diminished rate of high art production.

One practical justification for arts funding is that it may function as an economic stimulant, promoting prosperity by, for example, attracting tourists. Insofar as prospective arts funding can be pegged to the state of the economy, it would appear to be a legitimate state operation, since the maintenance of a functioning economy is related to the state's welfare responsibilities. Needless to say, it is often difficult to imagine the way in which grants to individual artists for new works—as opposed to city art centers—can engineer economic well-being, but there is no reason to think that such a connection could not be made in principle. Of course, an economic stimulation argument identifies the value of arts funding not with aesthetic or artistic value but with economic instrumentality.[10] But despite this, the economic stimulation argument seems acceptable, although it can only be mobilized where certain constraints are respected. Where prospective arts funding is employed to stimulate tourism or some other form of economic activity in a given area, the state must be convinced that no alternative form of intervention of comparable cost would yield greater prosperity in that area. Furthermore, where national rather than local stimulation is at issue, the nation-state must supply some rationale why it is undertaking to stimulate tourism in one geographical region rather than another. But when these conditions can be met, no obvious barrier to prospective arts funding appears to remain, though it is uncertain how often these criteria can be satisfied.

Connecting prospective arts funding to economic policy suggests another means for justifying state support, viz., employment. If state funding is not forthcoming, then many artists will be unemployed. Unemployment is clearly a matter of concern for the state. The massive unemployment of black inner-city youths is one of the great tragedies of our society, and we must demand that the state do something about it. Many would be in favor of New Deal-type programs to alleviate the program. Can we mount a similar argument in order to show that prospective arts funding can be seen as a way of averting massive unemployment among artists? My inclination is to think not. Artists do not seem to constitute a group that is comparable to black inner-city youths. Questions of justice and equal opportunity do not seem to bear on the issue of artistic unemployment. Moreover, the artistic unemployment we might envision involves artists' unemployment as artists rather than their unemployment simpliciter. That is, I may not be able to support my family as an unemployed poet, but that does not mean that I can't do it in another way, say, as a journalist or a copywriter. It does not seem to me that the state's responsibilities in regard to the unemployed extend to guaranteeing that everyone have the job he or she most desires. The case of artistic unemployment involves people not able to pursue the line of work they most covet, while inner-city unemployment involves people excluded from the workforce altogether. Our belief that the state has clear responsibilities in the case of innercity unemployment cannot ground claims to similar duties in regard to artistic unemployment. If artists are unemployed, the state will have certain duties to them, though it is not clear that those duties include finding them employment as artists.

It may be suggested that a certain conception of fairness can be used to ground government art support. If a given government subsidizes the building of sports arenas, then, in all fairness, arts production should also be supported. If the government facilitates the pursuits of sports fans, then it should, as a matter of treating people equally, also facilitate the pursuits of arts fans, perhaps by means of supporting the creation of new art. Of course, this argument presupposes a context in which some leisure activity, such as sports, is being subsidized. But what, in such a context, justifies that subsidizing of sports? If nothing does, then perhaps what is required is that neither sports nor the arts be subsidized.

Insofar as one objects to sports subsidies, one must forego art subsidies. Of course, a subsidy for a sport might be defended on the grounds that it stimulates the economy of an area, but then arts funding can, in principle, be similarly defended. Again, it does seem correct to say that if a majority, call them sports fans, demand sports funding in the face of opposition by a minority, call them arts lovers, then fairness urges that the leisure activity of the latter group also be supported, though perhaps not to the same extent. The deeper question, however, is whether any leisure activity should be supported. For if any is supported, then all should be in proportion to the allegiance to that leisure activity in the society. And yet this appears extreme. Suppose skateboard racers wanted a national stadium. Does that seem to be something for which the state should pay by levying taxes on the rest of us? Obviously, even wilder examples could be concocted—hopscotch stadia, a coliseum for Bocci Ball, a national gallery of toothpick sculpture. The advancement of the leisure professions may just not be an area the state should enter at all.

One of the earliest arguments in favor of government support of the arts is that the arts perform a moralizing function. During the period of the Second Empire, in nineteenth-century France, the Orpheon, a working-class choral society, was sponsored by Napoleon III's government on the grounds that it would introduce the proletariat to "moral amusements," which would not only cultivate their tastes but "moralize" them.[11] Similarly in this country in the nineteenth century the belief was widespread that through art the populace could be morally improved. These beliefs influenced both school reform and the founding of the great American museums.[12] In the era of state funding of the arts, faith in their potential to make people more moral—faith in the civilizing power of the arts—suggested a line of justification for the prospective funding of art, for surely the maintenance of the moral order in society is a legitimate state concern. Thus, if art can function as a means of improving morality, then the state is justified in supporting it. If art provides moral exemplars or deepens conscience, the state, it would seem, can avail itself of the devices of art to instill moral behavior in its populace.

One aspect of art that is related to its capacity to engender moral improvement is the tendency of certain kinds of art to develop our sympathies for others. Some art enables us to see the world from different points of view, thus promoting not only the acquisition of a formal requirement of morality but also enabling us to grasp vicariously the situations of different classes, races, creeds, and genders. Art, then, can foster greater tolerance within society and thereby bolster the moral order. A strengthened moral order is a goal that the state legitimately pursues, given, among other things, its responsibility to prevent harm from befalling its populace. That is, one way to prevent harm is to prevent people from harming each other by making them more moral. If art can serve the accomplishment of this goal, then the prospective funding of such art seems justified.

But this argument for prospective arts funding does have certain unhappy consequences. The argument assumes that art increases moral sympathies. We have no reason to dispute the contention that some art has this capacity. But it seems unlikely that all art functions this way. If the state is to justify its funding of art on moralizing grounds, then only that art which we can reasonably predict will increase moral sympathies can be funded. This will probably require some empirical research into the moral efficacy of different kinds of art. Art, indeed whole categories of art, that affords no moral uplift cannot be funded on the basis of this argument. Art that works against any increase in moral sympathy will also be problematic. Art devoted, for instance, to outraging the bourgeoisie or politically partisan art is likely to be debarred from funding insofar as it instills divisiveness rather than tolerance. That is, mobilizing this functionalist justification for arts funding, only grounds for certain types of arts funding have been secured. This raises problems like those encountered in our earlier discussion of the aesthetic environment argument. If the state is justified in funding only certain kinds of art and it enters the art world, putting its immense resources behind only moralizing kinds of art, then there is a great danger that the development of the art world will be skewed in certain directions. This violates our intuitions that the realm of art should be pluralist and relatively independent of considerations of social utility. Thus, though the state may be justified in funding certain types of art, we may be loath to have it exercise this prerogative because of the damage it would wreak upon art as we know it. Nor does it seem practicable to meet this objection by saying that the state should fund every type of art in order to fund the kinds of art it is justified to fund. For this will result in a kind of self-defeating schizophrenia: supporting antiaesthetic art in order to support aesthetic art; supporting divisive art in order to support art that expands moral sympathies.

A recent argument in favor of public art support has been advanced by Ronald Dworkin. He draws a distinction between two dimensions of culture. Culture "provides the particular paintings, performances, and novels, designs, sports, and thrillers that we value and take delight in; but it also provides the structural frame that makes aesthetic values of that sort possible and makes them values for us."[13] This structural frame includes a wealth of associations, references, images, and contrasts, which, like language, supply us with the tools with which we forge and map our common life. Dworkin insists that it is better for people to have a complex and multifarious cultural framework and that we owe future generations at least as rich a cultural framework as the one we inherited. Both these values can be achieved by promoting the creation of innovative art. Government support in this area is necessary because it "helps protect the fragile structure of our culture."[14] Admittedly, Dworkin uses this argument to endorse indirect rather than direct arts support by the government. But he does countenance situations in which government support could be direct. And someone other than Dworkin might attempt to use this argument in favor of direct support.

At least two problems, however, beset this approach. First, there is the assumption that the structure of culture is fragile. We have encountered this before. But as an empirical supposition we have argued that its truth is far from obvious. Moreover, when we look at the structure of culture, we note that it comprises many ingredients besides art—social dances, children's games, fashion, sports, religion, indeed the whole gamut of our symbolizing activities. When we think of the twenties, we recall the flapper and the Charleston; perhaps in the future people will think of the eighties in terms of punk haircuts and break-dancing. These images become part and parcel of our ways of thinking; they are the very weave of our common culture. But it seems dubious to consider them to be fit beneficiaries of public funding. Yet if art deserves public funding because of its contribution to our cultural framework, so does anything else that similarly contributes, including, potentially, every sort of symbolizing activity and notably some outlandish ones: hoola-hoops, comic books, Billy Graham, the Watergate break-in, and so on.[15]

One criticism that is apt to be directed at this essay is that we have repeatedly discussed prospective arts funding in terms of things other than art, i.e., in terms of some good consequences which would justify such funding. One may feel that this completely misses the point. Art is good in itself and does not require further validation in virtue of the further consequences it abets.[16] It may be true, though one has one's doubts, that art is intrinsically good. But even if the production of art is intrinsically good, that, in and of itself, would not warrant state funding of the arts. For the state does not and, in some cases, should not be taken to have a role in the production of whatever we conceive to be an intrinsic good or even of whatever is an intrinsic good (if there are such things). State intervention in these matters calls for justification.

In conclusion, there do appear to be theoretical justifications for prospective government funding of art. The two strongest justifications seem to be those concerning the aesthetic environment and the moralizing effects of the arts. However, though these arguments are available, it is not clear that they should be acted upon. For they endorse the funding of only certain types of art. Government support for the arts guided strictly by these arguments may indeed disturb the structure of artistic production and perhaps destroy the art world as we know it.

Notes

1. Edward Banfield, *The Democratic Muse* (New York: Basic Books, 1984), p. 4.

2. Carl Wellman, *Welfare Rights* (Totowa, N.J.: Rowman and Littlefield, 1984), p. 30.

3. Suggested in ibid., pp. 133-34, and by T. Benditt, *Rights* (Totowa, N.J.: Rowman and Littlefield, 1982), pp. 112-16.

4. William Rees-Mogg, "Paying for the Arts: The Political Economy of Art in 1985," *The Economist* 294, no. 7385 (9 March 1985): 94. It should be noted that Rees-Mogg uses this argument only to endorse indirect funding as a way of replacing declines in direct funding. However, I have heard arguments like this in discussions with proponents of direct funding.

5. Joel Feinberg, *Social Philosophy* (Englewood Cliffs, N.J.: Prentice-Hall, 1973), p. 111.

6. Derived from Wellman, *Welfare Rights*, p. 136.

7. Monroe C. Beardsley, "Aesthetic Welfare, Aesthetic Justice, and Educational Policy," in *The Aesthetic Point of View*, ed. M. Wreen and D. Callen (Ithaca, N.Y.: Cornell University Press, 1982), pp. 113-14. Originally published in *the Journal of Aesthetic Education* 7, no. 4 (October 1973): 49-61.

8. My disposition is to see state activity connected to state responsibilities or duties. My inclination is to think that state power is so awesome that, in contested contexts, only things as serious as duties should mobilize it. But others may not share my squeamishness. They will think that in stating the issue above in terms of state obligations to beneficence, I am asking too much. They might suggest that what is really at issue are not state obligations to beneficence but rather a prima facie license to the state to proceed in any area where it can do good or bestow benefit. This construal of the state's relation to beneficence, however, raises the same sort of problems discussed above in terms of an obligation to beneficence. Surely beneficent activity such as arts funding cannot be undertaken until the state has acquired its welfare obligations. And, furthermore, where the benefits in question are contested, it is not clear that the state can implement them over the protests of significant numbers of its skeptical citizens.

9. Quoted in Banfield, *The Democratic Muse*, pp. 68-69.

10. A similar point is emphasized by William J. Baumol in his remarks in "IV. Panel Discussion: Public Support of the Arts," *Art and the Law* 9, no. 2 (1985): 214-28. One kind of economic argument in favor of arts funding concerns the technical notion of a public good. I have not broached this issue directly in the article. Ronald Dworkin has dealt with the epistemological problems involved in considering art in this light in "Can a Liberal State

Support Art?" in his *A Matter of Principle* (Cambridge, Mass.: Harvard University Press, 1985), pp. 221-33. (This article is reprinted in *Art and the Law* 9, no. 2, 1985). I agree with Dworkin on this matter; for a differing view, see Baumol, "Public Support of the Arts."

11. Howard Becker, *Art Worlds* (Berkeley: University of California Press, 1982), pp. 181-82.

12. Banfield, *The Democratic Muse,* chaps. 4 and 5.

13. Dworkin, "Can a Liberal State Support Art?" p. 229.

14. Ibid., p. 233.

15. R. Nozick makes a related point in his remarks in *Art and the Law* 9, no. 2, 1985): 162-67.

16. T. Nagel seems to follow this line in his remarks in ibid., pp. 236-39.

Not with My Tax Money: The Problem of Justifying Government Subsidies

Joel Feinberg

The Taxpayer's Challenge

Most of us think of art as a worthwhile but often profitless kind of activity, worthy of whatever financial support it can get. Unfortunately, in this historical period few royal patrons or robber baron benefactors are available, and subsidies are more and more commonly expected from governments, drawing on their major source of income, tax revenues. Among those requesting government subsidies for art are, on the one hand, museum curators, repertory companies, and other groups who aim at preserving our cultural treasures, and on the other hand, creative artists hoping to add their own productions to the cultural treasury. Artists are not the only ones hoping for government aid. Scholars and humanists, like ourselves, are standing in line too, hoping that the modesty of their requests will improve their chances. In addition, the applicants include mathematicians and theoretical scientists whose projects are so esoteric, or expensive, or both, that they have little hope of finding funding without government help.

A few decades ago, Congress established the National Endowment for the Arts, the National Endowment for the Humanities, and the National Science Foundation, partly to ensure that art, humanities and

Joel Feinberg's article recently appeared in *Public Affairs Quarterly* 8 (2), April 1994, pp. 101-123. It is reprinted here by permission of the publisher and the author.

scientific research be removed from the prevailing pork barrel system, by which lobbyists persuade their own Representative or Senator that there would be great political advantage for him if he could produce funds for some favorite local project, by inducing powerful committee chairmen to attach funding for that project onto an otherwise respectable appropriations bill moving toward passage[1]. Brian Kelly tells us that "Some pork projects, like [a] North Dakota Senator's attempts to turn schlock entertainer Lawrence Welk's mud-walled birthplace into a museum, do not pass [what Kelly calls] "the laugh test."[2] Perhaps peer reviewers for N.E.A. are also capable of flunking the laugh test, but their procedures are somewhat more reliable, I should think, than the congressional pork delivery system.

The main challenge to the art and science subsidizers, however, is not *how* they spend tax money, but by what right they spend it at all. The problem raised by the indignant taxpayer is whether there is justification for using government funds derived from mandatory taxation of all citizens in order to promote the esoteric projects of a small number of people. Indeed there is a *prima facie* case for the proposition that such subsidies are unfair to those who are made to pay, not to protect their neighbors from harm, but to secure benefits for some of their neighbors that they (the complaining taxpayers) are not able to share. The principle invoked by the indignant taxpayer is that "Justice requires that persons pay for a facility in proportion to the degree they benefit from it." For convenience I shall call this proposed maxim of justice "the Benefit Principle." According to this principle, the approximate models of fair taxation are users' fees, so called, the price charged to visitors for their use of a zoo, or to drivers for their use of an expensive stretch of turnpike highway. Users' fees are paid voluntarily, and only by those who expect to receive benefits that are worth the price they pay.

Those defenders of public subsidies who accept the benefit principle must show that, initial appearance to the contrary, artistic endeavors supported by general tax revenues (instead of "users' fees") *are* somehow universally and equally beneficial, whether some philistine taxpayers know it or not. If, as I suspect, that is too great an argumentative burden to sustain, then the determined advocate of subsidies for the arts may have to abandon the benefit principle.

An alternative is to abandon one's advocacy of subsidies for all but special cases. Opera lovers and zoo users, for example, might very well be able to collect their own funds from private sources. They can receive certification from the I.R.S. as non-profit foundations that are genuine "charities" (that is, worthy causes) and thus be immune from taxation themselves, and also be eligible for gifts that are deductible from the taxable incomes of the donors. These measures, of course, are a considerable boost from the government. Moreover, they allow taxpayers to some degree to choose the direct beneficiaries of their own tax payments, and escape to some degree the requirement that they support causes from which they do not themselves benefit and of which they may even disapprove. The opera lovers and zoo visitors then could pay "voluntary taxes" in support of their favorite facilities and also users' fees on the many occasions they actually use those facilities, while other citizens, who are bored by opera and actually offended by zoos, could escape the compulsion that they support other people's pleasures.

I think that there is much to be said for this approach, but it cannot solve the whole problem by itself. There are exceptional cases in which the exclusive dependence on users' fees and "voluntary taxes" would clearly be insufficient. The more expensive the project, or the use of its finished goods, the harder it is to raise voluntary contributions for its support. Moreover, the more esoteric the project or its finished goods, the fewer the persons who can understand and appreciate it, and be willing to support it. A number theorist may need an expensive high-powered computer to help him establish some truth about prime numbers. I, as a typical taxpayer, might admire him, but there is no way I could "use" his results. The whole idea of a users' fee collapses in this example.

The homely case of the zoo provides a less *outré* example of how the costs of operation, for practical reasons, could exceed the capacity of patrons to pay for them by means of users' fees alone. Suppose that the entrance fee to the zoo is $5.00 a person, so that a family of four must pay $20.00. This leads to a shortfall, so the fee is raised to $10 a head. For a large percentage of regular patrons, the new fee has crossed the line of what they can afford, so *they* stop coming, and that in turn creates another deficit, requiring another price hike, leading to further customer alienation, and so on. We can imagine at least some circumstances in which dipping into the tax revenues is the only alternative to giving up the valuable facility altogether.

These are some of the reasons we might have in admittedly exceptional cases, for supporting facilities and projects, at least in part with tax revenues. But to acknowledge cases of this sort is not to solve our original problem so much as to transform its character. It is now less a pressing policy question than a philosophical one. In respect to those expensive and/or esoteric goods that we feel impelled to support out of tax funds, we still have a problem, though it may now seem only a theoretical one, like justifying induction, or justifying democracy, or the like. What can we say to the indignant taxpayer whose money we take to support things like zoos, which for the sake of the example, we can assume he never attends, doesn't like, secures no benefit from, and morally disapproves of?

The Search for Universal Indirect Benefits

The legitimacy of some tax-funded governmental activities, of course, is beyond all cavil. We all benefit from the protection of the police and the national defense, from public health agencies, from reliable treatment of drinking water, unpolluted air, sewer systems, highways, and so on. But only some of us benefit directly from school systems, museums, public parks, ballet troupes, opera companies, astronomical observatories, chess tournaments, mathematical treatises on number theory, and so on. Some of those who would not benefit directly from some of these activities can nevertheless be said to benefit indirectly from them. Single adults who have been educated elsewhere, childless couples, and couples whose children have grown up and finished their schooling do not themselves profit directly from the further maintenance of a public school system. Neither they nor their children will ever need further schooling at that level. But it is at least plausible to claim that *everyone*, even members of these groups, profits from living in a well educated society, and the better educated our fellow citizens are, the better off we are likely to be. Nondrivers, similarly, benefit indirectly from a network of good roads. It is clearly in your interest, even though you may be permanently confined to bed, that the transportation of responsible persons and essential goods be efficient, and that is true whether you know it or not.

It is less plausible, however, to claim that opera companies are indirectly in the interests of everyone, even those who are bored and uninterested, and that that is so whether the uninterested party knows it or not. At this point in the dialectic, the more thoroughgoing philosopher would have to decide whether a search for subtle *indirect* benefits will yield a justification for subsidizing the arts out of general tax revenues. She would have to survey the various dogmatic theories—aesthetic and moral perfectionism, aesthetic environmentalism, and so on, in her quest for the universal subtle benefit[3]. I am quite convinced that none of these theories is satisfactory, so I shall turn instead to the much more interesting arguments that proceed without the benefit of the benefit principle.

Imperfect Schemes of Rotational Justice

But first let us consider a highly indirect way of appealing to benefits and harms exclusively. Some of those in the great majority whose interests would not be harmed by the reduction of government support, say, for the Library of Congress, *would* be harmed by the withdrawal of some other government subsidy—the weakening of support for the visual arts, or highly theoretical sciences, or the loss of a tax exemption for churches (an indirect subsidy). This suggests that there may be a justification for the whole system of which these particular enactments are the products. When this system works with approximate fairness, it may make it seem tolerable to the citizens it represents that sometimes, because they pay the bill, they should be net losers, provided they have a fair opportunity to be net winners on other occasions. Almost everyone may have reason to prefer such a system of fluctuating benefits to its more cumbersome alternatives in which unanimity, for example, is always required for tax-supported appropriations.

When it comes to political institutions there is much to be said for the view that the primary subject of justification is the full institutional complex of rules and practices, not each small component or byproduct of it, considered in isolation from the rest. In our country, part of that complex consists of a democratically elected legislature, using majority rule to govern its procedures, making laws of which some confer powers, others prohibit or enjoin actions directly, others raise revenue, and still others set up programs to be paid for out of the revenues that were raised by virtue of the techniques and powers created by other rules. The system is meant to represent the interests and wishes of ordinary citizens and groups. Thus, if a given citizen is in the minority on one issue of how to spend money from a pool to which he has been forced to contribute, he will have a fair chance to be in the majority on another such issue. Different programs will create different patterns of protectees, beneficiaries, and indifferents, and each represented citizen will (it is hoped) "win some and lose some," never feeling as a consequence that he is completely overlooked and impotent. Individual tax-supported programs win their moral legitimacy by virtue of being the end product of a legitimate procedure, a complex institutional practice without which, in turn, everybody would be a net loser. That is the sort of justification for legally compelling people to pay for particular programs like the Library of Congress or the National Endowment for the Arts that they do not want and from which they may not benefit. Citizens pay their money and take their chances, knowing that they will not win all the time, but also that they may be protected from harm to some of their own valuable ulterior interests that are not widely shared.

The argument from rotational justice is admittedly imperfect. It does not guarantee that everyone will win and lose equally, and in fact even the best working of democracies will sometimes generate serious inequalities in the way tax funds are allocated. In our own Congress, projects that are genuinely worthy of government support on grounds recognized by the argument may in fact get caught up in the unfortunate pork barrel system of dispensations which for so long has been the scandal of our government operations. Moreover, in many or even most instances, the argument may prove to be unnecessary because the grievance of the nonbenefitting taxpayer can be obviated by the exercise of ingenuity in collecting users' fees and stimulating voluntary private contributions. Still, for the diminished number of cases that could not be supported privately because the project, though worthy, is too esoteric and too expensive to survive without government help, the argument from rotational justice often seems persuasive. It may well be the best we can hope to do if we restrict ourselves to the concepts of benefit and harm in our attempts to justify subsidies. On that level, it provides the best answer to the challenge of the taxpayer who disapproves in a particular case the uses for which his money is employed, who doesn't want his money used in that way, and who is unbenefitted himself by that use of it. Perhaps we can do better still, however, if we cease restricting our justificatory efforts to such values as harm prevention and benefit promotion, and appeal instead to values of a quite different kind.[4]

Benefit-less Values

In my book, *Harmless Wrongdoing*,[5] I argue that it is at least coherent to claim that some behavior is morally wrong even though it harms or threatens no one. Some might claim, for example, that homosexual relations between consenting adults in private, simply because they are condemned in the Bible, are morally wrong, even when they harm or wrong neither participant and offend no third party witnesses. Even if there are such instances of harmless wrongdoing, I argued, they are none of the state's business, since the coercive arm of the law can legitimately intervene in human affairs only to protect unwilling victims from harm, not to "enforce morality" whether harmful behavior is involved or not. Similarly, I argued that there are, or at least could be, so-called "free-floating evils," that is, intrinsically regrettable states of affairs that are evil for some reason other than that they harm or offend anyone. I cited as examples reputation-shattering false beliefs about the long dead (say about the Emperor Nero), voluntary contraceptively protected adult incest, hateful but repressed thoughts, and such single capricious acts as that of squashing a beetle in the wild. If there are such free-floating evils, I argued, they too are beyond the legitimate concern of the state.

But now, as we consider problems for government subsidy policies, we come to the mirror image of the problems about the proper scope of criminal prohibitions, and we discover some initially disturbing asymmetries. When we discuss the subsidy problem, we must inquire whether there are free-floating *values* or benefit-less good things, which is to ask whether a thing can be truly valuable for some reason other than that it benefits someone. Further we must consider, if there *are* some nonbeneficial values, whether it can be the proper business of the state, using tax funds extracted in part from the unbenefitted, to subsidize them. Liberal impulses on the question of the propriety of subsidizing nonbeneficial goods seem at odds with those on the question of criminal prohibitions of harmless evils, for characteristically the liberal approves of the subsidies for nonbeneficial goods though he opposes the criminal prohibition of nonharmful evils.

I see no contradiction, however, in this asymmetry. Sometimes the truth comes in displeasingly untidy forms, and at any rate, we might expect some stark and asymmetric contrasts when comparing concepts so opposed as good and evil.

I am happy to have as an ally in this inquiry so talented a philosopher as Tom Nagel, who attacks the assumption that "everything good is good only because it is *good for* . . . some person or persons, and that its value is simply the sum of its value for the people it benefits."[6] Rather, Nagel reminds us, "Some things are wonderful in a measure quite beyond the value of the experiences or other benefits of those who encounter them."[7] I suspect Nagel has in mind here not only such sublime works of art as the great medieval cathedrals, the Beethoven symphonies, and Shakespeare's tragedies, but also such natural wonders as the Grand Canyon, the one hundred twenty-five surviving Siberian tigers, and such relatively non-utilitarian projects and achievements as the ingeniously proved theorems of abstruse number theory, and the search for interstellar signals from possible intelligent beings in the Milky Way galaxy by means of an enormous radio telescope.

One needs little imagination to reconstruct the views of the fiscal philistines whom Nagel is attacking. "What do I care whether the Notre Dame cathedral falls into decay?" a provincial French citizen might ask. "Restore it if you wish but don't charge me with part of the bill. I don't profit, and most of the taxpayers I know don't benefit in any way from some pretty church in a distant place, so it is wrong that we should be compelled to pay in support of its restoration." *A fortiori*, such a person would protest against measures to use his tax money to help save the tigers, since the tigers directly benefit neither him nor the bulk of the human race sufficiently to balance the harm of the taxation required to save them. And certainly our hypothetical taxpayer would balk at the use of government funds to allocate time on enormous computers so that number theorists can list the first two billion digits in the value of *pi* (the ratio of the circumference to the diameter of a circle) as part of a purely philosophical study of the concept of randomness. As for radio transmissions of signals to outer space, our hypothetical taxpayer would be better off not knowing that "since 1974 a signal sent from the giant radio dish in Arecibo, Puerto Rico, describing our solar system, our DNA, our species, and our culture, has been speeding toward the constellation Hercules, dispatched in the hope that an 'alien being' there might apprehend it. But since Hercules is 25,000 light-years away, an answer would take at least 50,000 years to reach Earth . . ."[8] Because these time intervals are so great, the urgency of the project is decreased and the most recent version of the undertaking has been funded for only $100,000,000 over the next ten years.[9]

Not all or even most taxpayers are narrow-minded philistines. Many people would agree that there are precious objects and noble pursuits that are worth paying for even if their direct benefit to other citizens is an insignificant component of their value. But Nagel reminds us that even if these people "pay what the experience is worth to them personally, it may not add up to the value of the things themselves,"[10] and thus the remaining costs require some subsidy from other sources.

The Concept of Intrinsic Value: A Quick Sketch

If "value" is not simply a synonym for "benefit," what then can a value be? To be valuable, I suggest, is to be worthy of being valued, just as to be praiseworthy is to be worthy of being praised, and to be execrable is to be worthy of being execrated. The word "worthy" is the key term in the analysis, but we should expect that it will raise philosophical difficulties that must here be avoided. So I will not linger long with it except to point out two of its features. Judgments of worthiness, whatever response their subject is said to be worthy of, are often the occasion of controversy, but especially on those occasions we tend to think of them as objectively true or false, that is correct or incorrect in virtue of something other than the opinions people may hold about them. Secondly, worthiness in the present sense is a relatively weak normative term. When I say that Jones is praiseworthy for what he did, I do not intend anything so strong as a command that he be praised ("He is to be praised"), or that he *must* be praised, or even that he *ought* to be praised. More likely I imply that if there is a reason for withholding praise it cannot be that he does not *qualify* for it. To praise him for what he did would *not be inappropriate* even if on this occasion it would be inadvisable. Considered on its own terms praise would be an entirely *fitting* response to what he did, the response he *deserves*, even when there is an overriding reason in the circumstances for withholding it.

If to have value (or to be valuable) is to be worthy of being valued, what then does this response called *valuing* come to? To value a thing, I should think, is to have a relatively constant disposition to hold that thing in high regard, to appreciate, esteem, or admire it, and in the extreme case to revere, to cherish or to treasure it. None of these words are precise synonyms of valuing, but each stands for its own type or degree of valuing. We judge that a thing has a *great* value when we think of it as worthy of cherishing or treasuring. According to some theories this schematic definition is incomplete and will remain so until it specifies *by whom* the object is worthy of being treasured. Perhaps its character is such that it is worthy of being cherished by me (it is a photograph, say, of *my* grandmother), but not by you.

At this point we should add to our definition that the valuable object is worthy of being valued either for itself (that is for its own characteristics and properties) or for what can be done with it (that is for its causal or instrumental properties), or for both itself *and* its uses. The distinction between intrinsic and instrumental value of course goes all the way back to Plato's *Republic*, and was no doubt a commonplace earlier still. Nevertheless, many philosophers purport to find difficulties with it. Their main problem is understanding how anything could be valued entirely for properties that are noncausal or noninstrumental. To their understanding, even the paradigm examples of intrinsic value are objects worthy of being valued for their causal capacity to produce effects of a desired kind on those who value them. Some people, for example, value the experience of eating broccoli because broccoli promotes good health; it is beneficial or *good for* them, as we say. Others value the experience of eating broccoli because broccoli tastes good; they like it for itself, as they say, for what it is, rather than for what it does. Similarly, sexual intercourse can be valued as a virtually indispensable means to the creation of children. Producing offspring may be valued by some people as the sole answer to the question, "admitting that sex is good, what is it good *for?*" Others, most others, I should say, will value sex, at least in part, for its own sake, quite apart from its conducibility to some further end, like reproduction. But the skeptic about intrinsic value will point out that the broccoli appreciator, whether he values eating broccoli for its nutrition or for its flavor, values broccoli for what it produces: pleasant gustatory sensations in the one case, good health in the other. Similarly the sex appreciator, whichever camp he falls in, will value sex for *what it does*, producing children in the one case or erotic pleasure in the other. Why then, he might ask, is the one ground for valuing sex any more "intrinsic" than the other?

The questioner has a point. Most valuable things *are* valuable for what they do. But the distinction between intrinsic and instrumental value may nevertheless be usefully made. I suggest, in many cases, that we think of it as a matter of degree, a distinction of more and less. A pilgrim or an aesthete may value the Notre Dame cathedral for the infinite complexity and richness of its design, its stained glass, the texture of its stone, its soaring vaulted interior. All of this causes him aesthetic pleasure and/or religious awe. A Parisian city official from the bureau of tourism might equally value the cathedral, but primarily for the money it attracts from foreign visitors into the Parisian economy. The old-fashioned way of making the distinction was to say that the pilgrim values the cathedral "for itself," and the official "for what it does," its causal capacity to bring in revenue. The pilgrim assigns intrinsic value to it; the official assigns instrumental value. The skeptic, however, points out that even the pilgrim values the cathedral instrumentally. He finds it thrilling and awesome and treasures its capacity to cause these richly emotional responses. But there still is a point, I would say, in distinguishing *his* valuing from that of the city official. The end to which the cathedral is a valuable instrument for the official (namely, municipal revenue) is relatively remote, and many intervening causes and conditions contribute towards its realization; whereas the effect for which the cathedral is valued by the religious aesthete is relatively near and certain, intimately linked to the very perception of the valued object, and relatively independent of intervening causes and conditions. Most of the traditional examples of intrinsic value are like the cathedral in these respects. There may be some values that are in between the immediate causal effect and the remote consequence, and thus hard to classify as intrinsic or instrumental, just as there are moments at twilight that are hard to classify as day or night, but in neither case is the utility of the distinction seriously undermined.

There is another kind of reply that might be made to the skeptic who insists that all things worth valuing are so in virtue of their causal capacity to produce desired effects on users or observers. The second response is to insist on at least one class of exceptions to the skeptic's claim, namely those values for which the words "ultimate" or "final" are often used. Aristotle thought of ultimacy, along with self-sufficiency, as the marks of what he called "the good for man." That good is the ultimate one, in that it is never sought as a means to anything beyond itself. It is where the value theory buck stops. An ultimate value, then, is not merely chosen for its own sake, like other intrinsically valuable things. It is chosen *only* for its own sake, there being nothing else that it could be a means *to*, or that it could be good *for*, that would increase its total goodness one bit. Final values are just one class of intrinsic values, namely those that stand on their own feet and are not made better still by any further end to which they reliably lead. Not all intrinsic goods are ultimate in this sense, but all ultimate values must also be intrinsic.

The problem about intrinsic values that has traditionally divided philosophers is not whether there are such things but how many irreducibly distinct kinds of intrinsic values there might be. Pleasure, of course, is commonly counted as intrinsically valuable, an honor it shares with its near relatives, happiness and fulfillment, and also with virtue, even when virtue is its own and only reward. Knowledge too has its supporters, even though most knowledge is also valuable instrumentally, and therefore is ineligible as a candidate for ultimate value in Aristotle's sense. Knowledge of a difficult proof in number theory, for example, may have a value "in itself" way beyond any merely instrumental utility. Love has also been said to have an intrinsic value well beyond its incidental contribution to pleasure, happiness, knowledge, and such specific objectives as creating families with their own distinctive values. Some philosophers, departing from Aristotle's usage, are pluralistic. They are willing to attribute what they call ultimate value to all of the above candidates or to some subset of them. But if any of the other views are right, then there are some valuable things that are worthy of valuing for some reasons other than their causal capacities to produce relatively immediate valuable effects, since those effects add nothing to their total value. If there are *ultimate* values, then there are things that are valuable "in themselves," as we say, and not totally for, or not at all for, effects of *any* kind that they characteristically produce. And that is precisely what it means to be *intrinsically* valuable.

We come now to a fundamental question about our understanding of the concept of intrinsic value. In those cases in which an object's intrinsic value *can* be correlated with the value to a beholder of states of mind reliably produced in himself by that object, do we explain the object's value by reference to the states of mind it produces or do we explain the states of mind by reference to the independently grounded value? For example, suppose that we find the sight of *Notre Dame* predictably thrilling or its soaring interior awesome and inspirational. Do we thrill because of the value we apprehend (that value in turn derived from some features independent of our thrilled state) or do we value the cathedral, at least in part, because it reliably produces a thrilled state of mind in us? Could the value of the cathedral itself simply *consist* in the state of mind it characteristically produces in a large number of people or do those people experience their aesthetic-religious emotion in response to the appreciated architectural value of the cathedral? If the value either consists in or is derived from the thrilled state of mind of "consumers," then it is logically on the same footing, say, as a bottle of good wine whose value for some consists in its causal capacity to make people "high" or relaxed, or euphoric. In the example of the wine, others may value it on other grounds, for example its flavor, body, aroma, etc., but these too are effects produced in the drinker by the wine. In either case, therefore, the wine is valued by a large number of drinkers because of the effects it has on them.

But must all intrinsic values be that way? I think not. Consider examples of another type. Suppose one of our giant radio telescopes picks up signals of a patterned kind suggesting an attempt to communicate on the part of some distant intelligent beings. Cryptologists, after working for years on the project, finally succeed in deciphering it, and sure enough it *is* a kind of message. We send back immediately a response in the alien language, and then sit back to await a reply in 50,000 more years. Almost anyone would be excited by this sequence of events, but the excitement would be a consequence of our appreciation of the importance of the discovery that we are not alone in the universe. It would not be the case that the appreciation of this point was simply a response to its capacity to cause us excitement. In short, we value the message because of its cosmic implications; we do not value it simply as another reliable means of "getting high," that is of producing exciting mental states. Indeed, it is only because of those implications, as we understand them, that we can be excited.

Now, even though I have completed only the lightest sketch of the concept of value, we are in a better position to return to the main question. Are there valuable things that are valuable for some reason other than, or in addition to, the fact that they are beneficial? In particular, are some of these valuable objects and pursuits *extremely* valuable in the judgments of at least some persons, that is are they deemed worthy of that kind of valuing we call cherishing, treasuring, or venerating? The only way of proceeding at this point is to search for examples in our common judgments of objects or undertakings deemed worthy of *cherishing* for reasons other than their production of benefits. We have already considered some likely candidates. A cosmic message whose sequel can be expected in 50,000 years can hardly be of any direct benefit to anyone now, despite its instructive and understandably exciting character. Yet surely such a message would be a wonderfully good thing in its own right even in the absence of direct benefit. The discovery of some 10th century Arabic treatises on logic might be another example—a collection of overriding value, fit to be treasured by a small and narrowly specialized group of scholars. Those scholars can no doubt themselves be said to benefit, but their gain can hardly be the full explanation of why the ancient documents are objectively worthy of being cherished. A great amount of value remains to be accounted for even after we subtract that part that consists of benefits to specialized scholars.

Nor are all nonbeneficially valuable things treasured because they are surviving antiquities. Some are so new and so innovative that they neither interest, inspire, nor benefit anyone but their creators and a small circle of collaborators. Benefit then comes with time as belated understanding grows, until finally a later generation contains many who benefit by the existence of the formerly esoteric materials. But the original creators hardly have their remote descendants primarily in mind when they first cherish their own creations. Each historian of art will cite her favorite example of this process. Perhaps the most striking examples are from the history of music.

Philosophers who reject examples of the sort I have just provided usually do so, not because they deny that the objects in the examples are worth valuing, much less worth cherishing. Rather their denials are based on their judgment that these valuable objects and undertakings are really beneficial. They are able to hold their ground in this way, however, only because they employ an inflated sense of "benefitting." Typically, the objects and events we think of as beneficial are those that advance the interests of a beneficiary. But discovery of an intragalactic message with the promise of a once in fifty-thousand-year turn-around time does not obviously advance the interests of anyone we can now name.

Financial interests are the conceptual paradigm, I believe, for all talk of gain and loss, benefit and harm, though of course, people manifestly have interests other than their financial ones. The problem with talk of nonfinancial interest is that it gets fuzzy about the edges, since it sometimes tries to apply the exactitude of the accountant's ledger to subject matter that is too fluid to fit it. Suppose a number theorist discovers a monumental proof of a complicated theorem about prime numbers that wins the admiration of most specialists in that abstract and narrow branch of mathematics. The theorist himself might be an indirect beneficiary of his own work, if by boosting his reputation it leads to a higher salary or a better job. But we would hardly describe his work as benefitting humanity, or benefitting his countrymen, or even as benefitting his publishers, if any, since it is too esoteric to promise profit.

Why then would anyone want to say that the theorem proof, or the cosmic message, or the endangered species (say, of Siberian tigers), or the atonal sonata, though clearly things of great value, are also beneficial things, objects that advance the interests of specific beneficiaries? (We must remember, of course, that a valuable object can have some benefit for someone or other, but have an overall value that cannot be accounted for by those benefits alone.) The reason people insist that value must be a function of benefit, and that the counterexamples proffered above are themselves subtly beneficial projects, is that they count among the "benefits" of a valuable object or undertaking, the derivatively valuable states of mind they directly produce, particularly want-satisfaction, gratification, "excitement." The cosmic message is exciting, gratifying, stimulating to the imagination, and therein lies its "benefit." So the argument goes. Preserving the few remaining Siberian tigers has little direct benefit for people, since the loss of so few animals would not have an appreciable impact on the environment as a whole, and thus little consequence for human interests, but it would make most of us happy to think of these noble beasts remaining in existence, and the zoologists and environmentalists who work hard for this result will be especially gratified by the success of their own labors. The argument concludes that these effects—mental states such as want-satisfaction, self-satisfaction, and pride, are beneficial to those who experience them, and thus there is a necessary link between value and benefit, after all.

These arguments, I submit, will not withstand careful scrutiny. What is it in these examples that makes the original desire or ambition, a reasonable one? What makes self-satisfaction, etc., natural, fitting, and proper? Why is the successful result in these examples best described as an achievement? The answers to these questions about the grounds of the resultant mental states, must refer to something beyond the mental states themselves to something the mental states are *about*. We must already sense that the object or pursuit is beneficial (or valuable in some other way) if we are to experience any satisfaction at its production or occurrence. So the reason why it is beneficial cannot be simply that it produces satisfaction. Rather it produces satisfaction because it is deemed beneficial or otherwise valuable.

I propose therefore that we distinguish beneficial achievements from other achievements in the following way. A benefit to someone is something that advances her interests in such areas as wealth, security, power, and health. It is, as we say, something "good for her" whatever her conscious beliefs about it and emotional responses to it may be. To a person who has lost confidence in herself, for example, her production of a valuable thing of a kind not normally thought of as beneficial, may nonetheless *be* beneficial in her case by helping to restore her confidence. Her pride and self-satisfaction may be good therapy for her and therefore beneficial, even though production of the same kind of thing by a self-confident person, may produce a self-satisfaction for which he has no therapeutic need. In that case his achievement will have a value in itself equal to the value of the self-doubting person's creation, though his benefits no one, and hers benefits herself.

Consumers and creators of the arts, of all people, should need no argument to convince them that aesthetic value, at least, is not reducible to its beneficial properties. A painting might have a market value of a million dollars, and therefore be very beneficial to its owner who stands to gain enormously from its resale. But that beneficial capacity can hardly be the whole of its value, else it would be impossible to explain how it could have any monetary value at all. Surely, it is because some people judge it to be good *as art* that it can be good *qua* investment, that is, beneficial to its owner. A plain flat surface constructed from unfinished pine wood resting on a pile of bricks at each of its four corners can be a benefit to its owner in that it is a sturdy support for dishes or papers, and functions as a kitchen table or desk. An eighteenth century delicately carved and decorated classic of craftsmanship may serve equally "beneficially" as a kitchen table, but that doesn't explain how its total value, all things considered, is so much greater. Obviously it is valuable for some reason other than (or additional to) its beneficial utility. It is a cheat, I think, to identify that additional value as the pleasure in the minds of those who admire it, and then treat that pleasure as a "benefit" of the same order as its capacity to support papers and dishes.

Intrinsic versus Inherent Value

It may be useful at this point to complete our rough sketch of a theory of value by discussing briefly what might be called *inherent* (as opposed to intrinsic) value. While I think there are many things that are intrinsically valuable, although perhaps only a few *kinds* of such things, I don't think there are any inherently valuable things, in the sense I shall give that term, at all. What I mean by inherently valuable is similar to what G.E. Moore meant by "intrinsically valuable" when he wrote that an intrinsically valuable thing is one which would be good even if it existed quite alone. His model here seems to be the theory of primary and secondary qualities of physical objects, as expounded by Locke, and earlier by Galileo. Primary qualities are inherently part of the object itself—solidity, extension in space, figure, motion or rest, and number. An object's mass, in the sense of Newtonian physics, was thought to be a primary quality, that is a quality an object would continue to possess even if there were no perceiving beings in the world. Secondary qualities, on the other hand, such as color, taste, smell, sound, warmth, and cold, exist only when actually sensed, and then "only in the mind" of the one who senses them. What we identify as the smell of an object, for example, is the effect its vibrating molecules have on our olfactory nerves. A being without an olfactory nerve could not be affected in the appropriate way, and thus could never sense an odor, an aroma, or a stench. A world without properly equipped sniffers, then, would contain no smells. What then, would garbage lose its stench if all perceiving animals disappeared? No, the garbage would continue to smell as it does, but only in a hypothetical sense. The statement that decaying meat has a rancid smell, for example, can only mean that *if* any perceivers—animals equipped with olfactory nerves—were in the vicinity, they would have a rancid smell experience, and that hypothetical statement would remain true even if all perceiving animals were to cease to exist.

Inherent value (my term) is not like that, according to Moore. When Moore ascribes to an object what I call "inherent value," he will not settle for the hypothetical rendering of what he means. He explicitly denies that the inherent value of a thing is its worthiness to be valued by people in a position to value it, if there are such persons. The object's value inheres in it whether or not there are persons to value it, and it inheres in the object in a sense stronger than that of a causal capacity to produce effects on valuers, because those effects are already thought to be present in the valuable object itself. That is like saying that the vibrating molecules that can produce odors in the experience of observers with olfactory nerves, are themselves inherently smelly, quite apart from their capacity to produce smelly sensations in perceiving beings.

Sidgwick had found such talk about values incoherent, an opinion I'm happy, one hundred years later, to join. But G.E. Moore expresses his own theory in the form of a response to Sidgwick in a once famous passage. Moore begins by quoting Sidgwick:

> "No one," says Professor Sidgwick, "would consider it rational to aim at the production of beauty in external nature, apart from any possible contemplation of it by human beings." Well, I may say at once, that I for one, do consider this rational; and let us see if I cannot get anyone to agree with me. . . . Let us imagine one world exceedingly beautiful. Imagine it as beautiful as you can; put into it whatever on this earth you most admire—mountains, rivers, the sea, trees and sunsets, stars and moon. Imagine these all combined in the most exquisite proportions, so that no one jars against another, but each contributes to increase the beauty of the whole. Then imagine the ugliest world you can possibly conceive. Imagine it simply one heap of filth, containing everything that is most disgusting to us, for whatever reason, and the whole, as far as may be, without one

> redeeming feature. Such a pair of worlds we are
> entitled to compare: they fall within Professor
> Sidgwick's meaning, and the comparison is highly
> relevant to it. The only thing we are not entitled to
> imagine is that any human being ever has [lived],
> or ever by any possibility *can*, live in either, can
> ever see and enjoy the beauty of the one or hate the
> foulness of the other. Well even so, imagining
> them quite apart from any possible contemplation
> by human beings; still is it irrational to hold that it
> is better that the beautiful world should exist, than
> the one which is ugly? Would it not be well in any
> case to do what we could to produce it rather than
> the other? Certainly I cannot help thinking that it
> would.[11]

Moore cannot help holding his opinion, as he says, perhaps because he cannot help putting himself into the picture he imagines. He invites us to picture his two worlds not as they are in themselves unwitnessed by any human beings, not even ourselves. What we then succeed in imagining, of course, is a world observed by our own human, all too human, selves, quite contrary to the terms of the experiment.

Beauty and ugliness, I would prefer to say, are both in the "eye of the beholder" in roughly the same way that smell must always be in the nostrils of the one who senses it. If there are no beholders, there may still *be* beautiful and ugly things, in the sense that *if* there were qualified observers of the proper (that is, human) sort, in a position to behold the objects being judged, *then* those beholders would be affected in a certain way, and their responses to that predictable effect on their experience might be objectively appropriate. That hypothetical proposition, of course, can be true even if there are no such beholders. But Moore wishes it to be true of his unobserved worlds that they are beautiful and ugly in some categorical sense, just as if he were to maintain that unsniffed garbage is categorically smelly "in itself"—a claim I find impossible to understand.

My use of the phrase "eye of the beholder" may bring to mind the traditional formulation of a kind of value subjectivism, that "beauty is altogether in the eye of the beholder."[12] This saying has often expressed the view that one person's judgment that *x* is beautiful can be neither more nor less rational than another person's judgment that *x* is not beautiful. I do not hold that subjectivist theory; nor do I think it follows from a denial that beauty is a kind of *primary* quality of objects, like physical mass. To say that an object has any of the types of intrinsic value (including presumably, beauty), on my view, is to say that in virtue of its own characteristics it is worthy of being valued by some class of persons (possessors, beholders, creators, etc.). The key term, I repeat, is "worthy." That is the notion about which some of us are absolutist, some relativist; some objectivist, some subjectivist; some rationalist, some sentimentalists. I hold that the value of a thing is not a property of that thing independent of its effect on persons, but that claim does not commit me to the subjectivist view that disagreements over worthiness cannot be settled rationally, or that there can be no reasons supporting the claim that one of two opposed judgments of worthiness is correct, the other incorrect. But my present point is not that value subjectivism is itself false, but rather that it does not follow from a rejection of the concept of "inherent value."

The error in the "primary quality" theory can be expressed as follows. There are many examples of states of mind produced by a causal mechanism consisting of two necessary elements, one acting on the other. Intoxication, for example, may be produced by an intoxicating beverage acting on the brain (to which it has been transmitted by the circulating blood) of a human being or other biologically suitable animal. Without the intoxicating beverage there could be no intoxication. Without the appropriately receptive sort of nervous system there could be no intoxication. Both are necessary. Similarly, without molecular agitations of a certain kind and an appropriately receptive olfactory nerve, there could be no rancid smell, and without *some* kind of capacity to affect human beings as well as some human beings (valuing agents) to be affected, there could be no value. Sometimes one part of such mechanisms (the human receptor) is missing, but it remains true that the other part (with the causal capacity to affect the receptor) can still be said meaningfully to have value, but only in the sense that were the human receptor present, then she would be affected in a certain way. The mistake occurs when one infers from the presence of the affecting mechanisms that the usual effect (intoxication, aroma, value) is actually there anyway even when one necessary condition of its existence, the human receptor, is not. The same or parallel mistake in the example of the alcoholic potation would be to infer from *intoxicating* beverage to *intoxication*, even in the absence of an *intoxicated* (or *intoxicatable*) animal. As Santayana put it in discussing a closely related point, it would be to insist that "whiskey is . . . intoxicating in itself without reference to any animal; that it is pervaded, as it were, by an inherent intoxication, and stands dead drunk in its bottle!"[13]

For our present purposes it is not so important to argue that what I call inherent value is a conceptual muddle as it is to show that the thesis that there are inherently valuable things, which I reject, does not follow from the thesis that there are intrinsically valuable things, which I accept. Most writers use the words "intrinsic" and "inherent" interchangeably so that confusing the two distinct concepts is a mistake as natural as it is frequent. What I have been calling "intrinsic value" is simply a thing's being worthy of being valued in virtue of its own qualities, as distinct from the qualities of other things to which it can serve as an effective means or instrumentality. I have conceded that this distinction is imprecise, but there are ways of dealing with its vagueness that preserve its utility. People *do* value some things primarily for what they *are*, as opposed to, or in addition to, what they do, or what can be done with them. At least some of the time the things that are valued intrinsically are worthy of being so valued, even worthy of being *highly* valued in some cases, or cherished. These objects then are said, and sometimes correctly said, to have intrinsic value. But it in no way follows from these commonsense observations that intrinsically valuable things are *ipso facto* inherently valuable. One can rightly judge a thing worthy of appreciating or cherishing for its own qualities without interpreting those qualities as properties it would continue to possess in a categorical sense if it were all alone in the universe. Commonsense observations about how and why things are worthy of being valued do not generate this brand of metaphysical queerness.

The incoherence of inherent value has relevance for the problem of justifying subsidies for the arts out of tax funds exacted from those who are not likely beneficiaries. If the justification for this otherwise unfair practice invokes the idea of objects and pursuits that are extremely valuable at least partly for reasons other than their benefits, we can be tempted to fall into metaphysical obscurantism when we describe these precious objects. The confusion between intrinsic and inherent value once again can be the source of the trouble. Professor Nagel, after arguing that certain "treasures of human culture" have a value independent of, and superior to, the extent to which they are beneficial or actually appreciated, rushes to reassure us that he will not walk into the inherent value trap. "I am not suggesting," he writes, "that the existence of these things would be valuable even if there were *no one* to appreciate them. We don't have to conclude, for example, that if there were a nuclear war and human life were wiped out on earth, but New York hadn't been hit directly, it would still be a good thing that the paintings were hanging in the Metropolitan."[14] I agree with Nagel about this, though I should add that a hypothetical value judgment about the paintings would remain true even in the absence of human beings, namely that the paintings in the permanently deserted Museum are still things of great value in the sense that *if*, contrary to fact, there were human beings about, then the paintings would be worthy of being valued (appreciated, cherished) by those beings, and that is true for reasons not restricted to the actual benefits the paintings would produce. If it is exclusively benefits we want in the aftermath of a nuclear holocaust, we should probably be better off *eating* the wax paintings than "appreciating" or "cherishing" them.

Appraising Nonbeneficial Value

A final point remains to be made about nonbeneficial values. How are we to tell when an object or a project has such a value, especially when we are dealing with esoterica like research into number theory or electronic music? I have heard mathematicians praise proofs of theorems in terms that musicians would reserve for Bach or Mozart. I have no doubt, on their authority, that some of the highest flights of the human intellect have been made by mathematical theorists in areas that yield no particular benefits for humanity as a whole. I am sure that the more talented members of this group deserve support for projects that cannot be funded otherwise. But do I think that the project of using expensive giant computers to calculate the digits of *pi* up to the ten billionth say, so that number theorists might search for patterns of digit distribution in this endless number, is deserving of government support? Well, I am not a mathematician, so how should I know? If we are impressed enough by the nonbeneficial values produced generally by this kind of research to reserve some tax funds for their support, let the mathematicians themselves judge the worthiness of their colleagues' proposals. ("Peer review," I believe, is the jargon phrase.)

There are risks in this procedure. An occasional selection committee, reserving a small proportion of a small budget for experimental innovation,[15] a sensible practice in all fields, might budget tiny sums to underwrite an art museum exhibit of experimental works like that initially approved this year by the N.E.A. for $10,000 at the M.I.T. Museum and then vetoed by the director of the N.E.A. According to the newspaper, "The M.I.T. exhibit included works by four artists that portray body parts, including sexual organs, in various ways. The works include wallpaper imprinted with female and male genitalia, a glass sculpture of sperm and sculptures of disembodied breasts and buttocks."[16] This sounds to me interesting and I would be happy to go out of my way, to some degree, to see it. (You know—if I happened to be in Boston anyway.) The "risks" that I referred to are that such playful innovation will always be vetoed by overseers protecting the public morals, and fearful of doing otherwise on the good chance that politicians will retaliate by canceling all programs of support for the arts.[17] For all of that, however, once we have determined that an area of human activity, like art, (at its best) has a value beyond its benefits, then the projects in that area most deserving of support had best be determined by committees of leaders in the field in question. That will predictably lead, occasionally, to bizarre awards in the area reserved for experimentation, but the discovery of just one authentic genius otherwise certain to have been overlooked, is worth the cost of many dozens of bizarre failures.[18]

Future Business:
Dealing Anew With The Resentful Taxpayer

With the consent of my commentators, I have added this brief addendum to the paper they have seen and commented on. I find it striking, not to say a little embarrassing, that both of them, but especially Dr. Manning, point out that I overlook altogether a crucial strategic question my paper raises, *viz.* (partly in Manning's words) "why is the resentful taxpayer who objects to the state spending his tax money on benefits for others that he does not share, any more likely to accept the spending of his tax money for the production of intrinsically valuable objects that he is unable to appreciate?" (Or, one might add, if he does appreciate them, he does not appreciate them enough to be willing to pay a share of their costs." For Manning the question appears to be about motivation, rather than, or in addition to, justification. His question challenges us to motivate the person who doesn't give a damn about what we call "intrinsic value."[19]

My more limited aim was to distinguish benefits, direct and indirect, from benefitless intrinsically valuable things, to defend the latter conception by showing at least that it is coherent, and to sketch a possible analysis of it. But what makes me think that benefitless values will be any more effective than appeals to invisible benefits in motivating the philistine taxpayer, or justifying to him our use of his tax money? Could he not simply reply that he agrees that opera companies, for example, (at their best) produce intrinsically valuable experiences, yet deny that *that* is a good reason to tax unwilling citizens to support them?

If I had space to pursue this matter here, I would probably begin by developing in more detail my account of what intrinsic *value* is. It is important to emphasize that judgments of value are judgments of the worthiness or appropriateness of certain attitudes toward the object in question, characteristically expressed in language seeming to claim objective truth. If that is correct, then it would seem odd to admit that something is objectively worthy of being valued (esteemed, treasured, cherished, etc.) and then deny that the possession of such a property is any kind of reason—or a reason of significant weight—for requiring people to protect or support it. Even the egoistic philistine taxpayer, I should think, would have to admit that the possession in high degree of intrinsic value is not a gross irrelevancy, neither here nor there. Its relevance and cogency as a reason worthy even of the philistine's respect derives from the fact that the judgment of value is an appeal ultimately not to the taxpayer's actual attitudes and wants, sometimes called his "values," but rather to the worthiness and propriety of attitudes that he might not in fact share.

It would be exceedingly odd, for example, to protest taxation meant to enable purchase of a Civil War battlefield for perpetual preservation as a national monument, while eagerly conceding that the once fiercely contested fields are worthy of cherishing, treasuring, and revering. Suppose for example that one speaks as follows:

(c)   To prevent *harms*; that is, to rescue or protect persons
      from such harmful or dangerous conditions as malnutrition,
      disease, unemployment, and criminal violence.

This paper has been primarily concerned with limitations on the
first class of reasons listed above. I have been discussing the challenge
of the egoistic taxpayer who insists that fairness forbids taxing him to
support a result that produces no benefits for *him*. I have done this by
rejecting the ancient position that all worthwhile things produce
benefits, and produce them directly or indirectly for everyone. So I
show the liberal advocate of subsidies how to avoid a trap, and to do
it without reliance on any obscurantist notions, such as "intrinsic value"
is often thought to be, and "inherent value" really is.

But suppose that the quarrel is not between the egoistic philistine
taxpayer, on the one hand, and the liberal art-lover, on the other, but
rather between that taxpayer and people threatened with serious *harm*,
that is with the deprivation or loss of what they *need* (not just "want"
or "benefit from") in order to lead a good, or even minimally decent,
life. It would be quite unconvincing for the taxpayer to protest that it
is unfair to tax him in order to enable others to avoid starvation,
criminal violence, disease, etc. Other things being equal then, harm-
prevention trumps benefit-production. (Actually, "trump" may be too
strong a word here, because after all, elimination of a small harm
might not have priority over the production of a great benefit.) The
problem for liberal art-lovers, however, is that given the immense costs
of fighting harm, this priority-ranking of types of reasons would lead
to *no subsidies whatever*, either for intrinsically valuable things *or* for
benefits. The tax money would always run out before we could spend
anything on such luxuries as art and mathematical number theory. This
transforms our problem. In the light of the above, how can we justify
subsidizing any benefitless intrinsically valuable activities at all? Or for
that matter, any activities that are *merely* beneficial while not
preventing or curing harms? Even in the world of private funding
where private donors and charitable foundations must sometimes choose
between (say) donating a one-million-dollar painting to a worthy
museum or donating the money instead to cancer research, parallel
problems of choice arise. But the use of tax funds in the governmental
example adds a further level of moral complication. Our political
leaders struggle not only over what causes should be supported, and in

what order of priority. They must also choose whom to coerce into paying the costs.[20]

Notes

1. The local Representative, of course, can hope to succeed only by promising to vote in the committee for much more expensive projects in the *chairman's* home state, thereby adding to the chairman's already considerable clout. This is the process that brought us a 40 million dollar museum of the steam locomotive in Pennsylvania and an "authentic Bavarian resort" in the Idaho mountains, neither of which was much appreciated by the National Park Service. Leaders of both parties have condemned the pork system, and some have estimated that it "wastes" billions of dollars annually, but its momentum in the national Congress shows no sign of slowing.

2. Brian Kelly, *Adventures in Porkland: How Washington Wastes Your Money and Why They Won't Stop* (New York: Villard Books, 1992).

3. A very clearly written critical summary of these and other leading theories can be found in Noël Carroll's "Can Government Funding of the Arts Be Justified Theoretically?" in the *Journal of Aesthetic Education*, Vol. 21, No. 1, Spring 1987. It is a natural starting place for this whole subject.

4. The preceding three paragraphs are drawn from my book *Harmless Wrongdoing* (New York: Oxford University Press, 1988), pp. 314-15. The treatment of rotational justice in the book is more detailed than it is here.

5. *Ibid.*, pp. xxvii-xxix, 20-32, 125.

6. Thomas Nagel, "Symposium on the Public Benefits of the Arts and Humanities," *Columbia Journal of Art and the Law*, Vol. 9, No. 2, 1984, p. 236.

7. *Ibid.*, p. 237.

8. *Newsweek*, October 12, 1992, p. 67.

9. *Newsweek, Loc. cit.*

10. Nagel, *op. cit.*, p. 231.

11. G.E. Moore, *Principia Ethica* (Cambridge: Cambridge University Press, 1903), pp. 83-84.

12. *Bartlett's Familiar Quotations* attributes this familiar line to two sources: Lew Wallace in his *The Prince of India* (1893) and Margaret Wolfe Hungerford in her *Molly Bawn* (1878). The word "altogether" appears in the Wallace, but not the Hungerford quotation.

13. George Santayana, "The Philosophy of Mr. Bertrand Russell," in *Winds of Doctrine* (London: J.M. Dent & Sons, Ltd., and New York: Charles Scribner's Sons, 1913), p. 146.

14. Nagel, *Op. cit.*, p. 237.

15. The N.E.A., I believe, devotes 3% of its graphic arts budget to projects in this category.

16. The *Arizona Daily Star*, May 13, 1992.

17. The sadomasochistic Mapplethorpe photographs, I think, are a different matter. Depictions of unlikely objects jammed painfully into unlikely orifices are not exactly "playful." If the victim of this photographed abuse had been a woman rather than a homosexual man, Robert Hughes suggests, the Mapplethorpe show would never have gotten off the ground. See Robert Hughes, "Art, Morals, and Politics," *New York Review of Books*, April 23, 1992, p. 24.

18. Note that an object or facility can be *worthy* (deserving) of support, and yet there might be overriding reasons, in the present circumstances, for not giving that support. The money might better be used to support AIDS research, to end homelessness, to confront and genuine military danger, to reduce gigantic government deficits, etc. It is no contradiction to say that *x* is worthy of support (because worthy of being admired and cherished) and yet we ought to withhold support so as to reduce or prevent *harms*. See concluding section below.

19. Noël Carroll's similar concern, however, is quite explicitly about justification: "It may be true, though one has one's doubts, that art is intrinsically good. But even if the production of art *is* intrinsically good, that in and of itself, would not warrant state funding of the arts. For the state does not, and in some cases should not, be taken to have a role in the production of whatever we conceive to be an intrinsic good (if there are such things). State intervention in these matters calls for justification." See Carroll, *op. cit.*, note 3.

20. One final, ironic, footnote. I have learned, since completing this paper, that Congress did acquire the Manassas Battlefield from various private owners (developers) for $250,000 an acre for a 542 acre site. Many more old battlefields remain vulnerable, so Congress, unable to afford any more direct purchases, set up a fifteen-member Advisory Commission to cooperate with a new nonprofit Civil War Commission to raise *private* money for future purchases and maintenance. Projects whose costs are totally beyond private support remain "the exceptional case."

Should the Government
Subsidize the Arts?

Ernest van den Haag

The government always concerns itself with problems—usually by means of subsidies—when a constituency can be discerned or created. Now there is one for the arts. Hence presidents, congressmen, and senators can acquire cachet and reputations as cultivated and sensitive intellectuals by advocating more federal expenditures on the arts. President Kennedy started much of the rhetoric; President Nixon increased the budgetary appropriations. Ever since, the federal budget for the arts in all forms has grown by leaps and bounds. Although they deplore high taxes and huge benefits, the Congress and the executive branch have been remarkably generous to the arts. The matter raises some questions:

1. What is the role of the arts in American society, and what can it be? What should it be?

2. What is the role of the government in the arts? What should it be? Do Americans want their tax money to be spent for the arts by their representatives? Or, would they prefer to decide individually how much money to spend on works of art and on which works? What would happen without government subsidies?

3. If the arts actually do require a government subsidy, what or who should be subsidized and by what selection procedures?

Although major philosophers such as Plato and Hegel were doubtful about their value, much can be said for the arts. However, it is essential to distinguish arguments for the arts and for their support

Ernest van den Haag's article first appeared in *Policy Review*, 1979. It is reprinted here by permission of the publisher.

from arguments for government support of the arts. This essential distinction is seldom made. Yet, whatever can be said for the arts is certainly not sufficient by itself to justify any government subsidies. To be sure, the arts give pleasure to some—a special quality of pleasure or, better, desired experience—and employment to others. But so do whiskey and religion. Hence, an argument for government support of the arts must indicate not only what characteristics make the arts socially (and not just individually) desirable or necessary but also those characteristics that suggest why government subsidies to the arts are justified and needed while they are not for whiskey or religion. It must be shown that private funds are not likely to support the arts to the degree or in the manner justified by their social usefulness while government subsidies can do so.

The type of argument required is familiar; it is used to argue for public support of parks, or beaches, or police forces: they are needed, useful, and desired but differ from other nice things that may be purchased privately in that they benefit not only the individuals willing to spend money for them, but to a significant extent, the community as a whole, including those who would not volunteer to pay or cannot afford to. An adequate argument for federal support of the arts must show, then, that they yield indivisible collective benefits (as does the police force). If the arts do yield such benefits and they are of sufficient magnitude, the government is justified in compelling individuals to pay taxes, compulsory levies, to pay for the arts regardless of whether an individual taxpayer feels benefitted. Further, the collective benefit yielded by the arts must be shown to exceed the benefit to be expected if every person were to pay for whatever art he wished and could afford to buy. Finally, there must be good reason to believe that the government will not be (much) worse as a patron of art than private individuals are. Note that whatever arguments there are for public support of art probably could be made for subsidies to religion as well. Indeed religion is subsidized in most European countries. But, for historical constitutional reasons, no attempt is made to subsidize religion in this country. It has thrived nonetheless—which gives food for thought.

Historical Precedents for Subsidies

The argument for public support of the arts has been convincing since Pericles' time. Sculpture, architecture, music, painting, literature, as well as what today are called the humanities—historiography and scholarship have been very largely supported by public funds since antiquity. Temples and statues of the gods were erected with public funds. *Mutatis mutandis* public funds were spent for the arts in the Middle Ages. The arts were used to erect monuments to shared beliefs and to celebrate communal feeling they also celebrated royal houses (literally and symbolically) and the nations, regions, and religions of which they were emblematic.

Public expenditures for the arts have begun to be questioned only since the Industrial Revolution. Until then, public funds were disbursed by religious authorities and by the courts of the nobility; no one was able to question them. The distinction between the prince's (or the bishop's) personal funds and those administered by him was vague. He could dispose of either to foster the arts if it pleased him. His expenditure was accepted as it was in antiquity; tradition indicated that the arts, as did religion, bind together, help make into a cohesive whole, the society in which they flourish. They are an essential part of what civilizes, of the meaning-conferring essence, the soul of the culture of any society—as was the religion the arts used to celebrate. (The word, after all, came from *re-ligare,* to bind strongly.) With the Renaissance the arts became more secular. But the princes—of church or state—who supported them were still regarded as the embodiment of the polity. Their taste and their expenditure were not questioned, and the glorification of their reign through the arts was seen as the glorification of the polity.

Whatever their merit, these arguments scarcely justify tax-paid subsidies for the arts today, particularly in the United States. The arguments are relevant neither to modern art in modern conditions, nor to ancient art in modern conditions, nor to any art in the United States. Aristocracy and church have not been sufficiently dominant in our political history and mixed up with the nation-forming process to justify replacing their support of the arts with a government subsidy. Nor did the arts themselves ever play much of a role in sustaining our national cohesion. They do not now.

Whatever the value of opera (I happen to be a passionate opera lover), it cannot be said, as it may be said in Italy or Austria, that opera has contributed to our national cohesion, history, culture, or consciousness—or that it has any chance of doing so now. Opera was an exotic import of and for the rich who were also willing to pay for it. The educated middle class is getting interested in it now. But it is not clear why those who want opera are entitled to compel others to pay for it—even though these others, in the main, prefer unsubsidized movies or Broadway shows. A subsidy to opera supports or expands our national consciousness as much as a subsidy to the manufacture or the wearing of tails and top hats would.

What is true for opera is as true for classical music, for dance, including ballet, and, by and large, for the great works of art in our museums. They did not play an important role in our history or in forging or celebrating our national bonds—though they did in Europe (which, however, survived their export). We have marvelous things in our museums. But they did not get there through government activities and did not celebrate those activities or our national history, cultural or political. The contents of our museums have nothing to do with our national life, and they have not contributed to our national cohesion or identity. They are politically and socially irrelevant to us (whatever their aesthetic merit).

Tin Pan Alley, jazz, rock, or baseball are more important in the celebration of American values, not only in the working classes and among adolescents, but also in the upper classes and even among educated groups. They need no subsidy.

Subsidizations of Sports and TV

For quite a while, sports (and now TV) have been important elements in our culture and our cohesion, together with the automobile and the lengthening years of instructional and custodial care in schools imposed on the young. But the arts? Certainly not those in museums. Nor the modern artists the government is eager to subsidize. They may or may not be great. But they are at best marginal to American culture. It is not likely that this will change.

If TV or if sports do play the role I have attributed to them, should they be subsidized? They seem to do quite well, thank you, without government subsidy. If the exclusive support of TV by advertisers is regarded as a hindrance to possible informational or aesthetic achievements, there is no reason that TV could not be paid for directly by the viewers, as books or magazines are paid for by those who buy them or are willing to subsidize them. Unsubsidized literature has done well in the United States. The case for public TV is as questionable as the case for government-financed newspapers, magazines, or books, even though the federal and local governments insist on subsidizing public TV and radio.[1]

Unavoidably, public TV is biased. The values presented are not those prevailing among Americans at large, but those of the producers and of the public TV audience, both middle-class liberal. In its more political presentations public TV is definitely "left" of the public that pays for it. (No conspiracy: the people involved find it hard to take seriously values other than their own.) Apart from everything else it seems hard to justify publicly subsidized TV, for it simply amounts to a tax-paid subsidy to upper-middle-class viewers dissatisfied with commercial offerings addressed to the less educated.

To summarize: the arts are not among the activities which contribute enough to social cohesion, national identity, or shared values in the United States to justify support by the government. On the other hand, the activities which would deserve support on these grounds scarcely need it. Sports and TV and rock concerts are doing all right without government subsidy. The schools already are amply supported, and they do incidentally support the arts by supporting artists, writers, and other representatives of the arts directly and indirectly.

So far I have confined myself to denying that there is any justification for government subsidies to the arts under modern American conditions. The tacit assumption was that, whether or not a subsidy could be justified, the government could help the arts to flower by subsidizing them. This assumption must now be questioned: it seems unlikely that the government can help the arts by subsidizing them. Even though it does inflate the quantity of art produced, the government subsidy may actually harm the arts.

The most cogent argument against any form of censorship of art by the government[2] is, very simply, that the government is unlikely to be able to tell bad, worthless (pseudo) art from good. Wherefore, censorship would damage the arts by suppressing "good" as readily as "bad" art. If the government could distinguish valuable from valueless art and would get rid of only the worthless stuff, censorship would make everyone's life easier, as garbage removal does. But no one attributes such powers of discrimination to the government. Indeed, a major part of the general argument for freedom is that we cannot trust any government (democratic or otherwise) to tell vice from virtue, good from bad. If we could, we might not mind if the government subsidized virtue and suppressed vice. As it is, we prefer to leave such decisions to individuals (a few extreme cases excepted), because we have no reason to believe that the government could do better and much reason to believe it would do worse.

Well, if the government cannot be trusted to tell which art is so bad as to deserve suppression, how can it be trusted to tell which art is so good as to deserve subsidization? Either the government can or it cannot tell good from bad art. The answer is that it cannot. This seems to me just as conclusive an argument against government subsidies to art as it is an argument against government censorship of art.[3]

In practice the government's subsidies to art unavoidably become indiscriminate. (This is how the government protects itself against criticism and creates a wide, supportive constituency.) The government cannot actually subsidize art. At best it can and will subsidize a wide range of organizations or persons who claim to be producing art.

Supporting Fool's Gold

Now, a lot of ore has to be mined to get a little gold. One may argue that a lot of subsidy has to be spent on many unworthy artists so that the few worthy artists can be helped. However, there are relevant differences between mining and subsidized art production.

One difference need only be restated. Mining is not subsidized. It pays for itself—the purchasers of the metal pay more than enough for the necessary processes, including the mining of the ore that has to be discarded. Gold mining, thus, is analogous to the private purchase of art or, if you please, the private subsidy given to art producers. It is not analogous to government subsidies. Subsidies suggest that whatever worthwhile art they help produce is not worth enough to the public to persuade it to pay for the whole process, including the worthless art that is being subsidized. Thus, the government compels the taxpayer to do what he does not volunteer to do. I can find no justification for this policy.

There is an even more important difference between mining ore and art production. Payments to the mining industry may lead to more exploration and mining. But they cannot increase the total amount of gold-bearing ore that nature provided. Above all, such payments will not encourage the production of fake or imitation gold since consumers (and even the government) are quite capable of discriminating. Subsidies to art also may lead to more utilization of talent, although they cannot increase the pool of artistic talent provided by nature. But—and this is the decisive difference—a subsidy to art will attract people who would not have become artists without it. Art, unlike gold, is not definable so that the government could exclude subsidies to the untalented. We are forced to subsidize the mining of fool's gold as much as the mining of actual artistic gold, for the government cannot discriminate. The more we subsidize, the larger *the proportion* of fool's gold, of pseudo-art, in the end product being subsidized.

Normally, art production is self-selective. Few people produce art for the sake of money. The main reward is intrinsic —*ars gratia artis*. Artists are willing to risk foregoing income for the sake of self-rewarding achievement however much they hope it will be publicly recognized and become materially rewarding as well. Not that hungry artists are being artists. On the contrary. But the high risk of low income deters those more interested in income than in art and leaves mainly those who are artists for the sake of art, whether or not they are able to produce anything valuable.

Subsidies, however, will increase art production by attracting producers who, without the subsidy, would not have produced—those whose passion for art was not sufficient, without the subsidy, to induce them to risk sacrificing income. Subsidies may actually make it harder for true artists to succeed. Although more money is made available, there also is more competition for it. In this competition, the true artist is likely to be undone by those who, consciously or unconsciously, are interested mainly in money. They will be more worldly wise, better competitors. After all, they are not distracted by artistic concerns and ambitions.

Lacking original talent, the pseudo artist will be more imitative and therefore more easily understood and more appealing—and more eligible for subsidies. A subsidy to something or somebody actually original and valid is harder to justify than a subsidy to something appealing, unoriginal, and therefore more easily understood. Those in charge of subsidization will be safer by going with the fashion, not by helping unknowns who create new things. (This reasoning applies least to those matters which can be demonstrated, for instance, by experiment—and most to the least demonstrable things, foremost art.)

To speak of subsidizing art is, of course, to use a metaphor. One can only buy specific works of art or help specific artists. Since there are no generally accepted qualifications and no agreement on what or who is meritorious, government organizations must subsidize artists who have already been widely recognized—and need the subsidy least—or distribute their bounty so that every claimant supported by regional taste or by the taste of any major social group gets some. (This is, among other things, what Herbert Gans advocates in his *Popular Culture and High Culture.*)[4] Aesthetically this is counterproductive. Bad art, as does bad money, drives out good.

Government subsidies, finally, are biased in favor of the performing arts. Officials feel they can measure quality by the dubious gauge of popularity; this is easier to do with an orchestra than with a composer. The performing arts also involve far more people—performers, support personnel, and the public—than are involved in the lonely act of, say, composing a score or writing a critical essay. Hence, a large constituency. Wherefore, more and more subsidies go to the performing arts. The Metropolitan Opera or the Duluth Philharmonic is subsidized. The further natural bias of subsidies is toward popular performances and expansion of audiences at the expense of quality. It is in this way that political support can be secured.

Much more could be said along these lines. But the idea should be clear by now. (a) There is no good sociopolitical reason for the government to compel taxpayers to subsidize government-selected arts; (b) to do so compels all classes to subsidize the middle class; (c) to do so is more likely to harm than to help in the creation of actual, valuable art.

Subsidies to Museums

What would happen if the government—local and federal—were to cease supporting the arts?[5] What would happen to museums and galleries which have come to depend on subsidies?

Museums acquire, preserve, and display art both of the past and of the present. (They also engage in scholarly and educational activities incidental to their task.) Since much of the acquisition funds of museums now comes from private donations, government subsidies here are unimportant. Even if museums, left without subsidies, ceased to buy art and use acquisition money for maintenance, there would be no damage. The migration of old art from Europe and Asia into the United States and from private into public hands would be slowed. (The prices paid for ancient art would fall.) Since most museums have far more art than they are able to display, no less would be displayed than is now displayed. The egos of museum directors and curators would suffer greatly. But there would be no other damage. Failure to buy modern art would reduce its prices somewhat and its production. Again, no other effects are likely. Art is not produced for museums. Nor should it be. But, let me repeat, most acquisition would continue, since funding for this purpose is supplied by private donations.

Preservation of art, old or new, however acquired, is costly. So is the display of art under reasonable conditions. It is this cost, which museums incur unavoidably, that is largely paid for by public subsidies. There is an arguable social interest in preserving art for future generations; hence, some of the cost of preservation, as distinguished from the cost of display, may well be defrayed out of tax funds. However, there is no reason why those who are currently gratified by viewing art should compel others to pay for their gratification, no reason for museum visitors to contribute as little as they do now to the upkeep of the museums they visit. People are willing to pay, on the average, fifteen to thirty dollars to attend a Broadway show for two hours. There is no reason to pay less to attend a museum. (Preferred, habitual categories of viewers might be offered low subscription rates.) Would museums survive? Churches have survived by voluntary contributions without government subsidies. Museums could charge admission and expect donations. So could opera houses and symphony orchestras. They would survive—although their rate of expansion would be curtailed.

Raising the cost of attendance would thin the ranks of museum visitors (thereby reducing upkeep costs as well as paying a greater proportion of those costs). Lower attendance is regarded as a calamity by pedagogues who feel it necessary to make art available free of charge—even to stuff it down people's throats. Everything else—from bread to concerts—costs money. Why should art be free? There is, of course, no free art any more than there is a free lunch. Museum visits free to the visitor are paid for by taxpayers—largely by people whose incomes are lower than those of most museum visitors. I can see no justification for the shifting of the cost.

Reasonable entrance fees would solve a disturbing problem, deliberately neglected by administrators. Because they like popularity and wide support—which increase their power, their prestige, and their subsidies and salaries—administrators pay no heed to the problems caused by crowding for those who actually come for the sake of seeing art. The treasures of the past are finite; the number of potential viewers is infinite. In each generation only a few can actually see them. But since museums are costless to visitors, they now attract crowds so big as to make it nearly impossible for any individual to contemplate and experience the art they display. Their popularity defeats much of the serious purpose used to justify subsidizing museums. People are herded through galleries—they willingly trot by paintings driven by boredom and by others—so that everybody can satisfy his curiosity and gratify his sense of accomplishment.

If crowds were thinner, as they would be if a visit to the museum were to cost as much as attendance at a Broadway show, those who would still go to a museum would be able to enjoy it. They would find the conditions which make possible the aesthetic experience a museum can help them to achieve.

The absence of subsidies would have similar effects on the performing arts. The price of tickets would rise. Attendance would be reduced. Fewer performances would occur if people would not voluntarily pay for all the performances now subsidized. There would be an additional beneficial effect. The wages now paid performing artists and supporting personnel would decrease with the demand for them. I do not see much reason for a subsidy that leads them to earn far more than those from whom the money is taken. This redistribution is as involuntary as it is undesirable.

Notes

1. New York City, teetering on the edge of bankruptcy, insists on taxing business to support its own radio and TV stations. (The cost is negligible, but why is it needed? *As* a tourist attraction?)

2. Let me leave aside pornography here.

3. The traditional European subsidies (often combined with censorship) were given by taste-makers, by a cultural elite. Our government does not aspire to that status and we have no tradition of conferring it *(Deo gratias).*

4. Herbert J. Gans, *Popular Culture and High Culture* (Basic Books, New York, 1974). Gans has a populist point; rather than rely on the government's aesthetic discrimination, we might as well give up aesthetic discrimination, a middle-class prejudice, and replace it by some sort of popular vote.

5. I distinguish tax exemption (not taking money) from support (giving money) and do not oppose the first.

The Politics of Culture:
Art in a Free Society

Gordon Graham

To the casual observer of history the events of 1989 in Eastern Europe must appear as a clear triumph for the values of the free world. Everywhere, and contrary to all reasonable expectations, parties and people, who had decades in which to secure their political power and persuade their fellow citizens of the merits of the communist social order, were finally overthrown, and chiefly, it seems, because of the irrepressible attractiveness of individual freedom and popular democracy.

No doubt there is something correct in this superficial reading of these important changes. Equally undoubtedly historical investigation will in time uncover a more complex story, and reveal social and political forces at work of which both participants and contemporary commentators were largely unaware. But philosophical reflection suggests that there are also conceptual complexities here which any simple appeal to the values of freedom and democracy overlooks. Even if the proposition that Eastern Europe has finally opted for the freedom of the West is true, its implications are unclear. Just what the content of this freedom is, and how far it extends, is uncertain – a matter of considerable philosophical and political debate in fact.

Moreover, it is a debate which cannot be settled by appeal to the evidence of political practice in the West. For instance, whilst everyone agrees that the freedom of the *free* world includes freedom of religion,

Gordon Graham's article first appeared in the *History of European Ideas* 33 (6), 1991, pp. 763-774. It is reprinted here by permission of the publisher, Elsevier Science Ltd., Pergamon Imprint (Oxford, England), and the author.

many European countries continue to have established churches whose clergy are paid out of taxes which all citizens must pay, and some free countries still have laws giving special protection to the beliefs and sentiments of the Christian religion. Again, most people suppose that a free society such as obtains in the West and to which the East now aspires is one in which the coercive powers of the state are not used to endorse or enforce any particular morality. It is this belief in the limits of legitimate coercion that explains much twentieth century reform of laws on homosexuality. At the same time, Western 'liberals' did not hesitate to urge their governments to control and restrict sporting and trading links with Verwoerd's and Botha's South Africa, on the grounds that friendly acts towards a state based upon apartheid are immoral. Liberalism, it appears, is both against and in favour of moralising the law.[1]

This ambivalence has a parallel in another important sphere, the attitude of liberalism to the arts and ethnic culture. On the one hand, the repressive character of the communist world was frequently illustrated by its treatment of artist and the arts, the artists being persecuted when their creative work conflicted with the interests of party and state, and the arts being hijacked to serve the purposes of political propaganda just as they were in Nazi Germany. Bearing these facts in mind, a free society seems to require that the state leaves art and artists alone. On the other hand, Western governments use tax revenues to support art and artists selectively, and not infrequently the law is used to forbid the export of paintings or the alteration and destruction of buildings for aesthetic reasons. More generally, both laws and state money are used extensively to protect and promote minority ethnic cultures. The liberal belief in artistic freedom seems to imply that the state should keep out of the arts, but the practice of the West gives it a large and important role, and it is a role that liberally minded people tend to support.

It is this third context which is specially interesting, partly because, while the questions of religion in a free society and moralising the law have been widely discussed in liberal theory, relatively little has been said about the proper liberal attitude to the arts. But the question also has a certain topical urgency, best illustrated by a particular case. Until he was hounded out of his job and sent into internal exile by the Ceausescu government for his dissident views, Andrei Plesu was a professor of ethics and aesthetics in Bucharest. Following the revolution of December 1989 he was invited by the new National Salvation Front to be Minister of Culture. Plesu was committed to the ideals of a free society but he faced in practice the theoretical question which is the subject of this essay – what is it to be a minister of culture in a free society?

The English language is interesting here. While many Western governments are happily described as having a 'Ministry for the Arts', the title 'Ministry of Culture' already has an ominous, totalitarian ring. The first suggests an acceptable functionary in a free society, the second an unacceptable political overseer of artistic endeavour. Indeed we might use these terms to frame the question of this essay, and ask whether a Ministry for the Arts can stop short of becoming a Ministry for Culture. But to appreciate the force of this question we need to explore more of the philosophical background.

I

Liberal political theory has a considerable history, and it would be surprising indeed if in the course of it substantial differences between theorists had not emerged. There are in fact at least three distinct strands of liberalism, namely those that flow from Locke's appeal to the rights that obtain in a state of nature,[2] Kant's appeal to the value of autonomy in the moral 'kingdom of ends',[3] and John Stuart Mill's appeal to utility.[4] (Still other variations on basic liberal themes are to be found in Smith, Constant and von Humboldt.) However, the differences between these three, though important, lie not so much in their conceptions of a free society as in their explanations of why it is to be valued. All three strands of thought may be made to explain the value of the same sort of society. This is one of the elements they share which entitles us to call them all liberal theories. Thus, Mill's self-professed task in *On Liberty* is to explain why the freedom of the individual is of the first importance without appealing to what he calls 'abstract right' i.e. Lockean state of nature theory. But of course he still wants to defend just what Locke wants to defend – a sphere of individual liberty which the state cannot legitimately invade.

The relation between these different theories is not quite as simple as this way of putting it may suggest. Rival theories of the value of liberty can imply different liberties; it seems easier to found so-called 'welfare rights' on a Utilitarian than a Lockean basis, for instance.

Nevertheless, in broad outline liberal theories agree upon the sort of society we ought to want. That society, which I shall refer to as a 'free society', may be said to have three important features. First, there is within it a presumption of liberty. That is to say, in a free society an individual may be permitted to do anything, unless there is reason to outlaw it. This means that the burden of proof is always on those who wish to limit individual freedom, rather than those who wish to extend it, and in this a free society contrasts sharply with a totalitarian society in which everything is forbidden unless it has been expressly permitted. Secondly, the reasons for outlawing behaviour must rest upon criteria that can pass the test of publicity, that is to say, are acceptable when publicly stated and widely known. This aspect is captured rather differently in the rival theories; Kantian theory has generated a contractarian conception and with it the idea that the terms of political association must be acceptable to any impartially rational citizen, while Mill's Utilitarian theory appeals to the simpler idea that 'harm to others' is something everyone will recognise as a proper basis for constraint. Thirdly, all theories that the need for publicly acceptable criteria for limits on individual freedom rules out appeals to any one vision of the good life for a human being. Thus, we cannot properly appeal to Christian or Islamic morality, for instance, as the grounds of restrictive laws. Whether this last feature arises necessarily, as in some appeals to Kantian autonomy, or merely as a result of the historical development of pluralist societies, as in John Rawls' latest theory,[5] is a further matter for disagreement, but the principle itself is largely unquestioned.

Against this background it is easy to mount an objection to the treatment of art and artists in communist and fascist societies. In Nazi Germany or the communist China of chairman Mao, the work of artists was highly controlled. Artistic expression was forbidden unless it met the desired aim of presenting the public with a convincing version of the party's preferred vision of society and the future. Thus the painting and sculpture approved under the Nazis has a common character; its imagery portrays an ideological vision of Germany under the Third Reich. This vision did not bear much relation to reality. It was rather a political aspiration. Similarly, art in communist China served a similar purpose. The film *The East is Red*, for instance, made during the Cultural revolution, combined visual art, music, dance and drama in an impressive image of the new China, emerging from a backward history into the light of a gloriously new dawn. The unity, enthusiasm and progress it portrays again bear little relation to the cruel turbulence of most of the period under Mao, but it too illustrates how art may be used to represent a political vision.

Both cases are easily accounted for in terms of the liberal principles outlined above. The Nazis and the Communists restricted and coerced artists, which according to liberalism is tolerable only on certain grounds. The grounds upon which they did so, however, far from being publicly and impartially acceptable, consisted in the promotion of a single political vision. Indeed the use of art in this way was intended precisely to engineer public acquiescence in a highly partial vision of society. Of course, opponents of liberalism need not accept these principles. They may argue that the presumption of liberty is without foundation (as Mussolini did[6], that there is no standard that can meet the condition of impartial rationality, or (as proponents of Islamic republics do) that the vision they seek to enshrine in the body politic is the only right one. All these are familiar objections, and to them there are equally familiar replies. But to explore these issues further here would not be immediately to the point, though there will be reason to return to them. Rather, the aim here has been only to set out and illustrate the liberal's objection to state control of the arts in order to move on to the next question. If these are the grounds of the objection to the treatment of the arts under Nazism and communism, what legitimate interests can the state have in the arts in a free society?

II

Ronald Dworkin considers this question in 'Can A Liberal State Support Art?'[7] He contrasts two approaches to art in Western society. One, which he calls the economic approach, argues, in keeping with liberal principles (though not necessarily because of them), that the free market best reflects what level of resources people actually want to devote to the arts, and that public spending beyond that is an unwarrantable imposition. The alternative view, which Dworkin calls the 'lofty' approach, focuses upon the intrinsic merits of the high arts and supports state funding of them simply on the grounds that, whatever the general run of people may want, an intrinsically worthwhile object is being sustained. But as Dworkin observes

> the lofty approach seems haughtily paternalistic.
> Orthodox liberalism holds that no government
> should rely, to justify its use of public funds, on
> the assumption that some ways of leading one's life
> are more worthy than others, that it is more
> worthwhile to look at Titian on the wall than watch
> a football game on television. Perhaps it is more
> worthwhile to look at Titian; but that is not the
> point. More people disagree with this judgement
> than agree with it, so it must be wrong for the
> state, which is supposed to be democratic, to use
> its monopoly of taxing and political power to
> enforce judgements only a minority accepts.[8]

There are questions to be raised about Dworkin's exposition of this point. For instance, the coercion of the individual in accordance with an aesthetic judgement seems contrary to liberal conceptions of the free society even when that judgement is widely shared in a society. So the heart of the objection to such coercion cannot lie principally in its conflict with democratic values. But we can leave these points of difference aside, because Dworkin is certainly right in his claim that there is a conflict with orthodox liberalism here.

If this is correct, the arts appear to present liberalism with a dilemma. One possibility is that we accept what appears to be a basic principle of the free society, and leave the support of the arts to individual and group consumers. In this case, however, since enthusiasm for the high arts is usually a minority interest (albeit a large minority in some place), it seems likely that support for the arts will not be sufficient to sustain a society's cultural heritage. The anti-economic point of view fears cultural impoverishment. But is it impoverishment? Liberalism tries to leave aside the question of the relative values of Titian and football, but what Dworkin calls the 'lofty' view precisely rests upon the idea that artistic greatness must be protected, since, whatever its popular appeal, it has intrinsic merit. On this view, it is not just that the market is unlikely to sustain the arts, but that market attitudes are the wrong attitudes to apply to art. Such a view no doubt commands considerable support in contemporary societies that consider themselves to be both liberal and free, but there is indeed a tension here. If we endorse paternalistic attitudes to art, and thereby abandon a cardinal principle of liberalism, we may find ourselves without argument against the extension of paternalistic attitudes in other, perhaps more important, areas of social life. Many Christians sincerely believe that a life of monastic devotion has intrinsic merit and most Muslims sincerely believe that pictorial representations of the Prophet are intrinsically wicked. How can those who believe that the coercive powers of the state may legitimately be used to protect intrinsic *artistic* merit, deny the same support to *religious* merit.

What then should the state's attitude to art be in a free society? One way of trying to answer this question would consist in looking further at the principles of liberal political and social theory. Perhaps the foundations of liberalism are not as secure as they seem; perhaps government intervention in the arts is not contrary to liberal principles properly understood. But, given the several different liberalisms outlined above, this approach is as likely to raise additional difficulties as to provide a solution to the present one. An alternative route is to consider the question from the other side, to look more closely at art and to decide, on the basis of a proper understanding of its nature and value, what sort of role it is reasonable to expect government agencies to have. This is the approach I shall adopt in the remainder of this essay.

III

Those who are reluctant to leave the arts to the mercy of the market generally believe that something of great value resides in the paintings, music, drama, buildings and so on that a society possesses. But from whence does this value spring? What exactly is the value of art? One common answer is 'enjoyment'. The riches that a society possesses when it has strong artistic traditions lie in the fact that there is great and lasting pleasure to be had from literature, music, painting and so on. This explains, so many believe, the emphasis on the arts, especially the literary arts, in the curriculum of schools and universities. Individuals are taught to appreciate the great works of art, by which is meant 'taught to derive pleasure from them'.

In holding this view we need to think of the pleasure to be derived from art as mere amusement or titillation. Explanations of the nature of aesthetic pleasure differ, but generally they all try to account for the undoubted fact that, when we enjoy a work of art this is often not mere entertainment such as we might get from cartoons or detective stories.

Rather the enjoyment arises from, and is invoked by, the depth of intellectual and emotional involvement the work arouses. There is a contrast to be drawn between, for instance, farces and tragedies. We may properly be said to enjoy tragedies, but it is usually a different species of enjoyment from the amusement of farce. Still, though there is this difference to be made, the view that the value of art resides in the enjoyment we derive from it, must in the end hold that the fundamental difference between looking at Titian and watching football on television (to use Dworkin's example once more) lies in the respective pleasure or enjoyment that is to be derived from them. If this is true, the use of the coercive powers of the state to protect the arts amounts to the coercive protection of pleasure.

I shall call this view of the value of art 'the pleasure theory'. To examine its merits properly would require the exploration of quite a large number of philosophical issues, too many to be considered here in fact. However, only some of these relate to its implications for the question we are concerned with, namely the state's involvement with the arts, so it will be sufficient to focus upon these.

If the value of art lies in the pleasure we get from it, there seems to be nothing special about the *arts* which warrants state intervention, and the contrast between Titian and football on television is ill-drawn. This is because, rather obviously, people derive pleasure from football as well as painting, and football may as easily become a victim to market forces as painting. Nor is the pleasure to be derived from football or any other sport of a notably shallower kind. Though it is common for devotees of the arts to regard sport as nothing more than a pastime, great sporting occasions can provide the sort of intellectual and emotional involvement which transforms mere entertainment as much as great drama or music can. As far as enjoyment goes, we have no reason to deny that art and sport are on a par. It follows that if we have reason to subsidise theatres and art galleries on the grounds that they cannot attract sufficiently many paying customers, we have as much reason to subsidise football terraces.

This is not an implication generally drawn by those who favour state involvement in the arts. But there is nothing to step them drawing it, and indeed many free societies now have Ministers for Sport as well as Ministers for the Arts. But the extension raises a further question. Where is the subsidising of pleasure to stop? If it is legitimate to subsidise art and sport for the sake of the enjoyment of a minority, why not beer and skittles also? What is so special about *these* forms of enjoyment?

We might try at this point to make more use of the distinction between kinds of pleasure, and argue that there is reason to protect and subsidise "higher" pleasures while "lower" pleasures may be left to the market. This terminology of "higher" and "lower" derives from John Stuart Mill's famous essay *Utilitarianism*. There Mill is trying to explain the greater value that he perceives in the life of a Socrates dissatisfied compared with that of a fool satisfied while at the same time adhering to his view that the most fundamental of values is pleasure.[9] In my view his attempt at drawing the distinction fails, as do all such attempts, but however that may be, we can see in the present context, I think, that no such distinction is to the point. In the first place, so long as we try to explain the value of art in terms of pleasure, it remains the case that whenever arts are subsidised because they cannot attract sufficient resources in the market, one section of the community is being made to pay for the pleasures of another. This does not have the ring of a plausible social principle. Nor is it likely to meet the liberal 'publicity' requirement according to which the principles of social policy must be publicly stated to all who are obliged to respect them. To acknowledge that state support of the arts is nothing more than a matter of forcing some to subsidise the pleasures of others, however 'high' those pleasures are thought to be, is unlikely to meet with widespread support.

In the second place, application of the pleasure theory raises a doubt about the value of any pleasure that needs to be subsidised. *Utilitarianism* is also the place where Mill employs his famous argument that just as

> The only proof capable of being given that an object is visible, is that people actually see it. The only proof that a sound is audible is that people hear it. In like manner, I apprehend, the sole evidence it is possible to produce that anything is desirable, is that people actually desire it.[10]

The validity of this argument has been much disputed, but if we amend it so that it refers not to desires in general but to pleasure only, it is much less contentious. There is indeed some substance in the view that the only real evidence we can bring in support of the claim that something is pleasurable is that people actually take pleasure in it. In the present context this has an important implication. The pleasure theory, combined with Mill's amended 'proof', implies that the value of an art form is to be measured by people's reactions to it and its relative value by the strength of that reaction. The more pleasurable it is, the most people will seek it (*ceteris paribus*). But this means that an art form which needs subsidy is not sufficiently pleasurable to induce people to devote to it that proportion of their resources which will sustain it in existence. It follows that the pleasures in need of subsidy are not as pleasurable as those that need none, and consequently that the pleasure theory cannot justify state subsidy of the arts.

On all these counts the pleasure theory about art lends support to the economic theory about state involvement and undermines the more lofty view. If art is chiefly a matter of enjoyment, there seems little justification for the state favouring one form of enjoyment over another. But before we can draw any final conclusion from this about what the state's attitude to the arts should be, we need to ask whether the pleasure theory is well founded. This brings us directly to the question of the nature of art.

The pleasure theory warrants a straight comparison between art and sport,[11] since both are valued for the pleasure they give and both are vulnerable to changes of taste and fashion in the marketplace. But the fact that such a comparison is warranted on the pleasure theory may be said to count against it because it overlooks an important difference between the two, one almost certainly connected with the value of each. This is the fact that works of art have *content*, while sporting events do not. Certainly, it is true that in looking at a picture or reading a novel we may value it for the pleasure we derive from its contemplation and the skill that has gone into its making, and similarly we may value a game of football or a show jumping competition because of the pleasure we derive from the skills of the players and competitors. But whereas we can in addition value the picture or the novel for what it says or shows, there is no counterpart to this in a sporting event. Novels can be *about* something; football matches cannot.

This difference is regarded by many as crucial to the relative importance of art and sport. Major works of art are readily described as supplying insights into human nature and the human condition. This is how they assist us in making sense of our lives. Sport, though valuable, is essentially a release and distraction. Great art is directly concerned with human experience and with its ennoblement. It is this belief that inclines people to lend art an importance the pleasure theory cannot explain. Whereas on the pleasure theory the content of art is of instrumental value—a means of gratification—on this view there is a truth in art which, it presents itself in forms not susceptible to scientific investigation or demonstrable argument, is nonetheless to be valued for its ability to enhance our understanding. This is what I shall call the theory of art as understanding.

It would be a mistake to suppose that these remarks about the content of art amount to a refutation of the pleasure theory, or even that they supply an overriding reason to reject the view of art as entertainment. The issues raised by this dispute are much too deep-seated in the history of aesthetics to admit of such speedy solution. The chief point of raising them here is to demonstrate the earlier contention that our view of art in part determines our view of the place of politics in the promotion of art. The pleasure theory lends support to the economic theory. However, having seen that there is some reason to reject it, we must pass on to ask whether the idea that art is a form of understanding can be made to lend support to the more lofty view.

IV

If the pleasure theory suggests a comparison between art and sport, the theory of art as understanding suggests a parallel with science. This is because science is to be valued for the truths we discover and the improved understanding of the natural world that we arrive at, and not merely for the pleasure many undoubtedly derive from constructing theories and devising experiments. Most modern states, including those in liberal democratic societies, provide both institutional and financial support for scientific inquiry. The question is whether state support for the arts can be explained and justified in the same way.

One obvious and immediate doubt about the parallel between art and science arises from the connexion between science and technology. Since scientific research often leads to, and is frequently aimed at, technological innovation, it is plausible to argue that the state's support for science is justified by the benefits which advances in technology bring to all. Science can in this way be shown to play a role in increasing the health and welfare of a society, so that the state's role here is no more contentious than in the communal provision of sewers and water. Such a defence can hardly be extended to the arts however, which have only the most tenuous connexion with technological innovation and no obviously important role in the advancement of public health and welfare.

However, the true basis of the support for scientific research is obscured somewhat by this association with technology and the defence of science through technology is always somewhat unsatisfactory. To begin with, not all science does have practical application. Pure research must be undertaken for its own sake. Of course people, including scientists, often argue that pure science is to be valued for the technological innovations it might throw up. But this defence seems doubly mistaken. First, we know very well of some pieces of research that they are extremely unlikely ever to have practical application. Secondly, and more importantly, the suggestion that science is to be valued as an *instrument* to prosperity seems to mistake its secondary for its primary purpose, which is to increase knowledge and understanding for its own sake.

If, then, there is to be a satisfactory explanation of state support for science, that is, one which justifies support not merely for technological spin-offs, but for the advance of human knowledge and understanding in itself, this may well be expected to extend to other forms of knowledge and understanding. To see whether it does not we need to consider more closely just what the explanation is.

Traditional liberal conceptions of the state are conceptions of a limited, instrumental state. That is to say, Locke thinks of the state as the means whereby the natural rights and duties of individuals can be most effectively enforced; Kant thinks of the state as the means by which the purposes of autonomous beings may be harmonised; and Mill thinks of the state as a means of promoting general utility. All these theories think of the state as a means to some end rather than an end in itself. This instrumental conception of the state is an important part not merely of the political idea of liberal democracy, but also of its popular appeal. The political experience of the twentieth century, especially in Europe, has made people sceptical of any conception of the state as the realisation of a Utopian vision.

However, the liberal conception of the state as a mere means is often taken to imply further that the state may act to provide its citizens only with the means to further their own self-chosen purposes. So, for instance, the state is thought to have a duty to defend individuals against aggression, and may legitimately seek to promote general economic welfare, but may not direct the purposes to which citizens put the consequent peace and prosperity. Whether this further inference is also an essential part of liberalism we need not here inquire. It is sufficient to note that it is strictly invalid. Nothing in the instrumental conception of the state implies the restriction that it may only be a means to promoting *means* and never a means to promoting *ends*. Indeed it is doubtful if such a restriction is either coherent or desirable.

To see this, consider the idea of wealth creation as a goal for governments. Suppose we think of this as a matter of putting more money in citizen's pockets. It is plain that citizens whose purchasing power has thus been increased have not actually been *enriched* unless there is something for them to spend their extra money on. The provision of the mere means of obtaining wealth is not itself an obtaining of wealth.[12] In order genuinely to enrich citizens, governments must make sure that there are additional goods and services no less than additional means of exchange. It follows from this that a government cannot enrich its citizens by the creation of sources of instrumental value alone, but must create sources of intrinsic value also. Now the theory of art as understanding attributes intrinsic value to works of art and views the arts as the means of their production. Moreover, it is not merely an alternative form of enjoyment, but value of a distinctive kind, not the same (though dissimilar) to that which we find in science.

It is not difficult to see how this line of thought connects with the point about enrichment. If wealth creation (or at least its facilitation) is the proper business of government, and if wealth creation requires the maintenance of a variety of generating sources of intrinsic value, a state can have a legitimate role in the protection and promotion of the arts. If the government of a small barren country, say, has a duty to negotiate financially advantageous oil revenues on behalf of its citizens, it may as legitimately use some of these to enrich their lives with museums, galleries, orchestras and theatres, as well as hospitals and scientific institutes. Thus, just as the pleasure theory of art provides some support for the view that the arts should be left to the market, the theory of art as understanding provides support for the view that there is a proper ground for state support.[13] And the resulting picture of the state's involvement in the arts no more conflicts with commonly

accepted conceptions of the role of the state than does its involvement
in any form of wealth creation.

V

If this analysis is correct it supports my contention that the view we
take of state involvement in the arts depends upon our view of the
nature of art. Moreover, we have found some reason to think that a
proper understanding of the value of art will favour some measure of
state involvement. There is, however, one residual difficulty.

The point of the foregoing discussion of the nature of art was to
find a way of deciding what sort of state involvement in the arts there
should be, other than by an explicit examination of the principles of
liberalism. The question remains, however, as to whether anything said
in the last section in support of state involvement in the arts is in
conflict with the fundamental liberal conception set out at the start. On
the face of it there does not appear to be, especially since the
conclusion advanced there seems not to differ significantly from
Dworkin's liberal solution. In the essay already referred to, Dworkin
tries to 'define an approach to the problem of public support for the
arts that is not the economic, and yet is different from the more
unattractive versions, at least, of the lofty'.[14] His suggestion is that
there is good reason for states to support the *structures* within which
artistic endeavour may most readily take place, but this does not imply
any restriction on or endorsement of particular *content*. There is thus
still a radical difference between the sort of state involvement for which
we have found some support, and the wholesale domination of the arts
such as occurred under the Nazis or Chairman Mao.

But is this correct? Is there a radical difference, as opposed to a
difference of degree? The fundamental liberal principle is that the state
must not use its coercive powers to protect or endorse any particular
aesthetic vision. Dworkin's distinction between structure and content
aims to meet this requirement by providing for state support of
aesthetic visions in general, while denying endorsement of any
particular one. But ultimately any such distinction must collapse. If
resources are to be distributed and powers employed, sooner or later
these must invoke judgements of aesthetic merit. This means that
support will be given or restrictions invoked on aesthetic grounds, and

this means judgements about the aesthetic merits of particular works of art.

For example, if a government takes powers to prevent the construction or destruction of buildings, these powers may indeed be used to promote and conserve a wide variety of architectural styles. But the existence of such powers means that sometimes individuals will be forbidden to construct or demolish buildings on the grounds that the buildings in question are ugly or beautiful. Of course, governments may take advice on these matters, but this does not alter the fundamental fact that state powers are being used to enforce an aesthetic view against the free choice of individuals. Similarly, a government that awards or withholds export licences for works of art must at least sometimes interfere with the freedom of individuals on the grounds that one work of art is aesthetically more important than another.

What these examples show is that even the modest of state involvement which the second theory of art supports violates the fundamental liberal principle that individual action must not be restricted or constrained on grounds of aesthetic merit. What this implies is that we are faced with a choice – either we abandon a fundamental principle of orthodox conceptions of the free society, or we abandon the view of art as intrinsically important.

The starkness of this choice is somewhat misleading however, because violation of this orthodox liberal principle is quite compatible with a wide measure of artistic tolerance. Just as the existence of an established church is compatible, to a degree, with the toleration of dissent, so that state's involvement in the arts is compatible with a large artistic licence. But equally, just as proponents of the free society have not always rested content with religious toleration but have demanded an end to established religion, so they may not find artistic licence sufficient and demand an end to state sponsored art. In doing so, they are in my view calling upon a long established ideal of social freedom. But to insist upon this freedom, I have argued, may require them to reconsider the nature and the value they attribute to the arts.

Notes

1. One has to allow, of course, for a general measure of 'double-think' in political life. The Canadian Government introduced strict sanctions against South Africa on the very day it welcomed Nicolae Ceausescu as a distinguished guest.

2. John Locke, *Second Treatise of Civil Government*, ed. P. Laslett (Cambridge University Press, 1969).

3. Immanuel Kant, *Foundations to the Metaphysics of Morals*, trans. Lewis White Beck (Indianapolis, 1959) and *Kant's Political Writings*, ed. Hans Reiss, trans. H.B. Nisbet (Cambridge, 1980).

4. John Stuart Mill, *On Liberty and other writings*, ed. S. Collini (Cambridge, 1989).

5. John Rawls, 'Justice, political not metaphysical', *Philosophy and Public Affairs*, Vol. 15 (1986).

6. See B. Mussolini, 'The Doctrine of Fascism' in *Social and Political Doctrines of Contemporary Europe*, ed. M. Oakeshott (Cambridge, 1939).

7. Ronald Dworkin, *A Matter of Principle* (Oxford, 1985), Ch. 11.

8. *Op.cit.*, p. 222.

9. For a recent discussion of this distinction in Mill *see* Benjamin Gibbs, 'Higher and Lower Pleasures', *Philosophy*, Vol. 61 (1986).

10. John Stuart Mill, *Utilitarianism*, Ch. 5.

11. An interesting account of the value of art as a kind of play is to be found in Gadamer's *The Relevance of the Beautiful*. The best known attack on the idea of art as amusement is to be found in Collingwood's *Principles of Art*.

12. This is the form of contemporary impoverishment in the Soviet Union.

13. Neither provides anything like conclusive support. With respect to the first, since it is plausible to claim that pleasure is intrinsically valuable, it needs to be shown that there are no distinctive aesthetic pleasures, before the implication about support for the economic theory can be drawn. With respect to the second, it needs to be shown that what matters is the production and not consumption of intrinsic value. Is the state entitled to devote resources to the creation of intrinsically valuable works of art that none of its citizens actually wants, or is likely to want?

14. Dworkin, *A Matter of Principle*, p. 229.

V

Aesthetic Values
and Moral Values

Serious Problems, Serious Values:
Are There Aesthetic Dilemmas?

Marcia Muelder Eaton

People who argue, as have many during this century, that the aesthetic and the moral are totally separate and distinct, claim that several essential differences create and maintain this separateness. Behind the reasons given often lies the attitude that somehow aesthetic concerns are just not as important as other concerns, in particular not as important as ethical concerns. For example, Stuart Hampshire, attempting to support his assertion that "there are no problems of aesthetics comparable with the problems of ethics," has called artistic problems "gratuitous." Unlike the moral problems that confront us everyday and demand a response, aesthetic problems do not seem to impose themselves upon us in any comparable way.[1]

Although Hampshire himself takes aesthetics and art quite seriously, his remarks give aid to those who consider art a "frill," and take aesthetic considerations to be rather far down on the list of those things which individuals and societies should attend to. Who really cares whether concert halls or theaters stay open? Faced with problems of poverty and illness, what real difference is made if a museum shows a controversial exhibit or not? Could anyone seriously believe that teaching dancing is as important as teaching reading? When moral issues are settled the worst is over; aesthetic choices just don't pack the same wallop. Moral values are really serious, aesthetic values often appear less central to the pressing concerns of everyday life.

Marcia Muelder Eaton first presented this paper at the Annual Meeting of the American Society for Aesthetics held on October 26-29, 1994, in Charleston, South Carolina. Her paper is being printed here, by permission of the author, for the first time.

One way in which this belief or attitude has been examined in philosophical literature is in the so-called *overridingness debate* in which authors have argued over whether moral concerns do or do not always override aesthetic concerns.[2] However, it is not my intention here to try to show that giving money in support of medical research is not more important than giving money in support of the arts. Rather, I want to argue a more general point: there are some aesthetic problems that are marked with a kind of seriousness that characterizes some moral problems, or, to use Hampshire's language, there are some aesthetic problems comparable in an interesting way to some moral problems, namely in exhibiting the sort of features that one kind of moral conflict exhibits. The sort of conflict that I have in mind is that which is often referred to as "a dilemma." In our moral lives we often face agonizing choices when moral principles that we find equally compelling come into conflict, or when a single moral principle requires that we perform actions, both or all of which cannot be performed. I have to decide whether to be kind or honest. Or kindness demands that I do one thing for Dick, another thing for Jane, and it is impossible to do both. In this paper, I want to attempt to determine whether in the aesthetic arena there is anything analogous to what, in the moral arena, is known as the problem of moral dilemmas. In other words, I want to try to answer this question: Are there aesthetic dilemmas?[3]

There are two sorts of "tests" for determining whether a conflict is a moral dilemma, one logical, one emotional; and if there are aesthetic dilemmas one would expect positive results when these two tests are run on aesthetic conflicts. The first focuses on an agent's confronting separate, mutually incompatible or contradictory actions, both (or all)[4] of which are covered by competing moral requirements, neither of which is the clear winner.[5] The competing moral requirements create a logical puzzle. Using simple, straightforward rules of logic and apparently true statements, including the standardly accepted moral principles that "ought implies can," a contradiction (You are obligated to do A and you are obligated to do not-A) arises.[6] If a conflict is such that resolution is impossible, we have a full-fledged dilemma. Unlike the case of helping the homeless or teaching illiterates where one might conceivably do both, in dilemmatic situations it is impossible to satisfy two (or more) different obligations. "One but not both" is, as it were, built in. The now-classic example is "Sophie's

Choice."[7] Sophie is presented with two alternatives—she can save her son or she can save her daughter, but the *or* is exclusive; she cannot do both.

The logical (or incompatibility) test is often paired with an emotional test. Here a conflict becomes dilemmatic when one realizes that whatever one chooses, one will not "feel right" about it.

This remainder has been variously described as "guilt" or "remorse" or "regret."[8] In Sophie's case, the emotional remainder is so intense and agonized that she commits suicide. No assurances from friends and loved ones ("You did the only thing you could in the circumstances") provided relief.

Recently moral philosophers have been split on whether moral dilemmas actually exist. Full discussion of this debate is beyond the scope of this paper. However, most nonphilosophers are surprised when told about the controversy concerning the existence of moral dilemmas. "Of course they exist," is the typical response—and this remark is often followed with personal, "real-life" examples. The ordinary, nonphilosophic attitude seems to be that anyone with mature common sense will realize that life is so complicated that no a priori principle can rank different sorts of considerations, or certain kinds of moral requirements, above others. Any principle that Sophie might have articulated in advance could only be repugnant: "Always choose a son over a daughter," or "Always give precedence to your youngest child," or "When faced with such a choice, flip a fair coin," or "First choose the girl, next the boy."

Although I tend to side with those philosophers (and nonphilosophers) who believe in the existence of genuine moral dilemmas, I do not believe that the issue must fully be resolved in order to consider the possibility of aesthetic dilemmas. What cannot be denied is that some serious moral conflicts are marked by at least apparent incompatibility and intense emotional remainder. This intensity is one reason that the moral is granted such seriousness and importance. If one can show that there are aesthetic conflicts that also exhibit incompatibility and remorse, regret, or guilt, then there is support for the view that aesthetic values, like moral values, are really serious.

To my knowledge, no one has written specifically on the topic of aesthetic dilemmas. Unlike the moral realm, where nonphilosophers (and many philosophers) often believe that only someone from another planet would deny that dilemmas exist, I am not certain that there is a commonsense presumption in the aesthetic realm going in the direction of skepticism. But I am inclined to think there is. To a composer who says, "I have a dilemma—I could either end this sonata this way or that way—do A or not-A, but not both," one might easily and simply respond, "Where's the contradiction? You can just write two different sonatas; this isn't like Sophie's choice at all." (I'll say more about this kind of example below.) And there doesn't seem to be any obvious candidate for an emotional remainder that has anything like the force of guilt or remorse. Martha Nussbaum expresses this attitude extremely clearly and forcefully when she writes, (more or less in passing),

> Works of art are precious objects, objects of high value. And yet it is a remarkable feature of our attention to works of art that it appears to spread itself smoothly and harmoniously. I can, visiting a museum, survey many fine objects with appropriate awe and tenderness. I can devote myself now to one, now to another, without the sense that the objects make conflicting claims against my love and care. If one day I spend my entire museum visit gazing at Turners, I have not incurred a guilt against the Blakes in the next room; nor have I failed in a duty toward Bartok by my loving attention to Hindemith. To live with works of art is to live in a world enormously rich in value, without a deep risk of infidelity, disloyalty, or any conflict which might lead to these.[9]

But are these intuitions correct? Are there no real contradictions; is there no aesthetic emotional remainder? Are there, finally, no real *aesthetic oughts*? Only a close look at actual cases, i.e. at candidates for aesthetic dilemmas, will tell, I believe.

Many of the following examples were suggested to me in private conversations, both with philosophers and non-philosophers, artists and nonartists. I do not claim to provide a precise taxonomy for the examples. I have grouped them into rough categories of decision-making situations, some of which are more like morally dilemmatic situations than others.

I. Artistic Choices. Artists must constantly make choices with respect to the media in which they work and the goals they want to achieve. Should this area be red or blue, this poem in pentameter or hexameter, this composition divided into three or four movements? How should it end? The film classic *Casablanca* is legendary with regard to its ending—two different ones were in fact shot. While working on this paper, I was fortunate to be able to hear the British composer, John Casken, describe what he readily referred to as "a dilemma."[10] Working on a song-cycle for baritone and orchestra, using the words of the poet Rodney Pybus, Casken was "stuck" on what to do with the line, "Let me be whale and graze those unfenced acres of blue." The choice was between having the music fit into the context of the music that had just preceded it or providing a more literal sound imitation of "grazing" and "unfenced."

In all of these examples, the logical test does seem to be met in one sense. An artist cannot do both A and not-A, at least not in the same work. They can, however, create different works. And, like those theorists who maintain that dilemmas are really just not-yet-solved conflicts, one might be strongly inclined to treat all of these examples as problems that, once solved, will be felt to be "correct." "I've finally got it right," one can imagine the artist saying with relief. There simply does not seem to be anything like the emotional remainder we find in moral dilemmas—nothing that would qualify as aesthetic remorse.

II. Presenters' Choices. Art presenters—museum and theatre directors, anthology editors and other such decision makers—must obviously make choices about what to provide their audiences. Which of two equally beautiful works from a permanent collection or repertoire should be put before the public at a given time? Again the logical test is met; but only because the decision is space- and time-bound. One feels again that one can make up for what one doesn't opt for later. Bach in the first week, Bartok in the second. Again, one must ask, where's the real remorse?

A recent presenter's case does strike me as more genuinely dilemmatic. Picasso's famous *Guernica* was returned in 1981 by the Museum of Modern Art in New York to the Prado in Madrid because the artist himself had expressed his wish that it be displayed in that Spanish museum once the country was no longer a dictatorship. He wanted it to be housed under the same roof with such painters as Titian, Durer, Rubens, Velasquez, and Goya. Picasso's political and art historical intentions had finally been satisfied. In 1992, however, the painting was moved to the nearby Queen Sofia Center of Art—Madrid's first designated museum of modern art. It is in such a context that the painting actually belongs, decided the Prado's board of directors. The modern center is near the Prado (a five minute walk), and hence close to the art historical context Picasso desired, But is it close enough? Since a painting cannot be in two places at the same time, the logical test for a dilemma is met. The board did report that the decision was a painful one. To those who would feel bad no matter where it is housed, the emotional test also seems to be met. Though one could, perhaps, regularly move *Guernica* back and forth (on the faulty assumption that this could be done without harm to the work), we have here, I think, a candidate for a genuine dilemma.

A concern related to the "in which museum" problem is "in a museum or not in a museum"—an issue that has arisen recently in connection with quilts. Long ignored as "mere women's work," quilts have at last been duly recognized as genuine works of art largely because they have begun to appear prominently in major museums of fine art. Not everyone celebrates this, however. Many radical feminists argue that displaying quilts out of the contexts for which they were created diminishes, even erases, their aesthetic value. The true aesthetic value of quilts, they assert, can only be fully experienced when they are viewed on beds, preferably keeping bodies warm, better yet when the viewer knows that this piece of material came from Mary's blouse, that piece from Joe's overalls. Removing them from the bedroom amounts to acknowledging and acceding to the power of white, male museums directors to grant artwork status to an object. Suppose a curator invites me to display my mother's quilt in a museum. Surely there are good reasons to do so—the aesthetic properties will be accessible to many people under excellent conditions of visibility and preservation, for example. But there are also good reasons not to do so—the wrong sort of viewing conditions prevail and, some argue, seeing how quilts wear out (i.e. are not preserved) is part of the context required for full experience of their aesthetic nature. Again, both the logical and emotional tests may be met.

III. Ordinary or Everyday Aesthetic Choices. Which wallpaper should I put in the bathroom? Should there be a fountain or a grove of trees in the town square? If marooned on a desert island, which ten books (or musical compositions or paintings, etc.) should (would) I take? Some of these cases can be handled easily by the "one-now-the-other-later" strategy. Or by majority vote. Even tossing a coin doesn't carry the repugnance it does in the Sophie example. Someone who felt remorse about a wallpaper choice would be, I think, considered sick, not aesthetically sensitive or worthy. Again, my hunch is that cases like these are not strong candidates for genuine aesthetic dilemmas.

IV. Extraordinary Choices. The "desert island game" does suggest a more serious set of candidates, however. These examples are sometimes referred to as the "burning museum problem." Suppose you are in a museum when a fire breaks out and you can only carry out one (the "not-both" condition) artwork. You can take a da Vinci or a Picasso, say.

Now we begin to have something much more dilemmatic. The logical incompatibility condition is built it, and I believe that there will be an emotional remainder. Though not as excruciating as Sophie's forced decision about which of her own children to save, feeling regret when one cannot save both works of art that one values equally would surely be more appropriate than in the trivial wallpaper case,

V. Interpretative Choices. One nagging problem in philosophy and the theory of art has always been the problem of interpretation. Is there one and only one correct interpretation of a given work of art, or are there several equally (and perhaps incompatible) good interpretations? Clearly there is a close analogy here with the moral realm. Is there one and only one right thing to do in every situation, or are several equally correct (and sometimes incompatible) actions possible? In both the moral and aesthetic cases, belief in an all-encompassing theory covering all contingencies will require that one deny the existence of genuine dilemmas. Critical literature abounds with ongoing disputes over particularly troublesome cases. Some people believe that an adequate aesthetic theory supplies principles or strategies for making correct decisions. For example, intentionalists hold that the intention of an artist settles the matter: there is a correct interpretation of, say, *Hamlet* or *The Eroica Symphony*, namely the one intended by Shakespeare or Beethoven. On such a view, aesthetic dilemmas do not exist. But, needless to say, not everyone goes along with intentionalism (or with any other theory heretofore proposed).[11]

Another way of dealing with contradictory interpretations (e.g. Henry James' *The Turn of the Screw* is a ghost story and is not a ghost story) is tantamount to denying the logical incompatibility, namely, to accept a theory that enables one to have it both ways. One might take a relativistic stance: "*The Turn of the Screw* is a ghost story for J who loves supernatural thrillers and *The Turn of the Screw* is not a ghost story for K who loves psychological thrillers." Or one might (as I have done) claim that James intended to write an ambiguous work that, like a duck-rabbit figure, can be read in (at least) two ways.[12] But again, many theorists will not agree that competing interpretations can be dispensed with so easily. (I certainly think that *The Turn of the Screw* is a very special case; by no means can all works with incompatible interpretations be handled in the same way, i.e. with the "ambiguity solution.")

VI. Evaluative Choices. Your mission is to judge an art contest (poetry, singing, ceramics, etc.). You can give only one blue ribbon (the "not-both" condition). There may be some single-dimensional aesthetic judges who believe that some features always override—but I know of no serious critic or philosopher of art who take such a position. George Dickie has proposed a matrix system for evaluating art, but even his system allows for ties.[13]

Nonetheless, the emotional remainder test seems not to be met at all (at least when one is searching for aesthetic, not moral, remorse). Like feeling no guilt when one listens to Bach rather than Bartok, one just does not have to decide whether Bach or Bartok "deserves the blue ribbon." These examples seem so contrived that one feels that aesthetic evaluation begins to be made to appear rather absurd. Who cares? Even if I am supposed to award a prize, I can refuse, or insist on a tie. Sophie cannot refuse to pick just one child—or at least cannot do so without agony.

VII. Restorative Choices. I have saved for last the set of examples which I believe clearly do constitute genuine dilemmas. They preclude the "you-can-always-make-another-one" solution to incompatibilities and, for anyone who cares at all about such things, leave a significant emotional remainder. The most celebrated example is probably the cleaning of the Sistine Chapel, but there are others: particularly acute are those surfaces on which one painting has been done on top of another or decisions about whether to rebuild or leave a ruin. In Crete, for example, there has been a controversy about how to treat historical sites—to rebuild and even paint the stones so that a palace such as the one at Knossos looks like it did to Minoans, or simply to excavate the ruins as has been done at Phaistos. No matter which set of experts wins, something is inaccessible or lost—and in some cases lost forever. There are documented disasters. In June, 1992 in as careful a place as the Louvre, Veronese's *Marriage at Cana* was ripped in five places while undergoing restoration. It is unlikely that it can be completely repaired. Critics of what has been described as a "cleaning frenzy" in today's museums have formed an Association to Protect the Integrity of Artistic Heritage.[14] Comparable cases exist with respect to environmental decisions—one can build a dam at site A or at site B and flood (thereby destroying forever) beautiful valley A or beautiful valley B. There is "heated" controversy over whether or not controlled burning in forests should be carried out, and over whether or not naturally occurring fires should be allowed to follow their own course without interference.

The logical test is met in these cases—for one cannot, at least with existing technologies, have it both ways. And disappointment, I think actual remorse, may be felt. Some "clean/don't clean," "rebuild/don't rebuild," "burn/don't burn" proponents probably feel so strongly that theirs is the *right* way to go that there was, for them, no emotional remainder. I know some people who refuse now to go to the Sistine Chapel because they feel it has been ruined forever. But many of us are of two minds; and people of good aesthetic faith will be differently inclined—and feel that no matter what decision is made, restorative choices will occasion doubt and regret. Even the staunchest advocates of cleaning must have advocated extensive photographing of the dirty ceiling—as in frustration one grasps at straws in an effort to have it both ways.

In presenting the "desert island" choice above, I deliberately equivocated on 'would' and 'should'. Even if one is reluctant to go from the former to the latter in this particular example (agree that one can decide for oneself what one *would* take, but decline to say that there is anything that one *should* take) there are other examples where the move seems more natural.

How would/should you interpret a particular artwork?

To which work would/should you give the blue ribbon?
Certainly,

What would/should one do to the Sistine Chapel?

'Should', of course, implies the existence of an obligation. It is obligations that generate dilemmas by creating logical incompatibilities. If there are aesthetic shoulds, there must be aesthetic obligations. And if there are aesthetic obligations, aesthetic dilemmas become possible.

In the context of relating moral and aesthetic value, I have elsewhere argued that a parallel to moral obligation exists in the aesthetic realm.[15] The resistance to accepting the notion of aesthetic obligation rests, I believe, on our feeling that it is bad or wrong to fail to recognize and act upon moral obligations. Where is the badness or wrongness in the aesthetic realm? Can it really be wrong not to notice sunsets or to read poetry to appreciate jazz? It seems quite reasonable to claim that

(I.)   If S fails to consider moral features, then S is bad.

but less reasonable to assert that

(II.)   If S fails to consider aesthetic features, then S is bad.

But if we replace 'bad' in (II) with "leads an impoverished life," then I think we get a much more reasonable statement:

(IIa.)   If S fails to consider aesthetic features then S leads an impoverished life.

The problem now is that (I) loses much of its moral force:

(Ia.)   If S fails to consider moral features, then S leads an impoverished life.

Our moral actions, our failure to be morally sensitive, affects others in a way that aesthetic insensitivity seems not to do, and hence more than one's own life is at stake.

(Ib.)   If S fails to notice moral features, then S hurts others.

But not,

(IIb.)   If S fails to notice aesthetic features, then S hurts others.

Similarly, there is an asymmetry when one assumes a deontological moral theory.

(Ic.)   If S fails to notice moral features, then S will fail to do his or her duty.

But not

(IIc.)   If S fails to notice aesthetic features, then S will fail to do his or her duty.

However, if one believes it is one's duty to lead as full and rich a life as possible, something that I do not believe is farfetched, indeed I believe it is true, then (IIc) is no longer odd. And even (IIb) will be true in some cases. Failure to consider the aesthetic features of the

Sistine Chapel, to demolish it to build a parking ramp, for example, would hurt others. Thus both (I) and (II) may be true.

Individuals can substitute features in either statement that they think appropriate—e.g. duty or pain in (I), color or expression in (II). Although (I) is clearly true, it will strike many readers as odd to be told, following (II), that anyone has an «»obligation «» to consider the colors of a sunset or the expressiveness of a Beethoven symphony or the graceful lines of a statue. But the strangeness diminishes when one claims that one is obligated to consider colors, lines, or expressiveness when deciding what to do with the paintings in the Sistine Chapel.

Some may object that it is a *moral* obligation in the case of the Sistine Chapel—that one has a moral obligation to posterity (to preserve objects that will enrich others' lives), not an aesthetic obligation to the object. But suppose we have a case where we believe the moral value of two options is equivalent. Say we have a canvas on which two beautiful paintings have been placed, one on top of the other, and that peoples' lives will be equally enriched if either is saved, or equally harmed if either does not exist. For aesthetic reasons alone one must then make a choice. I do not believe a plumping, coin-tossing strategy would be satisfying here, anymore than it would be in the moral domain. Ultimately, of course, we are concerned about how people's lives will be affected—what will make their lives meaningful or worth living. Elsewhere I have argued that we keep the term 'ethical' for general question such as what sort of person one wants to be or what sort of lives are best, and use the term 'moral' for more particular, situation-bound questions.[16] Thus one might take the position that all choices about affecting people's lives are ethical. But that there are, within this general *ethical* realm, pure aesthetic/aesthetic as well as moral/moral dilemmas does seem possible. And therefore an analogic connection and comparability between aesthetic and moral problems and values is supported—one that allows us to claim that aesthetic values too, are really serious.[17]

Notes

1. Stuart Hampshire, "Logic and Appreciation," in *Aesthetics and Language*, edited by William Elton (Oxford: Basil Blackwell, 1967), pp. 162-3.

2. For examples of papers in this debate see, Philippa Foot, "Are Moral Considerations Overriding?", in *Virtues and Vices and Other Essays* (Oxford: Basil Blackwell, 1978); Michael Slote, "Admirable Immorality," in *Goods and Virtues* (Oxford: Clarendon Press, 1983); and Bernard Williams, "Moral Luck," in *Philosophical Papers: 1973-1980* (Cambridge: Cambridge University Press, 1981).

3. Many philosophers distinguish between conflicts of belief and conflicts of desire, and many assert that moral conflicts are of the latter sort. I do not want to prejudge the issue of whether moral (or aesthetic) dilemmas belong exclusively to the desire, not to the belief, category. But there is a useful distinction to be made—and, possibly, applied. Bernard Williams claims that when beliefs conflict, they either conflict obviously (i.e. are such that they clearly cannot be both true—'It is raining' and 'It is not raining') or are by themselves consistent but would not be consistent in combination with some third belief. 'The man is tall' and 'The man is the boss' do not conflict per se, but do if it turns out that 'the man' refers to the boss, and 'The boss is short' is true. Desires on the other hand, according to Williams, conflict when some contingent fact about the world makes it impossible for two desires both to be satisfied. I want a drink and I want to be warm—and the drinks are out in the cold. See Bernard Williams, "Ethical Consistency," in *Essays on Moral Realism*, ed. by Geoffrey Sayre-McCord (Ithaca: Cornell University Press, 1988), pp. 42-43. A moral conflict, he thinks, is simply "a conflict between two moral judgments that a man is disposed to make relevant to deciding what to do." (p. 45.) For example, one believes one ought to do two things, and cannot do both, i.e. one ought to do something in light of some features of a situation and ought to refrain from doing that thing in light of some other features of the situation. Moral conflicts, Williams says, are more like conflicts of desire than conflicts of belief, for the discovery that two beliefs cannot both be true weakens belief (in either one or both propositions), whereas the discovery that two desires cannot both be satisfied does not serve to weaken either or both desires. I am inclined to agree with Williams, but exactly how beliefs and desires contribute to moral choices will not be crucial to my discussion.

4. I shall for simplicity's sake discuss dilemmas in terms of only two options; clearly in some situations there may be more than two.

5. For this type of characterization, see Walter Sinnot-Armstrong, *Moral Dilemmas* (Oxford: Blackwell, 1988), p. 29.

6. Some philosophers believe that the contradiction can be avoided by rejecting this move. See Ruth Barcan Marcus, "Moral Dilemmas and Consistency," *Journal of Philosophy*, 77, March, 1980, p. 134.

7. William Styron, *Sophie's Choice* (New York: Random House, 1979).

8. Philosophers have tried to give precise definitions of and to distinguish clearly between the notions of remorse, guilt, regret, sorrow, etc. I do not think it is possible to do this. In ordinary conversation I have found that people differ considerably; some use 'remorse' only if they are personally responsible for what has happened, others use this term to express more "generic" sadness. The OED defines 'remorse' and 'regret' in essentially the same way. I shall use them interchangeably, often relying on the more neutral term 'emotional remainder'.

9. Nussbaum, op. cit., pp. 131-32.

10. This paper was first drafted while I was a resident scholar at the Rockefeller Study Center in Bellagio, Italy, March 6-April 8, 1992. I am enormously grateful for the opportunity thus afforded me to discuss my ideas with artists and scholars from a variety of areas. Casken was extremely patient and helpful.

11. Another kind of example is architectural choices, for example which plan for a new library should be selected. In some ways these examples are like the presenters' category and can be solved by a "this-one-here-this-one-there" strategy; or like ordinary choices architectural decisions may seem not to be serious enough to warrant anything like remorse (which standard design should be used in a particular housing development). But many architectural designs (perhaps all great ones) are site—and time—specific, and such examples seem to belong to the extraordinary choices category.

12. Marcia Muelder Eaton, "James Turn of the Speech-Act," *British Journal of Aesthetics*, Autumn, 1983, pp. 33-45.

13. George Dickie, *Evaluating Art* (Philadelphia: Temple University Press, 1988).

14. See, "Masterpiece is damaged at the Louvre," *The New York Times*, July, 1992, reprinted in *The Minneapolis Star and Tribune*, July 11, 1992, p. 10A.

15. Marcia Muelder Eaton, *Aesthetics and the Good Life* (Cranbury, New Jersey: Associated University Presses, 1983).

16. Marcia Muelder Eaton, Ibid., and "Integrating Aesthetic and Moral Value," *Philosophical Studies*, 67, pp. 219-40, 1992.

17. I am grateful to Jennifer Heaton for helpful discussions on the topic of moral dilemmas. This paper was presented to members of the Philosophy Department of Wayne State University; I am also grateful to them for helpful criticisms and suggestions.

Taste and the Moral Sense

Marcia Cavell

It has seemed to many philosophers that ethics and aesthetics, concerned as they both are with value, should have a common basis. Yet attempts to found a general theory have usually succeeded at the cost of sacrificing one kind of value or the other. From the vantage of the agent the ethical and the aesthetic points of view are clearly very different: As moral creatures we have to think of the effects of our actions on ourselves and others; we have to make difficult decisions which require us to consider and reconsider our commitments and often to sacrifice one moral good for another; we are confronted with problems in such a way that even to attempt to avoid them is to incur responsibility. To these dimensions of concern and obligation there is nothing parallel in the activity of the artist *qua* artist.

To some extent these differences are reflected in the role of the critic, that is, in the kinds of things we say about actions, on the one hand, and works of art on the other. As Stuart Hampshire has put it:

> A critical judgment is . . . noncommittal and makes no recommendation; the critic may reject the work done without being required to show what the artist ought to have done in place of the work rejected. But the moralist who condemns an action must indicate what ought to have been done in its place. . . . A moral censor must put himself in the place of the agent and imaginatively confront the situa-

Marcia Cavell's article first appeared in the *Journal of Aesthetics and Art Criticism* 34 (1), Fall 1975, pp. 29-34. It is reprinted here by permission of the publisher, the American Society for Aesthetics, and the author.

> tion which the agent confronted; that censor and
> the agent censored have so far the same problem.
> But a critic is not another artist, as the moral
> censor is another agent; he is a mere spectator and
> he has the spectator's total irresponsibility; it is
> only required that he should see the object exactly
> as it is . . . his purpose is to lead people not to
> look elsewhere, but to look here at precisely this
> unique object; not to see the object as one of a
> kind, but to see it as individual and unrepeatable.[1]

Moral judgments, Hampshire claims, are concerned with what actions
have in common, with their conformity to rules and principles;
aesthetic judgments are concerned with what is unique. His position in
sum, is "that aesthetic judgments are not comparable in purpose with
moral judgments, and that there are no problems of aesthetics
comparable with the problems of ethics."[2]

Though much of Hampshire's analysis is right, I believe he
overstates the case; and I will argue, first, that there is an activity
central to the moralist which bears as little relation to general rules and
principles as does the kind of aesthetic judgment Hampshire has in
mind; and second, that the aesthetic is no more able than the moral
point of view to concern itself with an object or event in isolation from
the environment and other events. While I agree, then, that a general
theory of value is not possible, my claim is that both in the kind of
things they say and in their reasons for saying them, the moralist and
the art critic have much in common.

I

Moralists, professional or lay, tend to be overly concerned with
principles, and inattentive to the difference between a moral point of
view and *moralizing*. ("Consistent policies are needed," Hampshire
writes, "in order to meet human predicaments; men may discuss the
reasons which have inclined them to solve their problems in different
ways. . . . Their arguments will lead them to general principles;
anyone, therefore, who moralizes necessarily generalizes.")[3] Moral
judgment, like aesthetic judgment, suffers the more rigid it is, the less
geared to this particular situation and person. As William Gass

remarks: "Ethics . . . is about something, and in the rush to establish principles, to elicit distinctions . . . and to discover 'laws,' those lovely things and honored people, those vile seducers and ruddy villains our principles and laws are supposed to be based upon and our ethical theories to be about are overlooked and forgotten."[4]

There is, of course, a kind of moral judgment which does derive from general principles. But moral thinking begins with a more particular awareness: Instead of "You ought not to do that . . ." or "That action is wrong . . . ," where the justification will appeal to a moral rule or to some likely consequence such as the happiness or unhappiness of the greatest number, the judgment goes: "That's an awful thing he did so hypocritical," or "Maybe you didn't think of it that way, but telling John about the other evening was an act of betrayal," or "What he said seemed perfectly harmless, but don't you see how cruel it was?" Moral values and principles are implied, but the obligatory and the immoral are not, per se, the issues. And we don't so much justify our judgments as explain them in much the same way as the critic explains why a character is badly drawn, or how a musical passage is more or less banal than it seemed on a careless listening, or why a poem is false and sentimental. In all these cases explanation takes the form of pointing out details we have missed, giving a new kind of emphasis, showing us patterns and relationships that put things in a new light. In fact, the sorts of moral predicates in question here are remarkably parallel to what philosophers have referred to as "aesthetic predicates":[5] "trite," "sentimental," "baroque," "tightly knit," among others. The same epistemological questions bother us in both cases: Is describing an action as disloyal, a piece of music as pretentious or banal, really to describe it? And if it is not a description, is it then, as I have been calling it, a kind of judgment? I have argued elsewhere[6] that it is both, and that there is a procedure by which it can be rationally defended. Whatever the answer, the point is that such remarks are in fact an important part of a process which frequently ends in a changed mind and perception. And essential to both moral and aesthetic judgment of this kind is a spontaneity that necessarily escapes formalization.

Aesthetic predicates have sometimes been defined as just those predicates whose application requires taste and perceptiveness. That is, if a critic merely followed a rule in describing a structure as tightly knit or delicate, we would not say that he was exercising taste. But equally if someone merely followed a rule in describing an action as generous or disloyal we would not say he was exercising moral sensibility. And as for the moral agent, if he tries to be generous by following a formula he will almost certainly fail. Hampshire has claimed that "to copy a right action is to act rightly; but a copy of a work of art is not necessarily or generally a work of art."[7] This argument is backward . . . a copy of a work of art is a work of art, though not an original one,[8] and to copy an action which treats another with respect, or gently, or compassionately, is not necessarily to treat another in those ways, unless the notion of "copying an action" is construed so broadly that it begs the question. That is, words which are kind in one situation and relationship may be unkind in another. To act towards a person with kindness or compassion or loyalty requires caring about that person and knowing something about his or her feelings. It requires, in short, a responsiveness to someone else and to the particularities of the present situation that is incompatible with repeating someone else's behavior, or one own, in another circumstance. One can mimic kindness. And perhaps, as Aristotle suggested, one way to become kind is to try to behave as if one were kind. But we ask for more than the form of kindness to say that it has informed a particular action.

There are many different sorts of moral judgment, and different sorts of things which concern us morally. The wider the reverberations of action—by which I mean the greater the number of people it affects and the more profound the effects are, the more the judgment will appeal to principles, precedents and probably consequences, and the less it will resemble the judgments of the "spectator critic." There is, however, a two-fold relationship between this sort of moral reasoning and the sort of moral judgment to which I have been comparing aesthetic judgments. First, the ability to reason morally in fact develops out of the sensitivity to particular people in particular situations. And second, the defense of one's position in regard to the large moral questions moves not only by appeal to principle and probable future consequences, but also by appeal to present fact, which is the sphere precisely within which moral sensibility functions. To put the two points in another way: we learn to become concerned with consequences on the large scale by becoming concerned with consequences, both actual and intended, on the small scale; and it makes sense to think in terms of precedent and principle because it is possible to perceive someone else's situation and to be able to imagine it as our own.

Hampshire is right to insist that in art criticism the quest for standards, conceived as universally valid rules or principles, is misguided. Aesthetic sensibility requires a spirit of play; but so does moral sensibility. To point out that an action which seemed open and aboveboard was devious, or that a remark which seemed simply honest was really destructive and cruel, is to look more closely at the tone in which it was said, perhaps, or at the history of the relationship between these two people, or at what one person can be presumed to know about the other, or simply at the meaning which the words have in the relevant context. It also reminds us that appearances are deceiving; that there is often a world of reference implicit in a single remark; or that we may be missing what distinguishes this situation from others superficially like it. The parallels between these processes and what the critic is doing when, for example, he asks us to look again at Blake's "Songs" for the irony which we may have missed beneath the innocence are, I think, obvious.

II

Hampshire claims that "the spectator critic in any of the arts needs gifts precisely the opposite of those of the moralists: he needs to suspend his natural sense of purpose and significance." What is true in this claim, it seems to me, is something like the following: The person who evaluates a play in terms of its probable effects on the behavior of the average theater-goer is judging the play from the moral point of view and not from the aesthetic. Looking at it as a work of art, he will be concerned not with its consequences for behavior but for perception, and he will discover these not in the future, but with a careful reading of the play itself. To describe a work as "revolutionary" or "shocking" or "sad" or "trite" is not to make a prediction about what it is likely to make the average member of the audience do, or even see. It's a shorthand way of saying things about the work itself, as judged, not by the average observer but, by the careful observer, who is perhaps qualified, or ready to be careful, in certain ways (the person who is unfamiliar with the art form in question will not be in a position to find it revolutionary; it can open doors on the world only if, as it were, one has already found his way into the antechamber).

But beyond this truth, I am not sure about the accuracy of Hampshire's statement as a description of either the moralist or the critic. What might it even mean to "suspend one's natural sense of purpose and significance?" We need to ask why Hamlet feigns madness and why he tells Ophelia to get herself to a nunnery. And though perhaps it's true that in a certain sense we look at works of art as individual and unrepeatable, it's just as true that we look at them, and should if we want to see them better, in terms of their relations to a style, a genre, a period, a culture, and often the "natural" world. The characters in a literary work, for example, aren't "real" people; but neither are they nonpeople. A play or a novel enlarges our experience by beginning with our experience. We recognize Hamlet as depressed, Uriah Heep as obsequious, Kate Croy as exploitative, because we know something about people and societies, and any discussion of the works in which these characters figure would have to be a discussion, in part, about such recognitions. (One of the things that distinguishes many of the art movements of the twentieth century is their refusal of interpretation: "nonobjective painting," "random" music, the novels of Robbe-Grillet, among many possible examples. These call for a different kind of aesthetic, an "aesthetic of silence" as John Cage has called it. Some of my remarks in this article would not apply, without considerable qualification, to these "postreferential" movements.)

Hampshire remarks that "a great part of a critic's work, in any of the arts, is to place a frame upon an object and upon its parts and features."[9] It's an ambiguous image: to put a frame around an object is to call attention to it; it is also to isolate it in space and even, to a degree, from the rest of our experience. A museum is itself a kind of frame. Museums are also, some would argue, a kind of mausoleum; for a frame helps us to see, but only if we can get rid of it when we need to. The critic's task is to frame, but also to unframe and reframe— to disturb the circles we have drawn around our experience. It is true that the critic wants us to look here, more carefully than we have done, seeing things we may have missed; but in order to accomplish this he may have to take us out of the frame and a very long way around—through the history of baroque music, or an understanding of myth, or of the eighteenth-century novel, and so on. Which means that while in some sense it is right to insist that a work of art must be seen and judged in its own terms and not by some external frame of reference, we have to add in the next breath that there isn't any Final

Frame, and that the question of what is "internal" and what is "external" to a work of art is very complicated.

Where is the in-itself of *Hamlet?* The consequences of that question are similar to the consequences of asking for the uninterpreted givens of our experience. And as soon as we see that we are driven towards answering "The black marks on the quarto pages," we recognize that we have lost *Hamlet* in the puzzle. A work of art is not created *ex nihilo*, but out of tradition, a style, a cultural moment, and conventions of all sorts. Originality in art is not opposed to conventionality, but it is rather like the creative process elsewhere: a matter of taking a convention or style and, under the exigencies of the artist's need to articulate what he feels has not yet been seen or said, moving conventions somewhere new.[10] While the work of art is the critic's focus, he is not supposed to forget everything he knows. The point is not to obliterate language and the past—assuming we could do so—but to allow them the new relations to the particular and present. The boundaries of *Hamlet* are more like horizon, ever-receding into other literary works and other experiences as our own position changes. In distinguishing between the manifest and the latent content of the dream Freud remarked that a full understanding of any dream would be tantamount to a full understanding of the dreamer's psychic to that point in his biography. "The full meaning" of any work of art posits an ever more difficult ideal. For it can only be displayed through the history of the human imagination which formed it and which it in turn informs.

What is being suggested here to the critic as a path between reductionism, on the one hand, and overreading, on the other, is by no means straight and narrow, and ease leads to self-indulgence. The guideline is that anything which helps unfold the meaning of the work of art has to be considered a part it and the underlying assumption is that though every work of art, like every human gesture or expression, is in itself a revelation we are often unprepared to receive it. Susan Sontag has argued that any act of interpretation is necessarily reductionistic. "Interpretation," she writes, "is the revenge of the intellect upon art. . . . To interpret is to impoverish, to deplete the world in order to set up a shadow world of 'meaning'. It turn *the* world into *this* world. . . ."[11] But this is true only of interpretations that are "intellectual" and self-preoccupied, and of the interpretation of "meaning" according to which every work of art *has* one, like a monogrammed briefcase which the object somehow possesses and which is separable from it.

Feeling puzzled about how to understand a friend's behavior or how to read *Hamlet* is feeling in need of a bridge between the person or the text and our own experience. It won't do to translate the behavior or the play into a statement of something we have already felt or known. In the case of my friend, that would be to deny that we are separate; and it would make of the play something incidental, uncreative and unilluminating. Friends and works of art do not move us by simply mirroring ourselves, but by giving us another hold on the world; by affirming our own experience while simultaneously modifying and extending it. The act of communication presumes duality and awareness of duality, and signals that we are going somewhere. Yet of course we begin from where we are; and since we are all in slightly different places, the necessary bridge will not be identical for any of us. The difficulty is that because there are no critical rules which allow one to say decisively and in every case that an image is trite or a design bold, so there is no rule to prevent the critic from going astray. Interpretation always requires tact; and tact, like compassion, is a virtue slowly won, requiring a closeness to one's own feelings as well as the willingness to be open to the experience of another. What will illumine a work for you may not for me, and may belong more to your autobiography than to the phenomenology of the work.

Hampshire has argued that the function of the moralist and of the spectator-critic are different. Yet works of art, like actions, have consequences. At its worst, art blunts sensibility, inhibits self-recognition, rewards mindlessness and rigidity; at its best, it expands vision and feeling. And here it seems to me that the immediate purpose of criticism of all kinds is identical: like art itself, it sometimes changes the way we see the world.

Notes

1. "Logic and Appreciation," W.E. Kennick, ed., *Art and Philosophy* (New York, 1964), p. 582.

2. Ibid., p. 581.

3. Ibid.

4. "The Case of the Obliging Stranger," reprinted in *Fiction and the Figures of Life* (New York, 1972).

5. See for example, Frank Sibley's "Aesthetic Concepts," in W.E. Kennick, ed., *Art and Philosophy* (New York, 1964).

6. "Critical Dialogue," in *The Journal of Philosophy* (1950).

7. Op. cit., p. 581.

8. See Nelson Goodman's argument in the section titled "Art and Authenticity," *Languages of Art* (Indianapolis, 1968).

9. Op. cit., p. 583.

10. Cf. Northrop Frye in *An Anatomy of Criticism* (Princeton, N.J., 1957): "The possession of originality cannot make an artist unconventional; it drives him further into convention, obeying the law of the art itself, which seeks constantly to reshape itself from its own depths," p. 132.

11. Susan Sontag, *Against Interpretation* (New York, 1961), p. 7.

The Inter-relationship of
Moral and Aesthetic Excellence

Ron Bontekoe and Jamie Crooks

Students of the history of aesthetics will know that until the nineteenth century the question of excellence with regard to beauty was seldom separated from the question of excellence with regard to the moral good. However, perhaps because of the growing uncertainty in the last century and a half concerning exactly what constitutes the moral good, and then again perhaps because of the gradual turning away of art from its earlier preoccupation with religious themes, in contemporary discussions of art it no longer seems natural or obvious to link moral and aesthetic excellence. Today the artist tends to be thought of as someone who is primarily, if not exclusively, concerned with exploring the formal properties of a medium. And the art viewer is enjoined to bear constantly in mind the preeminent importance of the purely formal characteristics of the artwork.

Thus we find Jerome Stolnitz, for example, writing in his *Aesthetics and the Philosophy of Art Criticism:*

> Any of us might reject a novel because it seems to conflict with our moral belief or our 'way of thinking'. When we do so, we should be clear as to what we are doing. We have not read the book aesthetically, for we have interposed moral or other responses of our own which are alien to it . . . We cannot then say that the novel is *aesthetically* bad, for we have not permitted ourselves to consider it aesthetically.'[1]

Ron Bontekoe's and Jamie Crooks' article first appeared in the *British Journal of Aesthetics* 32 (3), July 1992, pp. 209-220. It is reprinted here by permission of the publisher, Oxford University Press, and the authors.

To consider an artwork aesthetically, according to Stolnitz, is to contemplate it sympathetically and disinterestedly for its own sake—which is to say, 'simply for the sake of enjoying the way it looks or sounds or feels'.[2] Here Stolnitz, like many other modern aestheticians, echoes the sentiments of Clive Bell, the well-known formalist, who argued that 'to appreciate a work of [visual] art we need bring with us nothing but a sense of form and color and a knowledge of three dimensional space'.[3]

This emphasis on what might be called the surface qualities of the artwork does not go entirely unchallenged today, of course, but the challenges raised against it seem as often as not to have something half-hearted about them. George Dickie, for example, defends the critic's *right* to comment on such things as the moral vision contained within a work of art, but seems to leave open the question of whether there is any *need* to comment on it.

> Any statement about a *work* is a critical statement and, hence, falls within the aesthetic domain. To judge a moral vision to be morally unacceptable is to judge it defective and this amounts to saying that the work of art has a defective part. . . . Someone might still argue that even though a work's moral vision is defective and the moral vision is part of the work, that this defect is not an *aesthetic* defect. . . . *My* concern at this point is simply to insist that a work's moral vision is a part of the work and that, therefore, a critic can legitimately describe and evaluate it.[4]

Here Dickie seems implicitly to accept the separation of moral and aesthetic value even while he insists on the legitimacy of an art critic's venturing to comment on a work's moral vision. The authors of this paper would like to argue for a stronger claim than that which Dickie seems prepared to embrace. It is our contention that the expression of a bad moral vision does indeed constitute an *aesthetic* defect in a work of art, and that it is always necessary to judge a film, a novel, a painting or a poem to be flawed *as an artwork* because of its mishandling of moral themes.

I

Works of art traditionally have been regarded in one of two ways. Either they are understood to constitute a diversion from the world, a means of temporarily forgetting or displacing the burdens of everyday living, or they are understood to constitute a revelation in which the world itself somehow becomes thematic. In other words, the work of art has been regarded traditionally either as an entertaining lie or as a disclosure of truth. The 'choice' which we seem to be called upon to make here, however, is not an altogether serious one. After all, what we mean by calling the work of art an entertaining lie is rather obvious and uncontroversial: the novel we are reading describes events which never happened; the painting we are examining shows things which may or may not exist, but which quite certainly do not look exactly as they are represented in paint. To call a work of art a disclosure of truth, however, is to suggest something considerably more subtle—for the novel and the painting clearly are not (or at least not always, not necessarily) concerned with truths, if by 'truth' we mean anything like a description of things or events which corresponds to the way those things or events actually are.

What, then, do we mean by calling the artwork a disclosure of truth? We can begin to approach an answer to this question if we reflect on the fact that the 'lie' which is the artwork must be 'entertaining' or we would have no interest in it. To create a work that is entertaining, the artist must have both a mastery of her technique and an understanding of her audience. (Lacking either of these, she will merely confuse rather than entertain.) The artist must have knowledge, in other words. And because the novelist, the painter, the composer is a creator of original work, different in important respects from anything else that has been done, her knowledge will be unique in some respects—the product of a search for solutions to the particular artistic problems with which *she* was concerned.

It is not inappropriate to think of the artist as an explorer, an explorer who is making progress in two directions at once. On the one hand, she discovers through a long and sometimes difficult process of trial and error exactly what combination of notes played by which instruments, what shade of color placed *here* on the canvas, what arrangement of words in which metrical form, will most nearly enable her *to* capture what she is trying to convey in her work. The artist must discover *how* to accomplish what she wishes to accomplish. On the other hand, it virtually never happens that an artist knows in advance, that is to say, before her work is well under way, *exactly* what she wishes to accomplish. The second thing which the true artist has to discover, then, is precisely what it is that she is trying to say. This she discovers only in *the process* of creating the artwork. (The painter who has been commissioned to produce a portrait knows, of course, before she begins that the portrait *will* be of President X, but this is a very superficial description of the work and does not begin to express what the painter *will* have accomplished when the portrait is finished. The nuances of emotion that are discovered and revealed in the subject's face are noticed and fully articulated—even to the artist herself—only in the act of painting.)

The artist, of course, if she is going to present to her audience something worth their while, something that will repay them for the trust they have shown in her by attending her exhibit or purchasing her volume of poems, must first have found something worthwhile to show them. This principle holds even with respect to those art forms—non-programmatic music, for example, or abstract art—which do not seem to concern themselves with any specifiable content. As Wassily Kandinsky, the great pioneer and spokesman for nonrepresentational art, observes in his *Concerning the Spiritual in Art:*

> It is very important for the artist to gauge his position aright, to realize that he has a duty to his art and to himself, that he is not the king of the castle but rather a servant of a nobler purpose. He must search deeply into his own soul, develop and tend it, so that his art has something to clothe, and does not remain a glove without a hand. The artist must have something to say, for mastery over form is not his goal but rather the adapting of form to its inner meaning.[5]

What the artist has to say need not be expressible as a moral, of course, and even in relatively didactic art the moral of the story or painting *will* never encompass all that the artist has to say, for the artist is not, after all, a sage or a philosopher whose task it is to establish general principles of conduct. The artist is concerned, as the philosopher or the scientist also is, with 'getting things right', but in the artist's case this means clarifying and heightening some particular experience—the experience into which her audience is invited to enter. This experience is anticipated, explored and made available to her audience by means of the artist's own painstaking efforts to realize her artwork in accordance with the inner necessity which she senses and which, if she is successful, the responsive members of her audience *will* also recognize.

This is the sense, according to R. G. Collingwood, in which the artwork can be understood to involve a disclosure of truth: the artist is trying to 'get right' the particular experience which her artwork is intended to evoke. 'Art is not indifferent to truth', Collingwood writes; 'it is essentially the pursuit of truth. But the truth it pursues is not a truth of relation, it is a truth of individual fact'.[6] 'Art is knowledge; knowledge of the individual', he contends. And 'the individual of which art is the knowledge is an individual situation in which we find ourselves'.[7] The artist, on this view, is someone who has an unusual sensitivity to the inner structural necessity of a certain range of potential experiences. The true artist then reveals that inner necessity to her audience through the creation of her artwork. (On this point, as well as others, Kandinsky is in complete agreement with Collingwood. As he puts it, 'that is beautiful which is produced by the inner need, which springs from the soul'.[8]) The bad or pseudo-artist, on the other hand, is someone who, for whatever reason, fails to be guided by this inner necessity in the production of her work, and who invites the viewer, as a consequence, to enter into an experience which is 'muddy' or incoherent.

If this way of understanding the artist's task is correct, if she really is an explorer of the inner necessities which govern various experiences that are open to us simply by virtue of our being human, then the artist has an extremely important social function to perform. In the pursuit of her own particular form of excellence, the artist arouses in her audience an experience of exceptional clarity and intensity, and in doing so she shows us something about ourselves. She reveals something to us about the human condition: about how we respond to things given what we are, and also about what we might be—what we might be, of course, are artists ourselves, clearer-eyed and fuller-nerved than we are at the moment. Art as a disclosure of truth, then, on the one hand broadens our self-understanding and on the other hand challenges us to deepen our self-awareness.

There are two conditions, however, which the artist must fulfill if her work is to have this salutary effect upon others. Since it is only in the production of good art that the artist can be said to have genuinely found something worth showing us, the artist must first cultivate within herself an attentiveness to what we have been calling the 'inner necessity' of an artistic experience. And second, since sensing what one should do is one thing, but actually doing it is another, the artist must be dedicated to creating a work which realizes in its completed form as much of this 'inner necessity' as she can capture. In order to clarify what these two conditions amount to, let us consider more closely what is involved in the creation of a work of art.

Every beautiful object and every successful artwork is considered beautiful or successful by virtue of the extraordinary measure of 'fittingness' which is to be found among its various parts. It follows, then, that the artist, in order to be able to produce successful work, must somehow be able to sense the possibility of an exceptional fit between the parts of an object which does not yet exist. This anticipation of 'fittingness' involves an act of the imagination—which is to say, a marshalling of already existent resources and an arranging of those resources into a new and appealing pattern. It is during this process of the marshalling and arranging of resources, of course, that the artwork gradually emerges from the realm of mere potentiality and becomes a determinate object in the world. Now the point which needs to be stressed here is that, during the entire process of the artwork's emergence, the artist's anticipations of fittingness *will* be tested. Those anticipations *will* be confirmed in some respects no doubt, but they will also in many respects be frustrated: the anticipation of fittingness which arises when the work is still somewhat abstractly conceived will not be altogether borne out by the artwork when the paint is actually applied to the canvas, the words are actually written on the page, or the notes are actually sounded by the instruments specified. When this occurs, the artist *will* need to make adjustments to her conception of the work. She will need to cast about for a new way of arranging the parts—a way which, by restoring her anticipation of fittingness, allows her to continue the search for her finished work.

The process of artistic creation involves a series of such moments, each of which is distinguished by a particular anticipation of fittingness, which is to say, by a particular abstract conception of the meaningful integration of parts, followed by the concrete realization of that conception in the artist's chosen medium, and an evaluation of the measure of fittingness which actually results. Insofar as any given moment's anticipation of fittingness is successfully realized, the artist is freed in subsequent moments to focus on progressively more detailed aspects of the work's integration. The process of artistic creation, then, involves a constant shifting of the artist's attention as she pursues an ephemerally glimpsed vision of fittingness which leads her on and which yet seems always in danger of disappearing from her sight altogether. The artwork created is the record of her pursuit of that vision, and the progressive refinement of the artwork is broken off precisely at that point where the artist finally either seizes the vision in its entirety or loses sight of it once and for all.

In *Truth and Method*, Hans-Georg Gadamer describes the process of inquiry into the nature of things in terms of a logic of question and answer in which the most difficult task of the inquirer is the preservation of his 'orientation towards openness'. According to Gadamer, the skill of which the serious inquirer has the greatest need is the capacity to ask questions which open up, rather than obscure, the subject matter under consideration. A worthwhile question gets hold of the subject matter in the right way. Any question, of course, insofar as it can be formulated and asked, involves us in a commitment to certain presuppositions. Some questions, however, those that are 'distorted' or 'false', tie us fast to their presuppositions so that there is no real possibility of getting at the truth by means of them. Instead of enticing the subject of our inquiry to reveal its nature to us, the false question 'inhibits it by holding on to false presuppositions. It pretends to an openness and susceptibility to decision that it does not have'.[9] The true question, by way of contrast, only tentatively commits us to its presuppositions. Its concern is not to nail opinion firmly in place, but to establish the bounds of what remains open concerning the subject of inquiry.

Gadamer's description of what is involved in any process of genuine inquiry applies as well to the process of artistic creation, since the artist too is essentially an inquirer in pursuit of truth. Truth as the artist is concerned with it, however, needs to be understood in the Heideggerian sense of *aletheia*—of allowing the subject matter of one's inquiry to reveal itself as it genuinely is. The artist is an inquirer who tries to allow the particular aesthetic experience the possibility of which he has caught glimpses to reveal itself through his artwork. As with any

other inquirer, for the artist too, the most difficult task facing him is
the preservation of his 'orientation towards openness'—the finding of
questions which get hold of his subject matter in the right way. As was
suggested earlier, the artist's work is guided by his anticipations of
fittingness. But each such anticipation has the structure of a question:
the artist asks himself, in effect, *'Will this* way of arranging things give
me what I am looking for?' Insofar as this question is genuinely asked,
the artist has no hard and fast commitment to the answer which he
nonetheless hopes for. He does not assume, in other words, that *this*
way of arranging things *must* give him what he is looking for. His
interest, after all, is not finally in arranging things in *this* way, but in
realizing a particular aesthetic experience, and so he is prepared to
accept a negative answer to his question. Should the artist ever lose his
'orientation towards openness', however, should he ever lose sight of
the vision of fittingness which he is pursuing, he *will* find himself
without any means of answering his last question. For once he has lost
sight of his objective, the artist cannot possibly receive an answer to the
question, 'Will this way of arranging things carry me towards my
objective?' The artist who finds himself in this position has no real
option but to stop work, which is to say, to suspend his inquiry, until
the vision returns.

As Gadamer points out, there is a particular virtue that is
associated with inquiry, a virtue in fact which is the precondition of
inquiry—that being, of course, the Socratic virtue of knowing that one
does not know. So too there is a vice that is particularly associated with
inquiry, in that the possession of this vice precludes inquiry—the vice
of believing that one knows what one does not in fact know. The artist,
just as much as any other inquirer, has need of the Socratic virtue and
must avoid the temptations of its corresponding vice. He must
recognize, on the one hand, the degree to which his vision of
fittingness has yet to be clarified, so that he *will* not settle for the
achievement of a trivial, superficial aesthetic experience. He must
recognize, on the other hand, that insofar as the aesthetic experience
that he is attempting to define and evoke is unlike any other aesthetic
experience, the means of realizing that particular experience *will* have
to be discovered—that he is not *already* in possession of all that he
needs to know about how to realize his goal. The artist, in other words,
must be ruthlessly honest with himself. He must be, to use Gadamer's
phrase, 'someone who is radically undogmatic'.[10] At every stage in

his work his attitude is tentative, hypothetical. He probes possibilities on the basis of what he has already seen and felt, but the success or failure of his present probings is determined always by what they will cause him to see or feel, and this can never be known for certain in advance. The artist, like all inquirers, is searching for an adequacy of expression which *may* arrive, if he is diligent and fortunate.

II

The process that we have been describing in the past few pages, the progressive narrowing in on some worthwhile experience the possibility of which the artist has (in his moment of inspiration) caught a glimpse, *is the* defining characteristic of art, we wish to argue. It should be clear, after all, that one cannot define art in terms of some medium within which all artists work or in terms of some more narrowly conceived procedure of artistic production—the application of paint to canvas, for example. Nor can one take as the distinguishing feature of art the effect that it produces on the viewer, since, as Stolnitz has argued, we can take an aesthetic attitude towards many things— sunsets, driftwood, the stars at night, to name a few obvious candidates—and elicit in our aesthetic contemplation of such things effects that are indistinguishable from those produced in art.

On the other hand, it should be clear that all of the activities that we normally define as artistic—painting, sculpting, composing music, and so on—*do involve* the process that we have been describing. And if it happens that a number of other activities that one might point to also involve to some extent something like this process, this may just be why we sometimes speak of things such as the 'art of cooking' and the 'art of cabinetmaking'. How thoroughly and importantly something is an art, of course, is also a function of how thoroughly the activity is dominated by the process we have just considered. (Propaganda, pornography, and a significant amount of modern conceptual art, for example, often possess little in the way of aesthetic value because they tend to circumvent the artistic process: propaganda and pornography by subordinating the process of artistic inquiry to a predetermined end, the value of which is left unexamined; much of conceptual art by permitting the 'artist' to evade the responsibility of mastering some medium.)

So how does all of this relate to the expression of a moral vision, be it good or bad? First of all, it should be mentioned that the expression of a moral vision is not a *requirement* of art. The artist is never obliged to state what she feels about the nature of good and evil. In some art forms, moreover (consider the fugue, for example), the expression of a moral vision may not even be possible. In spite of this, however, it also seems clear that the creation of art invariably has a moral import. Morality, after all, is concerned with the improvement of the quality of human experience, and insofar as art aims at the clarification and heightening of particular moments in human experience, it can be said that to at least this extent art and morality share the same end. (On this interpretation, what distinguishes moral from aesthetic pursuits is not their originating impulse—the desire to improve the quality of human experience—but the type of relationship within which that impulse is expressed.)

Morality too, of course, is a subject of inquiry, and moral truths, like artistic truths, can only be grasped through the sort of dialectical investigation that we have seen Gadamer describe. That is to say, in the study of what is morally right, just as much as in the study of what is historically or scientifically true, and just as much as in the creation of genuine art, the inquirer must strive to preserve her open-mindedness. She must resist the tendency to allow her preconceptions about morality to substitute for moral thought, for if morality is concerned with the improvement of the quality of human experience, and human experience is as multivarious as we all know it to be, then clearly true morality has as little to do with the unquestioning application of a code, such as the Ten Commandments, as true art has to do with painting-by-numbers. This is not to suggest, of course, that there are no moral principles which ought to be respected. The point is rather that such principles are fairly obvious. The real task of moral thought, then, is to determine which principles should take precedence under which circumstances, and why.

The status of an action as moral or immoral depends in large part upon the context of human experience within which it occurs. The slicing open of an abdomen with a knife is, in one context, surgery, in another, attempted murder. Lying is clearly the *best* thing that one can do in certain circumstances. It is crucial, then, that the moralist understands the variety of contexts within which an action might be performed, and the significance of those contexts for the moral value of an action. This sort of understanding, however, is acquired only by the open-minded individual, and only when her open-mindedness is coupled with experience or the sympathetic exercise of her imagination. The point that we wish to establish here is that the advocacy of a particular moral stance can only be a completely responsible action when it is grounded in a clear understanding of the human condition. And the converse of this, we want to suggest, is that a bad moral vision is one that gets something wrong about the human condition, either by misrepresenting human nature or by refusing to acknowledge the significance of altered circumstances, but in either case, through inadequate attentiveness on the part of the moralist to the *full* complexity of the human condition.

The artist, again, has no obligation to concern herself as an artist with morality, but at the same time, of course, she is perfectly free to take moral issues as her subject matter. The only obligation she stands under as an artist is that whatever subject matter she chooses must be approached in the manner described above, that is to say, tentatively and with a commitment to capture the inner necessity governing her subject, for as was suggested in section I, it is precisely this approach that establishes her claim to *be* an artist. But if the artist *does* approach her subject in this way, filled with determination to capture the inner necessity governing some moral situation, the result of her inquiry *will* necessarily be the expression of a sound moral position in her artwork. Why? Why can we not imagine an artist, the Marquis de Sade, for example, about whom we might wish to say that, while his art is immoral, as an artist he is fully sensitive to the place of evil in the affairs of human beings?

The reason is that nothing about the accurate depiction of evil makes for a bad moral vision. Many great artists have chosen to show us unflinchingly some aspect of evil. Consider Iago or Stavrogin or Medea. We recognize the intelligence and worthiness of an Iago, and because of this are all the more disconcerted as he sets out cold-bloodedly to destroy Othello over an imagined slight. In spite of ourselves, we, like all of his acquaintances, are affected by the compelling attractiveness of a Stavrogin, who commits barbarous acts out of listless boredom. And even as we recoil from the details of her revenge, we understand the awful rage of a Medea when her husband, whose welfare and advancement have become the dominant motives of her life, casually discards her for another woman. Evil, accurately described, may disturb us intensely with its unmistakably human face, but it never recommends itself as something to be embraced.[11]

Simply put, a bad moral vision cannot be expressed by an artist who is fully sensitive to the significance of what she is saying because her moral vision, in order to be 'bad', must advocate a policy which is at odds with the significance of what her sensitive exploration of the human condition shows her. To cap a convincing artistic treatment of some moral issue by adopting an immoral attitude with respect to it would be akin to forcing a happy ending which rings false onto an otherwise well-wrought tragedy. It could not follow naturally from what had already been done. And if it followed none the less, we would be entitled to consider this as evidence of a lack of sensitivity on the part of the artist at an especially crucial point (the point of closure) in the creation of her artwork. In both cases, moreover, with respect to the tragedy which inexplicably ends happily, and with respect to the artwork which 'gets right' the nature of evil and then advocates something immoral, we can quite properly describe the failing involved as an aesthetic defect since in both cases the artist fails to exhibit that sensitivity to the inner structural necessity of her subject matter which we are entitled to expect from her.

Of course, it almost never happens that an artist tacks onto her work in this way a moral vision which is at odds with her (sensitive) understanding and portrayal of the human condition. What ordinarily happens is that the artist's moral vision *does* seem to follow naturally from the artistic investigation of her subject matter, but this is because her presentation of her subject matter is skewed from the beginning in such a way as to support her moral assumptions. This can, but need not, involve the artist's reading back into the human condition whatever is necessary to make her conclusions seem plausible. The artist who wishes to make a point may quite consciously simplify or exaggerate for the sake of her message. On the other hand, she may simply lack the sensitivity or intelligence needed to understand what actually transpires in situations involving characters such as those she is presuming to describe, and so her message, for all of its crudeness, may be the subtlest moral insight of which she is capable. (The writer of successful bodice-rippers, for example, who churns out three or four of these novels a year, no doubt feels perfectly at home in the sort of world that she describes, and one of the reasons why her work never rises to the *level* of great art, in spite of its value as escapist literature, is its moral shallowness.)

The artist, again, is an explorer. She searches for a way to 'get right' the particular experience that her artwork is intended to evoke. If she is to be guided by the inner necessity governing her subject, however, she requires freedom—the freedom to follow wherever that inner necessity leads her. For this reason there must be no topics, no directions that are in principle off-limits to her. *Everything,* all aspects of the human condition, should be thought of as potentially grist for her mill and open to her investigation. This freedom is granted the artist, moreover, in the confident belief that, if she succeeds as an artist, what she makes of her freedom *will* be morally as well as aesthetically sound. This is not to suggest, of course, that if she succeeds as an artist we will necessarily approve of her moral position, for her sensitivity to the human condition may well be subtler than our own, causing her to embrace a morality more refined than any we are capable of understanding.

By the same token, we have no guarantee that even a good artist *will* produce morally acceptable work, for the creation of an artwork almost invariably demands of us the exercise of many different types of sensitivity at once, and the artist may not be equally well endowed with all the requisite forms of sensitivity. A poet, for example, may be extremely sensitive to the demands of rhythm and have little talent for metaphor. A painter may be strong in composition and have only a weak sense of color. And so too, a filmmaker may be an excellent cinematographer, with a fine feel for plot, and yet lack the deeper insight into human nature which is a prerequisite both for convincing characterization and moral understanding. Each of these artists may produce work which is in some respects excellent, and to call them 'good artists' is thus merely to acknowledge the excellent effects that they *have* achieved. At the same time, of course, their failings in metaphor, in color, in characterization (and consequently in moral depth) count against their being considered 'great artists'.

One final consideration should make it especially clear that there is between moral excellence and aesthetic excellence this close connection that we have been trying to demonstrate. When we consider our experience of the moral 'ought' as it presents itself in situations where there is no question of clear obligation—of having to do something because the *rules* say we must—we discover that the moral 'ought' feels remarkably like the aesthetic 'ought'. We make a contribution to some worthy cause, cancer research, say, not because we must, or because it does not make sense to do anything else, but because under the circumstances it strikes us as being the best thing to do with *these* particular resources. So too, as we stand before the canvas and decide to make our brush stroke (with red paint) just *there,* we do so not because we must, or because it does not make sense to do anything else, but because under the circumstances defined by *this* painting-in-progress it strikes us as the best thing to do.

The fact that moral obligation presents itself at times in the guise of *duty,* of a simple adherence to rules which are not to be questioned, should not mislead us. True, there exist moral rules which, when followed, may in some sense *reduce* the quality of human experience. But this no more implies that moral obligation is *not* grounded in the impulse to improve the quality of human experience than the existence of 'laws' of perspective or conventions of realistic representation, which, when slavishly adhered to, may prevent an artist from achieving all that he is capable of, implies that the artist is not interested in producing the most successful work that he *can* produce. Rules and laws are merely shortcuts enabling us to arrive quickly at a place it once seemed to us worthwhile to revisit—worthwhile enough to devise a shortcut for getting there. Only if we periodically free ourselves of the tyranny imposed by these shortcuts, however, *will* we ever be able to recognize that there might be a better place to spend our time. And, of course, if we notice that there is such a place, the old shortcuts will cease to be of interest to us.

Notes

1. Jerome Stolnitz, *Aesthetics and the Philosophy of Art Criticism* (Cambridge Massachusetts: Houghton Mifflin Co., 1960), p. 36.

2. Ibid., p. 34.

3. Clive Bell, *Art* (New York: Frederick Stokes Co., 1913), p. 27.

4. George Dickie, "The Myth of the Aesthetic Attitude," *American Philosophical Quarterly*, Vol. 1 No. 1 (January 1964) p. 64.

5. Wassily Kandinsky, *Concerning the Spiritual in Art* (New York: Dover 1977) p. 54. Originally published in 1914 under the title *The Art of Spiritual Harmony*.

6. R.G. Collingwood, *The Principles of Art* (Oxford University Press, 1978) p. 288. First published in 1938.

7. Ibid., pp. 289-90.

8. *Concerning the Spiritual in Art*, p. 55.

9. Hans-Georg Gadamer *Truth and Method* (New York: Crossroad, 1975) p. 327.

10. Ibid., p. 319.

11. Of course it *may* be embraced in spite of this by an immature reader—in much the way that the Nazis because of their efficiency and success seem to infatuate a certain type of adolescent—but this incomprehension on the part of her audience is then no fault of the artist.

Contributors

Ron Bontekoe completed his Ph.D. in philosophy at the University of Toronto in 1988 with a dissertation on epistemology. From 1988 to 1990 he taught at the Ryerson Polytechnical Institute in Toronto. Since 1990 he's been a member of the philosophy department of the University of Hawaii—Manoa in Honolulu. His first book, *Dimensions of the Hermeneutic Circle*, will soon be appearing through Humanities Press. He is also coeditor, with Eliot Deutsch, of *A Companion to World Philosophies*, forthcoming from Blackwell Press.

Noël Carroll is Professor of Philosophy at the University of Wisconsin at Madison. His last book was *The Philosophy of Horror*.

Marcia Cavell completed her Ph.D. in philosophy in 1969 at Harvard University. She has taught at Brooklyn College, New York University, Queens College, the State University of New York at Purchase, and the University of California at Berkeley. Her published work includes numerous articles in aesthetics and the philosophy of mind, and a book titled *The Psychoanalytic Mind, from Freud to Philosophy* (Harvard University Press, 1993).

L.B. Cebik, Professor of Philosophy at the University of Tennessee, Knoxville, has written a number of articles on nonaesthetic issues in the philosophy of art. His latest book, *Art as a Social Realm*, will appear in 1995. His work in the philosophy of art continues a progression of studies that began with the philosophy of history (*Concepts, Events, and History*) and proceeded through the philosophy of literature (*Fictional Narrative and Truth: An Epistemic Analysis*). He presently serves as director of the Center for Applied and Professional Ethics at UT, one of a number of administrative posts he has filled while maintaining his philosophical studies. While Director of Research Compliances, he won the Society of Research Administrators Rod Rose award for his writings. Among his seven books and hundred-plus articles and reviews are a number in communications electronics, and he serves as Educational Advisor to the American Radio Relay League. Cebik's current philosophical projects include further studies in narrative theory, the establishment of nonaesthetic domains in the philosophy of art, an investigation of the concept of community, and the development of theoretical and practical properties of high frequency antennas.

Jamie Crooks completed his Ph.D. in philosophy at the University of Toronto in 1989 with a dissertation on Heidegger's interpretation of Nietzsche. From 1988 to 1990 he taught at the Ryerson Polytechnical Institute in Toronto. Since 1990, he has been a member of the philosophy department of Bishop's University in Lennoxville, Quebec.

Mary Devereaux teaches philosophy at Simmons College in Boston, Massachusetts.

Marcia Muelder Eaton is Professor of Philosophy at the University of Minnesota in Minneapolis. She earned her Ph.D. at Stanford University, where she taught. She also held regular appointments at Iowa State University and the University of Illinois at Chicago, and held visiting appointments at the University of Copenhagen, the University of Munich, and the University of Warwick. She is the author of *Aesthetics and the Good Life* (Associated University Presses, 1989) as well as two others books. Eaton was recently elected vice-president of the American Society for Aesthetics; she will serve as its president in 1995-97.

Joel Feinberg is Regents Professor of Philosophy and Law at the University of Arizona. He has also held regular appointments at Brown, Princeton, U.C.L.A., and the Rockefeller University. He has held numerous visiting appointments and fellowships, and was president of the Pacific Division of the American Philosophical Association in 1981-82. Feinberg is the editor or coeditor of *Reason and Responsibility* (Wadsworth, 1965), now in its eighth edition, *Moral Concepts* (Oxford University Press, 1970), *The*

Problem of Abortion (Wadsworth, 1973), *Philosophy of Law* (Wadsworth, 1975), now in its fifth edition, *Moral Philosophy* (Wadsworth, 1977), and *Philosophy and the Human Condition* (Prentice Hall, 1980). He is the author of *Doing and Deserving, Essays in the Theory of Responsibility* (Princeton University Press, 1970), *Social Philosophy* (Prentice Hall, 1973)—translations of the latter have come out in Portuguese, Japanese and Chinese—*Rights, Justice, and the Bounds of Liberty* (Princeton University Press, 1980), *Harm to Others* (Oxford University Press, 1984), *Offense to Others* (Oxford, 1985), *Harm to Self* (Oxford, 1986), *Harmless Wrongdoing* (Oxford, 1988), and *Freedom and Fulfillment* (Princeton University Press, 1992).

David E. W. Fenner teaches philosophy at the University of North Florida. He is the author of *The Aesthetic Attitude*, forthcoming from Humanities Press, and of articles in, most relevantly and recently, the *Journal of Aesthetics and Art Criticism* and the *Journal of Aesthetic Education*. He is a regular contributor of critical dance reviews to *Dancer*. Fenner is currently working on a manuscript in aesthetic naturalism.

Gordon Graham is Reader in Moral Philosophy at the University of St. Andrews in Scotland, and Chairman of the Department. He is the author of five books, including *Politics and its Place* (Oxford, 1986), *Contemporary Social Philosophy* (Blackwell, 1987), *Living and Good Life* (New York, 1990) and *The Idea of Christian Charity* (Notre Dame, 1990). He is also the author of over fifty papers on a wide range of topics in ethics, aesthetics and social philosophy. he was founder and first director of the St. Andrews Centre for Philosophy and Public Affairs, and is Direct of the Continuing Education Certificate in Professional Ethics. He has held special lectureships and visiting positions at several universities and colleges in the United States and Europe.

Ernest van den Haag was formerly John M. Olin Professor of Jurisprudence and Public Policy at Fordham University and is a retired psychoanalyst. He is well-known for his work in ethics and social philosophy, and has published several books as well as many papers in these areas.

Kenton Harris teaches philosophy at the University of Miami. He is also a dancer and choreographer with the American Dance Theatre. His recent work includes a currently unpublished monograph, *The Philosophy of Dance: A Groundwork for Dance Criticism*, and papers in the *Journal of Aesthetic Education* and *Dancer*.

Peter H. Karlen practices art, publishing, and intellectual property law, including the law of copyrights and trademarks, in La Jolla, California. He has taught art and intellectual property law courses for a number of years in law schools in Britain and the United States. In addition, Mr. Karlen is a contributing editor to *Artweek* and *Art Calendar* and is the author of hundreds of articles on art, literary, and intellectual property law which have appeared in art and legal publications. He holds a B.A. from the University of California at Berkeley; a J.D. from the University of California Hastings College of the Law; and an M.S. (Law & Society) from the University of Denver College of Law. Mr. Karlen has been listed in Who's Who in American Law, Who's Who in American Art, and Who's Who in the World.

W.E. Kennick is G. Henry Whitcomb Professor Emeritus of Philosophy at Amherst College. His book, *Art and Philosophy* (St. Martin's, 1964, 1979), has been a staple of aesthetic inquiry for many years; this is evidenced by the number of footnotes in this collection alone that reference this book. Kennick also co-edited/coauthored *Metaphysics: Readings and Reappraisals* (Prentice Hall, 1966) and has written articles for such as the *Journal of Philosophy*, *Philosophical Review*, *Mind*, *Review of Metaphysics* and *American Philosophical Quarterly*. His "Does Traditional Aesthetics Rest on a Mistake" has been very widely anthologized.

Richard Serra is an artist in New York City. He is known for his large-scale site-specific works in landscapes, urban environments, and museums.

Richard Shusterman received his doctorate in philosophy from Oxford University, after having been initially trained at the Hebrew University of Jerusalem. After writing *The Object of Literary Criticism* (Humanities Press, 1984), and *T.S. Eliot and the Philosophy of Criticism* (Columbia University Press, 1988), he edited *Analytic Aesthetics* (Blackwell, 1989) and coedited *The Interpretive Turn: Philosophy, Science, Culture* (Cornell University Press, 1991). Shusterman's recent book, *Pragmatist Aesthetics: Living Beauty, Rethinking Art* (Blackwell, 1992), has already been published in French (Minuit, 1992) and German (Fischer, 1994) translation. His forthcoming books include *Sous l'interpretation* (L'eclat, 1994) and *Practicing Philosophy*, forthcoming from Routledge. Shusterman is Professor of Philosophy at Temple University and at the College International de Philosophie (Paris).

Francis Sparshott was born and educated in England (King's School, Rochester; Corpus Christi College, Oxford—first class honours, Literae Humaniores, 1949). He came to Canada in 1950 and taught philosophy at the University of Toronto from 1950 until his retirement in 1991, specializing in ancient philosophy and the philosophy of art. He has been President of the American Society for Aesthetics; before that, he was president both of the Canadian Philosophical Association and of the League of Canadian Poets. He has published eight books of philosophy and nine books of poetry, most recent *Views from the Zucchini Gazebo* (poetry, 1994) and *A Measured Face: Toward a Philosophical Understanding of the Arts of Dance* (philosophy, 1995). He is married and has one daughter. Since retirement he continues to write, and "takes photographs when he can afford the film."

James O. Young is Associate Professor of Philosophy at the University of Victoria, in Canada. As well as contributing regularly to aesthetics journals, he publishes on philosophy of language, and he is the author of *Global Anti-realism* (Avebury, 1995). He is presently working on another book, tentatively entitled *A Cognitive Theory of Art*.